YEATS

Irish Studies

YEATS

Douglas Archibald

SYRACUSE UNIVERSITY PRESS

1983

Permissions to quote have been generously granted by Michael and Anne Yeats, A. P. Watt Ltd., Macmillan Publishing Co., Inc., Faber and Faber Ltd., Routledge and Kegan Paul Ltd., Columbia University Press, Indiana University Press, and Random House, Inc.

Library of Congress Cataloging in Publication Data

Archibald, Douglas N.
    Yeats.

    (Irish studies)
    Bibliography: p.
    Includes index.
        1. Yeats, William Butler, 1865–1939—Criticism and interpretation. I. Title. II. Series: Irish studies (Syracuse University Press)
    PR5907 .A72   1983   821'.8   82-19638
    ISBN 0-8156-2263-5

Manufactured in the United States of America

For Mitzi

Douglas Archibald is Dean of Faculty at
Colby College, Waterville, Maine.

Contents

Acknowledgments

I am grateful to Miss Anne Yeats and Mr. Michael B. Yeats, A. P. Watt Ltd., the Macmillan Press Ltd. of London, and the Macmillan Company of New York for permission to quote from the various works of W. B. Yeats.

Chapter 2 originally appeared, in a different form, in *The Massachusetts Review* (Summer 1974), and I am grateful to its editors for permission to reprint it here.

I have received generous assistance from The Society for the Humanities at Cornell University and from the Humanities Grant Committee and the Research, Travel, and Sabbatical Committee at Colby College and wish to thank both institutions for their support.

Neil Hertz, Philip Marcus, and Richard Fallis read the entire manuscript; it was improved by their criticism and I was sustained by their encouragement and remain deeply grateful. Colleagues at Colby — John Mizner, Ed and Susan Kenney, Pat Brancaccio, and Peter Harris — read parts and offered wise and helpful suggestions. The errors are of course poor things but my own. Two Colby students, Wendy Feuer and Tim Cross, cheerfully and efficiently helped to prepare the final manuscript. Typing was expertly done, at various stages, by Page Tyson, Julie Cannon, and Karen Bourassa. Dace Weiss prepared the index.

Particular acknowledgments are made in the notes. I would like at this point to thank those who have helped to shape this book in more general ways. For Irish history: W. E. H. Lecky and F. S. L. Lyons. For Yeats's life: Richard Ellmann, Joseph Hone, Philip Marcus, and George M. Harper. For textual matters: Curtis Bradford and Jon Stallworthy. For particular readings and insights into the workings of Yeats's imagination: Richard Ellmann again, Thomas Whitaker, Helen Vendler, Harold Bloom, Daniel Harris, George Bornstein, and Denis Donoghue.

Waterville, Maine   DA
Spring 1982

Introduction

In 1927 W. B. Yeats wrote "Blood and the Moon," his first poem explicitly devoted to Jonathan Swift and Swift's contemporaries, most memorable for those vivid and titanic portraits of them in the second section and for Yeats's imaginative excitement as he engages his predecessors. The opening stanza blesses Yeats's tower, anticipates his commentary on Swift's idea of liberty, and suggests his appreciation of Swiftian scorn. It is also an instance of Yeats's deceptively casual incorporation of Swift legend. In *Conjectures on Original Composition* Edward Young recalled an episode that was to become part of Dublin's ample lore about the Dean: "I remember, as I and others were taking with him an evening's walk, about a mile out of Dublin, he stopt short; we passed on; but perceiving that he did not follow us, I went back; and found him fixed as a statue, and earnestly gazing upward at a noble elm, which in its uppermost branches was much withered, and decayed. Pointing at it, he said, 'I shall be like that tree, I shall die at top.'"

Yeats converts the anecdote, as Swift had converted so much of his own experience, into an attack on modernism:

> Blessed be this place,
> More blessed still this tower;
> A bloody, arrogant power
> Rose out of the race
> Uttering, mastering it,
> Rose like these walls from these
> Storm-beaten cottages—
> In mockery I have set
> A powerful emblem up,
> And sing it rhyme upon rhyme
> In mockery of a time
> Half dead at the top.

xi

Swift is a compelling force in the conception and execution of "Blood and the Moon." Young's recollection must hover somewhere behind and within that powerful emblem of the first stanza. It is possible to estimate the degree of self-consciousness with which Swift's grim prophecy is invoked, the dimensions of his figure — what Yeats called "the half-symbolic image of Jonathan Swift"—in the poem, and the general significance of Swift to Yeats in 1927. It is possible, in other words, approximately to define and assess Yeats's encounters, what happens when his imagination meets the words or work, consciousness or presence, of another human being. Those encounters lie at the heart of his poetry. He may have been more gifted and fortunate in devouring and converting influences than any other modern artist save Picasso. To understand him we must take into account his extraordinarily athletic intellect and capacious imagination, his eclecticism, and his ability to transform everything to poetic use.

Throughout his life Yeats pondered the nature of personal identity and finally realized that an achieved identity is historical in two related ways: it depends not simply upon the individual, isolated ego but upon the interaction between that ego and the contingent moment, the social forces and ideas with which it makes its peace, truce, or battle. Further, personal identity is discovered and defined through that dialogue with history which all men semi-consciously conduct and which great men, especially great imaginations, actively pursue. Yeats is very serious in his continual search for historical continuity and coherence, his frequent claims that the true poet is "the last of a dynasty," his steady belief that "there is scarcely a man who has led the Irish people, at any time, who may not give some day to a great writer precisely that symbol he may require for the expression of himself." Thomas Mann, describing how his reading of Freud and apprehension of the past coalesce, called the completed search a "mythic identification." It is a deeply personal and open receptiveness to the past, whereby the creative mind intermingles past and present and so celebrates and reanimates both. A poet often discovers something of his own voice, and something of his autonomy, by a particular attentiveness to voices from the past. Yeats is unusually self-conscious about national or mythic identification. In the "Introduction" to *The Words upon the Window-pane* he is proselytizing, speaking to the "Cellars and Garrets" of Dublin about his, and as he claimed, Swift's idea of national life:

> If the Garrets and the Cellars listen I may throw light upon the matter, and I hope if all the time I seem thinking of something else I shall be forgiven. I must speak of things that come out of the common consciousness, where every thought is like a bell with many echoes....

This instinct for what is near and yet hidden is in reality a return to the sources of our power, and therefore a claim made upon the future. Thought seems more true, emotion more deep, spoken by someone who touches my pride, who seems to claim me of his kindred, who seems to make me part of some national mythology, nor is mythology mere ostentation, mere vanity if it draws me onward to the unknown; another turn of the gyre and myth is wisdom, pride, discipline.

He also knew the imagination's curious combativeness, its combination of receptivity and resistance:

I cannot discover truth by logic unless that logic serve passion. ... I must not talk to myself about "the truth" nor call myself "teacher" nor another "pupil — these things are abstract — but see myself set in a drama where I struggle to exalt and overcome concrete realities perceived not with mind only but as with the roots of my hair.

No matter how full the expression, the more it is of the whole man, the more does it require other expressions for its completion.

All that our opponent expresses must be shown for a part of our greater expression, that he may become our thrall—be "enthralled" as they say. Yet our whole is not his whole and he may break away and enthrall us in his turn, and there arise between us a struggle like that of the sexes. All life is such a struggle. When a plant draws forth and feeds upon the soil, expression is its joy, but it is wisdom to be drawn forth and eaten.

For an Irish writer the idea of thralldom is neither casual nor comfortable, and the sense of struggle, with its accompanying wariness and ambivalence, defines one form of imaginative interaction. But the relationship may grow, or be consummated, or spiritualized. The metaphors with which Yeats most often explores and adumbrates encounters are organic— an older writer nurtures a later one; or sexual—a tense but profound and productive union between two separate beings; or religious—the shock of recognition and affinity is a genuine revelation. The completed relationship, what Buber calls the saying of *Thou* across centuries and Eliot "a feeling of profound kinship ... or peculiar personal intimacy," is never achieved without struggle, and perhaps not without sacrifice; but neither is it, finally, competitive or predatory. It moves not so much beyond ambivalence as beyond defensiveness—to a special kind of mutuality and coherence which does not deny personal integrity or autonomy. Yeats, who felt that he could "hear Swift's voice," reflected often upon encounters and their value:

How much of my reading is to discover the English and Irish originals of my thought, its first language, and where no such originals exist, its relation to what original did. I seek more than idioms, for thoughts become more vivid when I find they were thought out in historical circumstances which effect those in which I live, or, which is perhaps the same thing, were thought out first by men my ancestors may have known. Some of my ancestors may have seen Swift, and probably my Huguenot grandmother who asked burial near Bishop King spoke both to Swift and Berkeley. I have before me an ideal expression in which all that I have, clay and spirit alike, assists; it is as though I most approximate towards that expression when I carry with me the greatest possible amount of hereditary thought and feeling, even national and family hatred and pride.

A study of that process, how the quest for "the originals of my thought" may lead to the achievement of "an ideal expression," is a useful and revealing way for us to encounter Yeats. It emphasizes imaginative growth and the many and various attempts to achieve a personal history, a realized self and a completed *oeuvre*. Some selectivity is necessary. So this book is organized around Yeats's interaction with the Romantic and modernist traditions in literature; his relationships with his family, especially his father, and his friends, especially Maud Gonne and Lady Gregory; the burden of his Anglo-Irish heritage and his celebrations of its major exemplars; his involvement with the occult, spiritism, and magic; his eclectic and willful historiography; his response to the turbulence of contemporary Irish and European culture and politics; his ardent desire to embody his belief that consciousness is conflict, to define and confront the antinomies of human experience, and occasionally to resolve them; and his need, at the end, to gather all the strands, to ready the achieved self for a new plunge into the void.

YEATS

1

The Last Romantic
Yeats and Coleridge

C oole Park and Ballylee, 1931," written under the pressure of Lady Gregory's final illness, concludes with one of Yeats's most assertive, plangent, and well-remembered stanzas:

> We were the last romantics—chose for theme
> Traditional sanctity and loveliness;
> Whatever's written in what poets name
> The book of the people; whatever most can bless
> The mind of man or elevate a rhyme:
> But all is changed, that high horse riderless,
> Though mounted in that saddle Homer rode
> Where the swan drifts upon a darkening flood.

It is possible to test those perceptions — Yeats's and many of his readers'—through a comparison of one of his most important poems, "A Prayer for My Daughter," with one of Coleridge's best, "Frost at Midnight," a meditation which defines one of the central types of romantic achievement. The poems are alike enough to permit us to call Coleridge's "A Prayer for My Son," and Yeats's (less happily) "Storm at Midnight"; both poems begin in an ordinary and therefore important domestic situation: Coleridge with his infant son Hartley in February 1798; Yeats with Anne Butler who was born in February 1919. Both begin with the composition of an actual and specific scene, Coleridge at Nether Stowey, Yeats in Galway. Coleridge is alone with his musings and his fire and his cradled son. Outside it is very still. He is anxiously aware of his separation from the landscape and his distance from the village, nervous about the solipsistic turn of his mind, reflecting on it all with an edge of self-contempt. His musings over the film on the grate recall his lonely and vulnerable schooldays in London, "pent 'mid cloisters dim," awed by the "stern preceptor's face," and beyond that his childhood in Devonshire and his beloved sister, "my playmate when we both were clothed alike," who provides this poem's definition of radical innocence.

In the third stanza the heard and felt presence of his son, his proper companion, leads to some hopes for Hartley: that his youth shall be rural, even pastoral, that his life in ordinary nature—lakes and crags and sandy shores—shall teach him about eternal nature, the visible language of God "who from eternity doth teach/ Himself in all, and all things in himself."

Stanza four returns to the scene—but it is an idealized scene, a scene of the imagination and of sacramental meaning. It is still very quiet, but the quiet of earned serenity rather than solitary uneasiness as paternal hopes discover their concrete embodiment in the sweet seasons to come to Hartley, and in "the secret ministry of frost" which "shall hang" its "silent icicles,/ Quietly shining to the quiet moon."

Yeats begins in storm-ridden gloom and anxious pacing. His cradled infant also slumbers peacefully—"sleeps on"—but the presence of Anne is no more soothing or sustaining than the presence of Hartley; and the repetitions in the first two stanzas emphasize gloom and anxiety and lead to nightmare excitement:

> Once more the storm is howling, and half hid
> Under this cradle-hood and coverlid
> My child sleeps on. There is no obstacle
> But Gregory's wood and one bare hill
> Whereby the haystack-and roof-levelling wind,
> Bred on the Atlantic, can be stayed;
> And for an hour I have walked and prayed
> Because of the great gloom that is in my mind.
>
> I have walked and prayed for this young child an hour
> And heard the sea-wind scream upon the tower,
> And under the arches of the bridge, and scream
> In the elms above the flooded stream;
> Imagining in excited reverie
> That the future years had come,
> Dancing to a frenzied drum,
> Out of the murderous innocence of the sea.

The third stanza abruptly switches to prayer—"May she be granted beauty..."—but it is social prayer, and a little banal, perhaps redeemed by its yearning for "The heart-revealing intimacy/ That chooses right." It also provides the first hint of the presence of one of the other females of the poem, Maud Gonne, a long-term obsession, who is to become its presiding evil genius, or demon. He then returns to admonition—"In courtesy I'd have her chiefly learned." And again the banality is redeemed, or almost redeemed, by yearning: in this case for a productive union between domesticity and sexuality. This is a marriage poem, too, though an altogether unconventional one whether considered generically or biographically.

The sixth stanza introduces the poem's second dominant image (the wind being the first), the laurel tree with its linnets, an emblem of art which carries the wish for music, magnanimity, merriment and location—rootedness.

By Yeatsian antithesis the seventh stanza admits the lack of those qualities, his own estrangement and contentiousness, and the absence of any genuinely fertile soil. The eighth goes on to attack Maud Gonne's intellectual hatred which perverted sexuality, preempted domesticity, and earned her not a perpetual laurel, but her own Paris/Hephaestus, Major MacBride whom she married in 1903, from whom she was soon separated, and who was executed by the British in 1916. Yeats had managed a rather qualified generosity in his poem on those events; but not now, as the hostility of "A Prayer for My Daughter" is political as well as personal:

> My mind, because the minds that I have loved,
> The sort of beauty that I have approved,
> Prosper but little, has dried up of late,
> Yet knows that to be choked with hate
> May well be of all evil chances chief.
> If there's no hatred in a mind
> Assault and battery of the wind
> Can never tear the linnet from the leaf.
>
> An intellectual hatred is the worst,
> So let her think opinions are accursed.
> Have I not seen the loveliest woman born
> Out of the mouth of Plenty's horn,
> Because of her opinionated mind
> Barter that horn and every good
> By quiet natures understood
> For an old bellows full of angry wind?

Stanzas nine and ten begin with the imagined disappearance of those conditions of hatred; then, like "Among School Children," the poem moves to a symbolic and visionary embodiment of its major assertions: the recovery of innocence, the discovery of self-sufficiency, the creation of Custom and Ceremony:

> Considering that, all hatred driven hence,
> The soul recovers radical innocence
> And learns at last that it is self-delighting,
> Self-appeasing, self-affrighting,
> And that its own sweet will is Heaven's will;
> She can, though every face should scowl
> And every windy quarter howl
> Or every bellows burst, be happy still.
>
> And may her bridegroom bring her to a house
> Where all's accustomed, ceremonious;
> For arrogance and hatred are the wares
> Peddled in the thoroughfares.
> How but in custom and in ceremony
> Are innocence and beauty born?
> Ceremony's a name for the rich horn,
> And custom for the spreading laurel tree.

Coleridge's meditation leads through recollection of innocence to a prayer that God, the Great Universal Teacher, "shall mold thy spirit, and by giving make it ask." Yeats's meditation leads to a prayer that his daughter shall recover the soul's innocence and learn that "its own sweet will is Heaven's will," that the soul's endeavors are the same as God's. For Hartley the necessary prerequisite is the perception of nature. For Anne it is the realization of Custom and Ceremony. The last stanza of each recapitulates the poem, but also redefines it. Coleridge's uneasiness has become serenity. The windbent trees have become the rich horn and the spreading laurel.

There are some clear differences between the surfaces of the two poems, most notably perhaps their dramatic situation and response, their weather. With Coleridge "The frost performs its secret ministry,/ Unhelped by any wind.... 'Tis calm indeed." With Yeats the wind howls and screams. But they are also symbolic landscapes—psychological, historical, moral—and a poem which places itself in the midst of a gale suggests a different state of being from a poem which places itself in "extreme silentness."

A second difference is Yeats's much greater allusiveness, which may seem odd as Coleridge is the more learned, more systematic, and more original thinker. Yet, except for the bit of folklore about the film and the stranger, we do not need any footnotes for "Frost at Midnight." Yeats, on the other hand, invokes a considerable range of reference: Helen's choice of Paris, Aphrodite's of Hephaestus, Apollo chasing Daphne, the cornucopia itself, which Jupiter tore from the side of a goat and which has become the traditional emblem of abundance. But Helen masks Maud Gonne, Aphrodite masks her daughter Iseult, and the "glad kindness" of stanza V delicately incorporates Mrs. Yeats into the poem. So there is a good deal of personal mythmaking. To put it another way, Yeats, far more than most lyric poets, assumes the existence of an *oeuvre* and our knowledge of it. His first letter has generally been read as the charming bravado of a timid teen-ager: "My dear Mary Cronan, I send you the verses you asked for I have very few poems under a great many hundred lines but of those I have this is the shortest and most intelligible its subject was suggested by my last visit to Kilrock. I am afraid you will not much care for it — not being used to my peculiaritys which will never be done justice to until they have become classics and are set for examinations. Yours truly, W. B. Yeats. PS As you will see my great aim is directness and extreme simplicity."

But I don't think bravado is the right word. In fact he did have mostly long poems; and I think he knew — knew what he was about and what the consequences were likely to be. It is true that all poetry is better read with the knowledge of other poems; but some poets are more self-conscious and aggressive about it than others. "Frost at Midnight" can be read in isolation; "A Prayer for My Daughter" demands that we know something else about Yeats, especially if we are to understand the vision of the future years in stanza two and the self-born qualities of the soul in stanza nine.

The substantial formal difference is that Yeats's poem is rhetorically loose and structurally tight. The voice is not wholly disparate; it slides rather than jumps, works modulations rather than juxtapositions. It has a fixed rhyme scheme and stanza form, Yeats's version of *ottava rima,* derived from Cowley's "Ode on the Death of Mr. William Harvey," and used for "In Memory of Major Robert Gregory" and "Byzantium," which gives it a termination and tightness that the more open-ended blank verse lacks. The five-beat line is flexible but does provide a sense of regularity. And the poem's images, especially those of wind and tree, are very carefully organized. We begin with the howling wind of nature and history, the murderous Atlantic and chaotic times which batter Yeats and his home. In the seventh stanza that wind becomes assault and battery, the angry wind of political disputation and intellectual hatred. And that wind has been exchanged — "battered" — for the cornucopia which becomes by the last stanza an emblem for ceremony and the beauty it sustains. In the first two stanzas the trees are bent by the screaming wind. They are contrasted with the laurel of stanza six, firmly rooted in the earth with the linnets in its upper branches "dispensing round/ Their magnanimities of sound." And these trees become, also in the last stanza, the emblem for custom and the innocence it protects.

Attending to the images defines two ways of attending to Yeats and describing his distance from Coleridge. A cabbalistic reading will say that this tree is the tree of life of various hermetic and esoteric traditions, that Yeats probably found it in McGregor Mathers' *The Kabbalah Unveiled* or was told about it by Madame Blavatsky, and that Custom and Ceremony are particular sacred rituals. Rosicrucianism and the occult do matter in ways that we shall have to investigate. Only in this poem—and in most of Yeats's major poetry—they matter rather distantly. The drafts make clear that the trees are first of all real trees at Coole Park, individually seen and even named ("Stand at the garden on the western side/ Near the Katalpa tree and call").

A more familiar view, or at least one held by more conventionally literary critics, is that Yeats is not the last Romantic, but the first Irish Symbolist poet, tutored by George Moore and then Arthur Symons, befriended by the Rhymers and watching them become "the Tragic Generation," struggling to understand Mallarmé in spite of inadequate French. For such a poet, necessarily isolated or estranged from ordinary society, symbols do not contain truth; they are truth, "radiant truth out of space and time." In this reading, Anne does not matter; Maud Gonne does not matter; Ireland does not matter—what matters is Yeats's creation of the symbolic equivalent of his own state of being, or consciousness, or desire. Yeats frequently wished for this to be true, and sometimes wrote as if it were. He wanted to believe that words alone are certain good, but was too badgered and battered to be sure. He wanted Maud Gonne to be Helen or Beatrice, but he knew that he was not Paris and that a spiritual marriage hurt too much. He did not live in Axel's castle, but in a Norman Tower in the west of Ireland, the place where invasions or liberations — both bloody—begin. It is surely a mistake, as Dennis Donoghue has said, to see Yeats "merely as Mallarmé's ephebe or a slightly more robust Symons.... There are moments in which he is satisfied with whatever the subjective will chooses to do, but there are other moments in which he is satisfied with nothing less than the truth, conceived as independent of his will." If he wanted to think or read or write as a Symbolist, he still had to face his empiricist or phenomenologist scruples. And after all, he stated the case emphatically at the end of "The Circus Animals' Desertion":

Those masterful images because complete
Grew in pure mind, but out of what began?
A mound of refuse or the sweepings of a street,
Old kettles, old bottles, and a broken can,
Old iron, old bones, old rags, that raving slut
Who keeps the till. Now that my ladder's gone,
I must lie down where all the ladders start,
    the foul rag-and-bone shop of the heart.

Return to the opening landscapes. Coleridge is aware of the owl, the frost, the fire; sea, hill, and wood; and the populous village beyond. Yeats is pummeled by a storm, by the "haystack- and roof-levelling wind/ Bred on the Atlantic." The phrase is not simply descriptive. Yeats often complains during these years about the urban wind of revolutionary or socialist doctrine that will break up the old alliance between aristocrat and peasant, landlord and tenant, between the haystack and the roof of the big country houses. The only protection against that wind is "Gregory's wood and one bare hill"—a tradition, the Anglo-Irish founders and planters like Sir William Gregory, and an eminence, that of the whole Gregory family, old friends of Yeats. But Gregory is long dead, Lady Gregory old and infirm, the hill barren and insufficient, the house and lands soon to be sold. The pathos of the poem comes from its over-riding sense of loss, as Yeats combatively celebrates a moribund culture from which he did not quite come. The complexity of the poem comes from the fact that this is an imaginative landscape as well as an actual one, that Yeats peoples it with good and evil spirits. We can discover the same sort of symbolic associations for the tower, the bridge, and the stream, as well as for the wind, trees, and birds. The elements of that landscape are a good deal less natural, public, conventional than Coleridge's.

The landscapes set the terms of the meditations and their resolutions. Coleridge's landscape is disquieting and leads to recollection. Yeats's is threatening and violent and leads to a vision of the coming destruction—a vision most emphatically drawn in "The Second Coming," which was written in January, 1919, a month before Anne's birth, and placed just before "A Prayer for My Daughter" in *Collected Poems*.

The global references in "The Second Coming" ("the world," "everywhere") may invoke the Great War and the Russian Revolution, but they also require a *caveat:* in spite of periodic gestures towards international politics, Yeats is really only interested in Irish politics, and steadily, intensely interested in that. "The Second Coming" and "A Prayer for My

Daughter" do have public as well as personal occasions. They are probably
the arrest and imprisonment of Con Markiewicz and Maud Gonne for
their alleged part in the "German Plot" against conscription, Sinn Fein's
victory over a coalition of moderates and loyalists in the election of 1918,
England's imposition of military rule in Ireland, increased guerrilla activities by the I.R.A., all the destructive beginnings of the Troubles which
Yeats was to confront in "Nineteen Hundred and Nineteen." His
apocalypses are also local. The deterioration of Irish life is the point of
departure for all three poems; what Yeats thought of as his conservative
revival is one of "A Prayer for My Daughter's" conclusions.

The terms are not only local, but domestic: What can one do? What
can I hope for my child in the face of social anarchy and personal willfulness? A prose paraphrase of Yeats's program is not very satisfactory. He
wants his daughter to be beautiful, but not too beautiful; courteous; free
from opinions and intellectual fire; settled in a comfortable and orderly
house. It is not very invigorating, and it may be reprehensible—snobbish,
escapist, ridden by male chauvinism and reactionary nostalgia. All those
qualities are there, overwhelmingly there if we think of the poem as a letter
(say to Lady Gregory) about his daughter's prospects. Some of Yeats's
letters do sound flat and shallow; and so do some lines from the early
drafts: "Grant her an even temper and good health/ A husband, children,
and a little wealth." But this is a poem not a letter and it is not simply or
primarily about what he would like his daughter to be.

It is a prayer for the recovery of the soul's innocence, a fact which too
many readers have managed to overlook. The New Critics have characteristically granted too much to Anglo-Irish snobbery (though they like to
call it *sprezzatura*) and too little to spiritual questing. Politically-minded
critics have attacked the snob and ignored the quester. "A Prayer for My
Daughter" asks—how can the innocent survive the chaotic forces of 1919.
To recover and sustain its innocence the soul must learn that

> it is self-delighting,
> Self-appeasing, self-affrighting,
> And that its own sweet will is Heaven's will.

Innocence must be *learned,* a strenuous discipline that helps to redeem the
banality of the fifth stanza. The burden is on the self. Nature is threatening
and history is destructive, moving out of murder into frenzy. The single,
vulnerable individual soul must create and maintain its own innocence.
How?

The poem suggests and dramatizes three very characteristic Yeatsian processes; the first is rooting, digging in. Radical innocence (contrasted with murderous innocence) means rooted innocence. Like the tower and the tree, Anne will, Yeats hopes, be sustained by "one dear perpetual place." What else is there to do if you are born in Sligo and settled in Galway, bound to the north by dour Ulster, to the east and south by the Catholic majority, and to the west by the wild Atlantic?

The second process is recovering, reinvesting, establishing value where the poem finds chaos; turning the screaming and angry wind back into the ceremonious and plentiful and mythological horn; turning the exposed and shaken trees back into the fruitful and musical and rooted, into the customary. So nature becomes art, and ceremony and custom — cornucopia and tree — are, like "Gregory's wood and one bare hill," defenses, barriers against willfulness and chaos.

The third is that centrally Romantic act, which Coleridge does so generously and movingly, blessing — casting out remorse, overcoming despair and repression, discovering a self that can give to a loved other. Yeats's plainest statement of this is the fourth poem of "Vacillation"; his most rhetorical is the last stanza of "A Dialogue of Self and Soul."

Action, not icon: ceremony, custom, and blessing are processes, and the poem which tries to create them is a process; The kind of life Yeats asserts is precarious and courageous and certainly most privileged — an elaboration of forms and formalities — just as the poem is both a demonstration of and insistence upon form. If "A Prayer for My Daughter" is to be compelling, Yeats has to start from scratch, from nothing, or perhaps from worse than nothing because he begins with an immense and pervasive threat. His response is to realize his symbols, to make them real. By the time he is through, his management of the symbols is altogether inseparable from the kind of life they represent. The act of the poem—its existence *and* its formalness — is the kind of act the poem itself is trying to make possible.

Some of the differences between Coleridge's poem and Yeats's are clear: a difference in scene and response which defines a difference in situation and attitude; an allusiveness on the part of Yeats which suggests that he feels he has to create a tradition, that the more or less public and available experiences to which "Frost at Midnight" alludes are not appropriate to him, that he must make his own experience public; so he is familiar and wayward with classical myth and does not hesitate to invent his own; a different apprehension and manipulation of forms and formalities.

The major difference is ultimately teleological; it has to do with assumptions about the nature of the world and experience. The third stanza of "Frost at Midnight" perceives a pattern: lakes, shores and crags; clouds which image lakes and shores and crags. The repetition of sea, hill, and wood in the first stanza had signalled a turning inward, the moment when the external scene was absorbed into consciousness. This repetition marks the realization of connectedness. Nature becomes NATURE, the visible language of God, which reveals divinity. Coleridge assumes the innocence of the child and the beneficence of nature. He assumes that significant and creative experience depends upon a coalescence of mind and nature. The poem is an act of discovery: of Hartley, of nature, of God. The anticipated relationship between God and Hartley of the third stanza —"he shall mold/ Thy spirit and by giving make it ask"—is a regenerative recapitulation of the troubling relationship between Coleridge and the film —"Echo or mirror seeking of itself" — of the first. Superstition and solipsism have become substantial faith and paternal generosity.

Because the poem is an act of discovery Coleridge can be more generous and less prescriptive and contentious than Yeats, who fights to recover the innocence of his child and then to protect it. Recovery and protection take place in the face of a nature and history that are equally capable of destruction. The poem denies neither nature nor God, but the soul must transform nature and create its own innocence. It must, by an act of will and imagination that the poem imitates and dramatizes, make its endeavors the same as God's, "its own sweet will Heaven's will." In the early drafts Yeats was willing to grant more beneficent activity to God ("Trembling for this child's peace unless/ Heaven pour abounding sweetness on his child") and able to imagine the return of Anne to Coole Park after his death. But the revisions removed both the divine gift and the sense of a secure future. "A Prayer for My Daughter" concentrates on the present moment, and the act of the poem is not discovery but making. It claims to create the correspondences rather than perceive them.

When Yeats talks about correspondence, which he most often does by talking about Symbolism, he plays out the full range of possibilities implicit in Romantic epistemology and in late nineteenth century reanimations and revisions of it.

At times he sounds like a thorough-going *Symboliste,* accepting the slogan—"To name is to destroy; to suggest is to create."—urging his readers "to dwell upon the element of evocation, of suggestion, upon what we call the symbolism in great writers," usually associated with "wavering, meditative, organic rhythms," and "the substance of ... style." He may invoke states of mind detached from particular words but located in individual consciousness: dreams, dream states, trances, "deep meditation," even madness. Sometimes he uses Imagination, like the eighteenth century, as that mental faculty which is not Reason. More often he follows

Blake: "'Vision or imagination'—meaning symbolism by those words—'is a representation of what actually exists, really or unchangeably. Fable or Allegory is formed by the daughters of Memory.'" He can claim creation *ab novo*, emphasizing the subjective will in conflict with, and at the expense of, external reality. He insists on perceptions not only of a redeemed and transformed nature, but of "something that moves beyond the senses," "disembodied powers," "invisible life," "a part of the Divine Essence." He may refer meaning to the *Anima Mundi* of his occult research, "traditions of magic and the magical philosophy." He may invoke what Jung called the collective unconscious and Yeats himself "the sudden conviction that our little memories are but a part of some great Memory that renews the world and men's thoughts age after age, and that our thoughts are not, as we suppose, the deep, but a little foam upon the deep." That transcendent reality may be carried and suggested by literary history (a "sacred book"), cultural history (an emblematic moment from the past defining both unity and fulness of being), even a particular historical personage.

So the making in "A Prayer for My Daughter" is a characteristic process; and it defines some major moments in Yeats, like the conclusion of "Among School Children" or the profoundly moving last letter, written to Elizabeth Pelham on January 4, 1939, three weeks before his death at age 73:

> I know for certain that my time will not be long. I have put away everything that can be put away that I may speak what I have to speak, and I find "expression" is a part of "study." In two or three weeks—I am now idle that I may rest after writing much verse—I will begin to write my most fundamental thoughts and the arrangement of thought which I am convinced will complete my studies. I am happy, and I think full of an energy, of an energy I had despaired of. It seems to me that I have found what I wanted. When I try to put it all into a phrase I say, "Man can embody truth but he cannot know it." I must embody it in the completion of my life. The abstract is not life and everywhere draws out its contradictions. You can refute Hegel but not the Saint or the Song of Sixpence. . . .

"Expression" is a part of "study"; making is a way to truth. If it can be done at all, it can only be done when the poem acts it out, when it embodies the ways in which ceremony and custom are recovered, innocence achieved, blessing given, form elaborated and insisted upon — when the poem makes the same qualities it protects.

Yeats may not have been the last Romantic, but "A Prayer for My Daughter" is a deeply Romantic poem, a poem with a difference as well as a debt, however, because it presupposes the loss of Romantic optimism and faith. That was not, of course, an easy optimism or a facile faith, and far too much has been made of "Romantic innocence." But there was, for Coleridge and his great contemporaries, a belief, often won out of pain, in the possibility of discovery, a hope that with strenuous effort and some luck the imagination could discover ultimate truth, and that the truth would be benevolent and sustaining. Yeats is less sure. He searches for assertion without belief, assurance without doctrine, conviction without dogma. "'One has had a vision,'" he turned away a skeptical and importunate questioner in London; "'one wants to have another, that is all.'" From his determinedly unideological father he learned to value personality rather than character, confidence rather than opinion, amplitude of being rather than logical consistency. This relentless quester long remembered that "even when I was a boy I could never walk in a wood without feeling that at any moment I might find before me somebody or something I had long looked for without knowing what I looked for." Experience often failed him, leading to "a kind of fright, a sense of spiritual loss," so that he finished *Reveries over Childhood and Youth,* months spent with his own past, "sorrowful and disturbed...when I think of all the books I have read, and of the wise words I have heard spoken, and of the anxiety I have given to parents and grandparents, and of the hopes I have had, all life weighed in the scales of my own life seems to me a preparation for something that never happens." He never ceases to strive, however, and almost always couples imaginative strength and artistic achievement with "faith in an unseen reality." He pushes Romantic or Kantian idealism into subjective idealism, as in his revisionary conflation of Berkeley and Blake, the astonishing claims of "The Tower," the heroic failure and loneliness of "The Man and the Echo," the attempt to accommodate history in "Meditations in Time of Civil War," and the personal appropriation of the myth of Cuchulain. Sometimes he surges past idealism and into solipsism, which becomes his great resource, and his great problem. That is why Yeats's most compelling poems and plays exist in the midst of conflict and on the edge of disaster—the disaster of the personal and social conditions in which they begin; *and* the possible disaster of the imagination's response and renovation. His victory is to transcend those disasters, his burden is to be overwhelmed by them. After much attentive waiting, Yeats understood that if the veil of the temple was going to tremble, he would have to do it himself.

2

Father and Son
John Butler and William Butler Yeats

A good deal has been said about the relationship between JB and WB Yeats, though much of it has been set in a context or seen from a perspective that is partial and misleading. The first context, inescapably, is Freud—often incompletely understood or unimaginatively applied. So JBY, in one account, is the "dusky demon...hung with slime" in Book II of *The Wanderings of Oisin*. So a few famous, nearly violent incidents have been accepted as the totality or the definition of their relationship—JB impatiently trying to teach WB to read and humiliating him in the process (*everybody* was worried about Willie's early education); the quarrels about Ruskin that led to an angry shove and an invitation to box. But those are isolated events and the hostility has been exaggerated. Elizabeth Yeats lived with the situation and her diary entry for September 1888, probably finds the right note: "Sept. 9....Papa and Willie are arguing something or other. Sometimes they raise their voices so that a stranger might fancy they were both in a rage; not at all, it is only their way of arguing because they are natives of the Emerald Isle....Sept. 18....Papa and Willie had a hot argument on metaphysics."

The second context is the characteristic, now mythic, Victorian pattern of filial revolt and self-discovery. It has been difficult not to see the Yeats family drama being played out on that very British stage. There is young Matthew Arnold distancing himself by being "Parisian"—jaunty, casual, and a touch wild—but then lamenting in one moving and incomplete poem after another a world that could not be as directed and orderly as his father's Rugby. There is Edmund Gosse emotionally and intellectually strangled by the rigid fundamentalist father who "prided himself on never having read a page of Shakespeare, and on never having entered a theatre but once." There is, especially, the intensely concentrated education of John Stuart Mill, where children's books, like other playthings,

13

were only sparingly admitted; an education of deep-rooted antipathy to verse and to "the English idolotry" of Shakespeare, a utilitarian sense of language and mind, an aversion to pleasure and playfulness as well as to error, and starved or constricted feelings.

JBY is not part of that pattern. He is one of the first rebels against it. He is always hostile to Puritanism, indifferent to organized religion, and skeptical about systematic education. He never thinks he is "the mortal vessel of truth" and so provides his eldest son neither the burden of obedience nor the open invitation to revolt. He most values what James Mill most disparages. It seems likely that some of his own educational views come from Mill's *Autobiography,* not so much because he endorses the son, but because he forms his ideas in direct and self-conscious antipathy to the father. He does everything he can to counter adolescent loneliness, to bridge the chilling and limiting generational distance. He will be for his sons what Wordsworth was for J. S. Mill in the crisis of 1826.

But WBY coming of age in the 1880s needs a Wordsworth as well as a father. He subscribes to the Victorian convention of revolt before any of his biographers do, and so creates the third and most pervasive context of misemphasis. The son of a rebel (or even of a simply unconventional father) is in a slightly awkward position, needing a battle but not wanting to sound reactionary, or silly, or fantastic. So "my father's unbelief" serves as the patriarch's restrictive belief; surface disagreements are made to seem substantial and agreements are tipped into differences: "I had come to think the philosophy of his fellow artists and himself a misunderstanding created by Victorian science, and science I had grown to hate with a monkish hate." His own retrospective sense of an unhappy childhood—a tricky combination of fact, convention, and need — gets attached to his father. As a young man WBY seems often to be searching for the liberation that Mill felt on tearfully reading the passage in Marmontel's *Memoirs* about the father's death. But JBY was not James Mill and he would not die.

Their relationship is alive and complicated, and there are important shifts and modulations as well as impressive continuity; it is unwise to be too schematic, but the pattern is clear enough to permit a chronology and some categories. From 1865 until about 1887 (WB's birth until his majority, when JB is 26 to 48) JBY is "Papa" or "Father," the vigorous presence of *Reveries.* The father is protective, supporting, impatient; the son is dutiful, awed, resisting. Between 1887 and 1908 (WB is 23 to 43, JB 49 to 69), the newly published poet discovers other fathers—O'Leary, Morris, Henley and Lady Gregory—and his resistance becomes liberation, sometimes deliberate and sometimes exultant; the father is usually enthusiastic, frequently corrective, sometimes edgy and resentful. After JBY's removal to New York (1909–1922; JBY is 70 to 82, WB 44 to 58), the roles often seem reversed; as WB assumes increasing financial responsibility for his father, he becomes protective and sometimes patronizing. JBY is anxious, a bit touchy, genuinely proud and grateful. Father and son talk to each other, by letter, more equally and openly than ever before. After his death in 1922 JBY joins his son's expanding mythology and becomes — like Synge, Lady Gregory, and Maud Gonne—a vital image of the later writing.

The early years were not promising. Until 1874 JBY was often away from his family trying to acquire skill and commissions in London. Susan Yeats — burdened with nerves, anxious about money, indifferent to his painting—remained in Sligo with the children. Robert's death in 1873 was a severe strain. JBY's sporadic attempts to educate his eldest son (though their grimness has been exaggerated) were no more successful than his own father's attempts to teach him mathematics. His frequent complaints about the Pollexfen-Middleton pressure, stern grandfathers and "dictatorial aunts' likely to break his son while trying to mold him, express the uneasiness and yearning of the too-absent father. A letter to his wife in 1872, written from Regent's Park, concludes with this brief and plaintive paragraph: "Tell Willie not to forget me."

At Bedford Park, Howth, and York Street, between 1876 and 1887, father and son are continually together. The sense of trust, so crucial to the growing boy, and the strong influence, so much a part of his maturation, form and develop. (Sixty years later, acknowledging congratulations on his seventieth birthday, WBY said that his achievements were "those things that accident made possible to me, the accident being I suppose in the main my father's studio.") JBY begins another of his careers—helping, advising, encouraging the young poet. His judgment of the early writing is confident, clear-headed, and high-hearted (to Dowden in 1884): "There was evidence in it of some power (however rudimentary) of thinking, as if someday he might have something to tell. ... So far I have his confidence. That he is a poet I have long believed, where he may reach is another matter." He organizes a subscription for *Mosada* in 1886 and presents a copy to G. M. Hopkins ("For a young man's pamphlet this was something too much; but you will understand a father's feeling."). He recognizes the need for an audience but tries to lessen the concern with a reception, mitigate hostile criticism, and provide accounts of informal praise. He is very astute about work and writing, urging his son not to find regular employment even though conventional opinion expects it, and the family needs money. He suggests writing fiction rather than criticism when poetry doesn't come, is immensely relieved when WBY declines a newspaper post ("You have taken a great weight off my mind"), and is steadily skeptical about WB's seeking or accepting a position at Trinity College — the colleagues would be dull, students preemptive, and politics conservative.

Oedipal tensions and divisions emerge in the late 'eighties and accumulate during the 'nineties. JBY is diligently though haphazardly the father of a family; WBY is making a self. He discovers new mentors ("dominating men like Henley and Morris," he later wrote Quinn), creates new activities, and explores new ideologies—theosophy, Blake, the Rhymers' Club, the Celtic Twilight, nationalist politics. He removes himself from the family circle, falls in love with Maud Gonne, has an affair with Olivia Shakespear, and gains the friendship and support of Lady Gregory. He remains primarily a writer, but becomes something of a literary man of the world as well—lecturing, editing, founding societies, managing a theatre, travelling to Europe and the United States. His letters, until now full of domestic details, rarely mention his father, and then casually. JBY's centrality to *Reveries over Childhood and Youth* is defined by his absence from *The Trembling of the Veil* and *Dramatis Personae*. When he does talk about his father, there is a new and dismissive note, as in his response to O'Leary's reservations about the occult: "The probable explanation however of your somewhat testy post card is that you were out to Bedford Park and heard my father discoursing about my magical pursuits out of the immense depths of his ignorance as to everything that I am doing and thinking."

On his part, JBY is struggling with the role of *paterfamilias*. Susan Yeats's strokes and incapacitation have left him a real burden, lost support, and increased, child-like need; rents from the family property ceased in 1888; painting did not produce income. He is a shaky and stumbling father, but responsive and caring, not so much determined to hang on to parental authority as anxious to have WBY fulfill his idea of the eldest son. Sometimes the results are comic. When he insists that Willie take the girls with him to French classes at William Morris' they cannot contain their giggles over the poet's pronunciation, and he quickly, resentfully, retires. Sometimes the consequences are more severe. In 1906 WB and Elizabeth quarrelled over the management of the Dun Emer Press when he tried to prevent the publication of book of poems by AE. JB interceded in the name of family affection; when WB replied that he did not need it, on the authority of Nietzsche, his father wrote two strong letters, punctuated by angry questions:

> As you have dropped affection from the circle of your needs, have you
> also dropped love between man and woman? Is this the theory of the
> overman, if so, your demi-godship is after all but a doctrinaire demi-

godship. Your words are idle—and you are far more human than you think....

The men whom Nietzsche's theory fits are only great men of a sort, a sort of Yahoo great men. The struggle is how to get rid of them, they belong to the clumsy and brutal side of things....

I never show your letters to them at home. Women are always apt to treat every utterance as if it is something final—and I don't think anything you say at present or for some time to come *if ever* is to be treated as final....

Did you stay too long at that English School, and have you a sort of airy contempt for women? If so cast it from you, it dishonors you as a man and a poet.

In spite of some real distance that has grown between them, JBY continues to encourage his son, and to correct and challenge him. He wonders if Swinburne might be right in one thing only, that the Celtic Twilight "puts fever and fancy in the place of reason and imagination." He interprets his son's various roles, insisting that "you are a public man in the Irish movement" and not "a Caliban publishing a volume of decadent verse." His skepticism about occultism and psychical research is not as thorough-going as the poet (and his biographers) think, and it is animated less by resentment over lost influence than by a concern that "magical pursuits" are often nonsense, and bad for the intellect. His letters consistently assert the fundamental values of intellectual energy, strenuous devotion to the truth, and a widely sympathetic sense of humanity. He perceives one drift of his son's mind into the hermetic and the esoteric, and another into the conservative and the authoritarian, and he tries to counter both.

Naturally, there is tension and pique. In WB's singlemindedness his father sometimes sees, and marks, egotism, selfishness, and ruthlessness; in JB's unambitious independence and sympathy his son often discovers drift, failure, "infirmity of will." Both are more often without funds than with them; JB has to suffer the indignity of asking his son for small loans and WB the awkward impatience of granting or refusing them. Worries become demands and short-tempered refusals which generalize into a defensive edginess not quite resolved by tacit apology. It is not necessary to keep score, but it is wise to remember that fathers, too, feel humiliation: "I wish Willie had Jack's tender, gracious manner, and did not sometimes treat me as if I was a black beetle"—a description glossed five years later when JB wrote that "German women are to their lords like so many black beetles."

The reversal of roles after 1908 is not surprising. WBY has arrived and JBY has departed to live across the Atlantic—lonely and lively and optimistic, fathering Van Wyck Brooks and John Sloan but ardently hoping for grandchildren, consulting sooth-sayers about the prospects, but never being sure until WB marries and Anne and Michael Yeats are born. WBY's interest in family history—how the Yeatses, Pollexfens, and Middletons connect with the rest of Ireland—antedates that marriage by a few years. In 1912 he urged his father to begin an autobiography; in 1914 he wrote *Reveries over Childhood and Youth* and published *Responsibilities,* with its familial and ancestral preoccupations; in 1917 he purchased Thoor Ballylee which became such a rich emblem of self and family and their complex relationship to national history. By now he is financially settled though not wealthy and takes on an increasing share of his father's support, conspiring with Quinn for a while and assuming formal liability around 1920 ("At last," JBY replied, "I shall be able to put aside money-making and acquire skill, as a palmist advised me to do years ago.").

Now it is the son who is protective, impatient, and a bit patronizing. JBY is grateful to and proud of his famous son, worried that he has been "an unconscionable burden," and hopeful that the self-portrait will redeem it all. He is also steadfastly unwilling to be merely the father of his son and aware of the perils that await his reputation: "I wrote to Willie some time ago and said it was as bad to be a poet's father as the intimate friend of George Moore. If you listen to Shelley his father was a monster, in reality his father was a well-intentioned and kind father, however mistaken he may have been in the handling of that rather strange person, his son.... all poets have a tendency to see facts metamorphosed. They will sacrifice anything to a tyrannous need of self-expression.... I am rather dreading Willie's forthcoming autobiography."

He nevertheless continues, through all the years in New York, to maintain his role of critic and guide—encouraging, optimistic, angry at attacks on WBY and careful to report praise; he has real confidence in his own judgments and continued confidence in his son's work. He sustains the old, corrective and challenging note, concluding one late letter with a complaint that poets have lost the courage of their imaginations: "How are they to get back their courage?—Please tell me Mr. W. B. Yeats." For WBY—fifty-six, famous, enjoying the satisfaction of refusing a knighthood —these questions must have been a little disconcerting.

WBY felt that his father's portraits of him were sentimental, seen "through a mist of domestic emotion." Perhaps—but two letters written during the summer of 1921, six months before he died, are impressively clearheaded. There is a very sharp recognition of the dynamics of the Oedipal situation, its sublimation as well as its aggression:

I am reading those chapters by you in the *Dial. I am grateful to you....*
[although] the unfortunate phrase "enraged family" may be thought
to mean something different from what I thought. There never has
been a moment in my life of meeting you, even though it was by chance
in the streets of Dublin, that it did not give me pleasure. As you will
find out, there is a feeling that of itself unbidden and of necessity
always springs into actuality when a parent meets his offspring, a sort
of animalism that defies control, for it is animal and primitive.

There is an assured claim of his own significance and a prophetic criticism
of his son's work:

When is your poetry at its best? I challenge all the critics if it is not
when the wild spirit of your imagination is wedded to concrete fact.
Had you stayed with me and not left me for Lady Gregory and her
friends and associations, you would have loved and adored concrete
life for which as I know you have a real affection. What would have
resulted? Realistic and poetical plays — poetry in closest and most
intimate union with the positive realities and complexities of life. And
that is the world that waits, so far in vain, its poet.... The moment you
touch however lightly on concrete fact, how alert you are! and how
attentive we your readers become!.... Every artist, poet and painter,
should have many visions—first the poem itself or the picture... and
then as part and parcel of that the vision of the man or woman or
landscape....

Am I talking wildly? Am I senile? I don't think so, for I would
have said the same any time these 20 or 30 years. The best thing in life
is the game of life, and some day a poet will find this out. I hope you
will be that poet. It is easier to write poetry that is far away from life,
but it is *infinitely more exciting* to write the poetry of life.

That is not biography and too casual for literary theory, but it is
strong and valiant. The language is dated but the perceptions are sound
and do in fact describe something very close to the mature W. B. Yeats, the
pre-Raphaelite and *symboliste* who grew up to become the last Romantic.
The letters were written just as the poet began his most breath-taking
decade, the years which produced *The Tower* and *The Winding Stair*. JBY
celebrates what he has helped to create and what will not bear full fruit
until after he is dead.

JBY's ideas do not form a coherent body of thought. His mind is
more derivative than original, more responsive than creative, more casual
than systematic. The life is brilliant and fruitful, but it is not so much a

monument to intellect as a triumph of personality. He not only survived his
burdens, but defeated them. The last letters poignantly reveal a sense of his
own death and of the fact that he will not go home. Yet he can misquote
Hamlet convincingly:

> Rough hew them how we will
> there is a providence that shapes our ends.

> I have no belief in what is called a personal God, but I do believe in a
> shaping providence—and that this providence is what may be called
> goodness or love, and that death is only a change in a world where
> change is a law of existence

and can finish a worried letter six months before his death with the voice of
Edgar after his, his king's and his father's holocaust: "'Ripeness is all.'"
   There are few lives that more movingly embody what Erik Erikson
has called the final stage of the life cycle, or "integrity": "It is the ego's
accrued assurance of its proclivity for order and meaning—an emotional
integration faithful to the image-bearers of the past and ready to take, and
eventually to renounce, leadership in the present. . . . It is a sense of com-
radeship with men and women of distant times and of different pursuits
who have created orders and objects and sayings conveying human dignity
and love." Shortly after Anne Butler Yeats was born, JBY wrote to
Elizabeth that he "would like to see Willie playing with his own child.
From the first, whenever American people came up to me in their American way and shouted: 'How you must be interested in your grandchild,' I
replied 'No, not a bit, but very much so in seeing my son as a father.' Is it
because I shall never see her grown up?" Some years later, Padraic Colum
asked WBY if it were inevitable "that a great figure should be succeeded by
lesser figures? It was, he asserted, and recalled Wellington's saying when
his son appeared: 'There is the only caricature that gets under my skin.'"
The old man's health and generosity of spirit is a great gift, and one that the
poet did not—could not—fully understand until many years later.
   The extent of JBY's creation—the precise nature of his influence upon
his son—is difficult to define. The poet lived a long life, and his father was
alive for all but seventeen years of it. It is important to explore the
interaction of their imaginations, though it cannot be done in quantitative
ways. JBY is unsystematic, abundant, and generous, scattering his wisdom
throughout three countries; WBY is eclectic and wayward, taking his ideas
and perceptions from all sorts of odd places, revising, transforming, and

always trying to integrate them. There are important matters that WBY does not discuss with his father, and there are moments when one feels that JBY does not quite understand what is happening in his son's mind, and how exciting it is. They exchanged hundreds of letters, but some have not survived and many are unpublished, and both men are notoriously cavalier about dates. WBY's letters are likely to be more newsy and less philosophical than JBY's; his responses are often brief, slightly distracted references; but this does not mean that he has not heard or will not use his father's ideas. Both men repeat and transform the other, and it is sometimes impossible to say who said what, and when. It is not a matter of cost-accounting, of intellectual debits and credits, but of suggestive patterns of influence, incorporation, and reciprocity.

There is, first of all, the father of *Reveries over Childhood and Youth* — the vivid teacher and strong example whom WBY at first self-consciously emulated and whose consequence he could never shake off. In 1910 he wrote to JBY that he was working on three lectures which formed "a plea for uniting literature once more to personality.... In the process of writing my third lecture I found it led up to the thought of your letter which I am going to quote at the end. It has made me realize with some surprise how fully my philosophy of life has been inherited from you in all but its details and applications." The "all but" is an important *caveat*. Nevertheless, the essential shape of that inheritance can be perceived. WBY, for all his urgent will to believe, never overcame his father's nineteenth-century skepticism and was frequently admonished and sometimes chastened by his liberal humanitarianism. JBY's enthusiastic sense of English and European literature, as well as his artist friends in London, was a permanent buffer against the various pressures towards Celtic insularity. His casual fascination with national and individual character types works its way into the psychology of *A Vision*. The "accident" of "my father's studio" is surely decisive in WBY's interest in painting and important to the visual, myth-making qualities of his imagination. His immensely attentive revising is a kind of transformation of JBY's endless retouching; when he wrote that bold quatrain:

> The friends that have it I do wrong
> When ever I remake a song,
> Should know what issue is at stake:
> It is myself that I remake.

he might have added that the issue is also generational, that sons remake their fathers as well as their selves.

He learned from his father, before he learned from experience, the burden of his anomalous Anglo-Irishry, the strain of living on both sides of the hyphen (or the channel) at once, which means not quite living on either side. JBY's uncertain national identity, though it never felt as precarious as the poet's, helps to shape his son's desire to reconcile the two Irelands, his estrangement when the Ireland that emerges is so different from the Ireland of his hopes, and his late, combative efforts to bring Protestant Ireland "back into the tapestry" of national life. The most substantial legacy is probably that strong sense of intellectual freedom and artistic independence — the one unequivocal commitment that both men make. JBY is likely to be carefree and ironic about it, and his son aggressive and hyperbolic; but the steel is always evident, and there are moments when the poet sounds like no one so much as his father. That most astonishing thing about WBY's life—its strong purposefulness and awareness of *œuvre* from the very beginning — develops partly in reaction to his father's frustrated career, but it is also deeply in his debt.

When WBY sent a copy of *Ideas of Good and Evil* to John Quinn he wrote in the inscription: "There is a good deal of my father in it, though nothing is just as he would have put it." That suggests the pattern of incorporation, the ways in which an increasingly confident WBY absorbs his father's ideas ("personality"), language ("a tongue to the sea cliffs"), or roles (the *Playboy* controversy) — and transforms them. JBY wrote, for example, two enraptured letters about Isadora Duncan: "dancing in the biggest theatre, and on the biggest stage in N. York—a figure dancing all alone on this immense stage—and there again you felt the charm of the self-contained woman. ... she stood still, she lay down, she walked about, she danced, she leaped, she disappeared, and re-appeared—all in curious sympathy with a great piece of classical music, and I did not sometimes know which I most enjoyed, her or the music" and it is difficult not to feel that this experience, much transmuted and in complex ways, reappears in "Among School Children."

Perhaps the most resonant instance of incorporation begins in July 1913 when JBY writes his son about a disturbing encounter in New York. Characteristically, it has impelled him to aesthetic generalization:

> Poetry is the reaction from the imperfect to the perfect—to a perfect grief as in Synge's *Riders to the Sea* or to a perfect joy as in your earlier poetry—the accompanying melody whether of prose or verse the effort to keep the heart soft and wakeful, portraiture in art or poetry the effort to keep the pain alive and intensify it, since out of the heart of the pain comes the solace, as a monk scourges himself to bring an ecstasy.

Some time ago I saw a young mother with a sick infant in her arms. I need not go into the circumstances, but I know that I put the question to her and that I was haunted by what I saw and heard for days and days. Why did I put these questions and why did I try constantly to recall and keep alive the incident? I regretted that I could not take my canvass and paint a portrait of her and her child. She was soft spoken, Irish and young and very pretty, from Donnybrook, and all her children had died in infancy. She was *ashamed* of her sick child and *tried to hide it from me*. She was not many years over and her father and mother dead since she left Ireland—her face full of goodness. I would fain scourge myself spiritually, and it pained me that the image should fade. The medieval artists lived among such sights and sounds and had nothing to console them but their religion, unless like Raphael they averted their eyes.

On August 5th WBY replies, nudges a bit about the autobiography, and, affected by the episode and his father's interpretation, suggests "a volume of criticism and philosophy extracted from your letters and lectures": "I thought your letter about 'portraiture' being 'pain' most beautiful and profound. All our art is but the putting our faith and the evidence of our faith into words or forms and our faith is in ecstacy. Of recent years instead of 'vision,' meaning by vision the intense realization of a state of ecstatic emotion symbolized in a definite imagined region, I have tried for more self portraiture. I have tried to make my work convincing with a speech so natural and dramatic that the hearer would feel the presence of a man thinking and feeling."

About a year later JBY returns to the experience and extends his interpretation: "I came away, and for days and weeks almost to this hour I am haunted and oppressed by the feeling of grief, of poignant depression which suddenly assailed me as I talked to that poor young woman. Had I been an active-minded philanthropist or a suffragette indignant with a man-managed world, I'd have got busy and never rested till I eased my heart by doing something to help." But he did not. He observed intently, asked questions, left reluctantly yet "hoping in a cowardly way never to see her again," and then spent two years trying to recall every detail. Why?

The answer is that every feeling and especially it might seem the painful feeling, tries to keep itself alive, and not only that but to *increase in strength*. This is the law of human nature and is what I have called the spirit of growth—in other words, I would have given worlds to have painted a careful study of her and her sick infant and carried it away with me to keep my sorrow alive.... all art begins in portraiture. That is, a *realistic* thing identified with *realistic* feeling, after which and because of which comes the Edifice of Beauty—the great reaction.

Two and a half years later, in February 1917, WBY completed the "Anima Hominis" part of *Per Amica Silentia Lunae.* At the center of that important testament is one of his most plangent, Paterian passages—and at the center of that passage is his father. Section V begins with the famous assertion, "We make out of the quarrel with others, rhetoric, but out of the quarrel with ourselves, poetry." (JBY had written, at about the time he first saw the girl from Donnybrook, "art embodies not this or that feeling, but the whole totality... when everything within us is expressed there is peace and what is called beauty—this totality is personality.... rhetoric expresses other people's feelings, poetry one's own.") "Anima Hominis" develops the contrast between the rhetoricians, sentimentalists, practical men and the artists, singing amid their uncertainty and their solitude: "They find their pleasure in a cup that is filled from Lethe's wharf, and for the awakening, for the vision, for the revelation of reality, tradition offers us a different word—ecstasy." He then recalls his father's letters: "An old artist wrote to me of his wanderings by the quays of New York, and how he found there a woman nursing a sick child, and drew her story from her. She spoke, too, of other children who had died: a long tragic story. 'I wanted to paint her,' he wrote; 'if I denied myself any of the pain I could not believe in my own ecstasy,'" and offers one of his most telling definitions of the imagination's integrity: "He only can create the greatest imaginable beauty who has endured all imaginable pangs, for only when we have seen and foreseen what we dread shall we be rewarded by that dazzling, unforeseen, wingfooted wanderer....He is of all things not impossible the most difficult, for that only which comes easily can never be a portion of our being. ... I shall find the dark grow luminous, the void fruitful when I understand I have nothing, that the ringers in the tower have appointed for the hymen of the soul a passing bell."

The old artist's encounter has become one of the texts of modern romantic consciousness — and the revisions matter. "The quays of New York" is rather too picturesque (JBY had said "on the west side as close to the Hudson as possible"). The young mother has lost her Donneybrook particularity and become suffering humanity, the object of the transforming imagination. JBY is made anonymous and so merged with Shelley and the romantic tradition. The sentence as recalled is not quite accurate: it makes JBY a little more single-mindedly the artist and a little less the compassionate old man, not yet a grandfather, trapped in his own pain and

impotence, what he called "my terrible sincerity in presence of any sufferings." The triumph of art in "Anima Hominis" is heroic, but triumph and
transformation are achieved at some cost. JBY's imagination is manifestly
less visionary and strong, but there is in his experience and account an
impressive human sympathy for particular beings, and a nagging awareness, conventional but salutary, of the irremediable differences between
art's makings and life's offerings.

If JBY is a teacher and a resource, he is also a partner in a continuing
dialogue. When he died WBY wrote to Olivia Shakespear: "I find it hard to
realise my father's death, he has so long been a mind to me, that mind
seems to me still thinking and writing." He remains a living mind and it is
possible to discern the pattern of reciprocity between father and son, that
shifting complex of assertion, revision, accommodation and (occasionally)
acknowledgment. Reciprocity sometimes transcends, but never elimi-
nates, the old Oedipal tension. So JBY writes a Christmas letter in 1913
about "my theory that the beautiful is the lovable made sensible." It has the
edge of neglect ("Again I am writing. ... Another important matter to
which I have drawn your illustrious attention. ... ") but it concludes
generously, urging his son to use whatever he wants without acknowledgment: "My individuality must not 'get in the way' — *nothing should
intervene between a lecturer and his audience* and there never can be any
question of egotism between you and me." WBY replies that "your last
letter came just in time to give me a most essential passage"; it is in fact a
rather qualified compliment since JBY's contribution has been to recall
one of the poet's own essays; but the appreciation is genuine enough: "The
curious thing is that this thought, which I feel certain of, has always, until I
got your letter, refused to relate itself to the general facts of life." Later on,
WBY concludes an extended argument about imitation and subjectivity
with a small but real concession characteristic of their best exchanges: "I
write all this not because I think it particularly striking or because I think
you have no answer to it, but to suggest to you some new thoughts which
will come to you from meeting it."

The dialogue includes extended conversations about art, style, and
intellect; about Anglo-Ireland, Celtic Ireland, the literary movement and
political events; about other national literatures and characteristics. They
correspond regularly about the relationships between belief, conviction,
and commitment; though the terms fluctuate a good deal, both men seek
personal assurance without the confinement of systematic doctrine, and
support each other in that search. Both like to recount and explore dreams
and value dreaming as an approximate visionary experience and as a
metaphor for subjective integrity. In 1914 JBY wrote that "a people who

do not dream never attain to inner sincerity, for only in his dreams is a man really himself. Only for his dreams is a man responsible—his actions are what he must do." *Responsibilities,* the volume of Yeats most preoccupied with family, published the same year, has as one of its two epigraphs, attributed to an "Old Play," the assertion — "'In dreams begins responsibility.'"

That vivid conversation of the York Street Studio continues for forty years. Father and son frequently wrote of an attitude towards human experience that combines tragic heroism, romantic optimism, and Anglo-Irish pride. Its points of reference are extensively literary, sometimes philosophical, occasionally political, and it appears in few men as strikingly as it does in either Yeats.

Painter and poet share the urge to denounce and rejoice, a yearning fascination with heroic proclamation in the face of chaos and loss. Right after the Easter Uprising and in the midst of the Great War, JBY writes from New York, "a man fighting at the Front, were he endowed with an absolute immunity from bullet and bayonet thrust and poisonous gas, would become in spite of himself a humorist. In the midst of the tragedy he would laugh. In any nation where the solitary abound there will be this kind of humor." In poems like "A Dialogue of Self and Soul" and "Lapis Lazuli," WBY celebrates that heroism with more imaginative fullness and capability than his father achieves—but the perception is the same, and even the poet's resolution is temporary and uncertain.

Behind tragic gaiety and heroic indignation, and allowing for their fleeting moments of perfect expression, lies what is probably the central doctrine of each man — that combination of unified culture, integrated intellect, and harmonious emotions that JBY calls "personality" and which WBY develops into "Unity of Being." In *The Stirring of the Bones* he writes that "true Unity of Being" exists when "all the nature murmurs in response if but a single note he touched," a figure elaborated in *A Vision's* description of Phase 11: "Unity of Being becomes possible.... Personality seeks personality. Every emotion begins to be related to every other as musical notes are related. It is as though we touched a musical string that set other strings vibrating." In *Four Years* he recalls that, around 1890, he "thought that in man and race alike there is something called 'Unity of Being,' using that term as Dante used it when he compared beauty in the *Convito* to a perfectly proportioned human body. My father, from whom I had learned the term, preferred a comparison to a musical instrument so strung that if we touch a string all the strings murmur faintly. There is not more desire, he had said, in lust than in true love, but in true love desire awakens pity, hope, affection, admiration, and given appropriate circumstance, every emotion possible to men." WBY is here recalling and conflating his father's remarks before the turn of the century, his own extended responses to them, and various letters from New York, like one JBY wrote during the summer of 1914: "Art achieves its triumphs great and small by involving the universality of the feelings—love by itself is lust, that is primitive animalism, and anger what is it but homocide? Art lifts us out of the sphere of mere bestiality, art is a musician and touches every chord in the human harp—in other words a single feeling becomes a mood, and the artist is a man with a natural tendency to thus convert every single feeling into a mood."

WBY replied in September, "I think with you that the poet seeks truth, not abstract truth, but a kind of vision of reality which satisfies the whole being." The idea of feelings and ideas integrated into moods had long been a kind of doctrine for both men. One of JBY's first philosophical letters—to Dowden in 1869—and one of WBY's last—to Elizabeth Pelham in 1939—make similar assertions. Both letters are marvelous and, in the context of the lives which produced them, very moving. Almost seventy years, two full careers, and countless achievements separate them; yet, they are not only compatible but complementary statements, and an appealing affirmation of generational continuity.

WBY is a stronger writer than his father, more the formalist, less happy about the Irish character, and more aggressively insistent on the autonomy of the imagination and its transforming powers. He is also, in *Estrangement* and *The Death of Synge* (the published passages of a diary for 1909), much more bitter: "Style, personality — deliberately adopted and therefore a mask—is the only escape from the hot-faced bargainers and the money changers." That is paternal wisdom squeezed into a rage by frustration and alienation. For JBY, personality—or "human nature when undergoing a passion for self-expression"—is also style, and style is ironic defense or intermittent achievement; for his son, during these grim years around Synge's illness and death, it is a weapon. Later on, under the different and intense pressures of civil war, in a poem that meditates upon it, he will make his legacy a curse as well as a gift.

JBY was still in Dublin during the *Playboy* controversy and the other events that contribute to the fury of *Estrangement*. His own account is characteristically relaxed and self-deprecating:

> Of course I did not make a speech in favour of patricide. How could I? Here is what I said. I began with some information about Synge which interested my listeners and then: "Of course I know Ireland is an island of Saints, but thank God it is also an island of sinners — only

unfortunately in this Country people cannot live or die except behind
a curtain of deceit." At this point the chairman and my son both called
out. "Time's up, Time's up." I saw the lifted sign and like the devil in
Paradise Lost I fled. The paper next morning said I was howled down.
It was worse, I was pulled down.... The sentence about the curtain of
deceit flashed on my mind at the moment, and was a good sentence,
but manifestly a blunder, although, I did enjoy it.

In his diary for 1909, WBY makes his father both more effective and more
detached: "No man of all literary Dublin dared show his face but my own
father, who spoke to, or rather in the presence of, that howling mob with
sweetness and simplicity. I fought them, he did a finer thing—forgot them."
Years later, well after his father's death and close to his own, the poet
returned to the event among the other reverences and recapitulations of
Last Poems and the late prose. His father has become, at the end, an image,
mythic, a member of all the heroic company. His personality—as being and
as doctrine — has *become* his son's utterance, an emblem. of domestic concern, artistic integrity, Anglo-Irish identity, and other beautiful
lofty things:

> My father upon the Abbey stage, before him a raging crowd:
> "This land of Saints," and then as the applause died out,
> "Of plaster Saints"; his beautiful mischievous head thrown back.

3

Friends and Friendship

Mrs. Yeats once told her husband, "'AE was the nearest to a saint you or I will ever meet. You are a better poet but no saint. I suppose one has to choose.'" It is a distinction Yeats seems to have endorsed in a short poem written in 1931:

> The intellect of man is forced to choose
> Perfection of the life, or of the work,
> And if it take the second must refuse
> A heavenly mansion, raging in the dark.

Critics, especially formalist critics, have taken the lines as a mandate to ignore the life while interpreting the text, or at least as a justification for making their own choice. It is certainly a mistake. Yeats rarely makes clean choices, presents us instead with a career of vacillations, or attempts—always willful and often heroic—to have it both ways. If he does make a choice (or if we must choose in order to decide how we are to understand him), he selected perfection of the life. Perfection means energy, intensity, and multiplicity, and in a few rare moments what he describes as ecstasy or beatitude. No less than Keats he thought that the poet leads a life of allegory and that his works are comments on it. Before comment, and as part of the process of perfection, comes transformation. "A poet," he said in one of his last and most comprehensive essays

> writes always of his personal life, in his finest work out of its tragedy, whatever it be, remorse, lost love, or mere loneliness; he never speaks directly as to someone at the breakfast table, there is always a phantsmagoria. Dante and Milton had mythologies, Shakespeare the

29

characters of English history or of traditional romance; even when the
poet seems most himself, when he is Raleigh and gives potentates the
lie, or Shelley "a nerve o'er which do creep the else unfelt oppressions
of this earth," or Byron when "the soul wears out the breast" as "the
sword outwears its sheath," he is never the bundle of accident and
incoherence that sits down to breakfast; he has been reborn as an idea,
something intended, complete.

It is possible to attend to that rebirth, to the process by which
accident and incoherence become complete, by which life, passing through
phantasmagoria, becomes meaning, and personal history becomes myth.
Friends and friendship provide a useful focus. Yeats was both purposeful
and lucky in this choice of friends: they are vivid and talented; most are
also articulate and productive so that we can achieve a reasonably clear
sense of them that is independent of Yeats's sense, and try to understand
the lives that he is transforming, and the nature and purposes of those
transformations. He is altogether self-conscious about the imaginative
uses of friendship. Writing in his journal after an Abbey quarrel in which he
had lost his temper and made an enemy, Yeats urged upon himself more
discrimination and exercise of will, for "a perpetual choice of the element
of friendship, being a daily creation, would be a perpetual exultation, and
is not all strength and faculty an exultation?"

As that sentence suggests, friendship is also a demanding discipline
and friends must be worthy of the choice. The journal continues: "We
artists suffer in our art if we do not love most of all *life* at peace with itself
and doing without forethought what its humanity bids it and therefore
happily. We are, as seen from life, an artifice, an emphasis, an uncompleted
arc perhaps. Those whom it is our business to cherish and celebrate are
complete arcs." If the difference between Coleridge and Yeats is the difference between discovery and making, the difference between a raconteur
(even a very good one, like his father) and Yeats is the difference between
reporting and summoning. When Yeats summons up objects and friends in
his poems and in some of his prose, he is peopling the world of his
imagination. To summon is to honor the reality of the beings summoned
while at the same time making them part of a rendered imaginative world,
part of a mythology. The poems about friends are a special and valuable
mixture of social history and poetry, neither art following life, nor life art,
but life and art informing each other, an achievement and a pleasure we are
invited to share. They are also autobiography, as Dennis Donoghue says,
"the perceiving subject takes itself as object, ponders his own case." As
Yeats realizes his people, and peoples his world, he is creating a self, his
own realized figure as man and poet.

Maud Gonne and Lady Gregory, along with J. B. Yeats, were probably the most important persons in Yeats's life, certainly those who most fully enter his poetry. We can begin with a relationship which, while less important, is relatively brief, contained, and well documented, and hence provides a model of the pattern and process of Yeats's cherishing and celebrating. In 1912 Yeats began visiting Mabel Beardsley who was dying of cancer in a nursing home in Hampstead. It was a sad and affecting situation. Mabel had been, from childhood, the most intimate companion of her brother Aubrey, who had died of consumption in 1898, but who was still a figure of scandal because of his startling and erotic drawings, his association with Oscar Wilde, and his involvement with *The Yellow Book* and *The Savoy*, the two most notorious journals of *fin de siècle* aestheticism. For much of the British public he was the quintessential figure of the Decadence; for Mabel he was the source of vitality and significance. She was the model for many of his drawings, his first teacher about sex, his partner in transvestite dressup. Whatever their sexual preferences and experience, about which there has been considerable speculation, it seems clear that their feelings about one another were incestuous.

Her life apart from Aubrey and his circle was less vivid. She was, briefly, a teacher at the Polytechnic School for Girls and a marginally successful professional actress, usually playing the other not-so-good woman and yearning to achieve that Edwardian status, the Society Beauty. Her long decline began with the trauma of Aubrey's death in 1898 and continued until 1916 when she died at forty-four. Those years were filled with melancholy, pain, and trivia — affectation and shallowness transformed by suffering; life's meaning sustained by devotion to the memory of her dead brother whose images (photographs of him, drawings by him) surrounded her; life itself lengthened by the ministrations of her mother Ellen, dutifully repeating the final nursing she had done years earlier for her other child.

Yeats wrote two letters to Lady Gregory about the visits, their effect on him, and some poems he was writing about both:

> Strange that just after writing those lines on the Rhymers who "unrepenting faced their ends" I should be at the bedside of the dying sister of Beardsley, who was practically one of us. She had had a week of great pain but on Sunday was I think free from it. She was propped up on pillows with her cheeks I think a little rouged and looking very beautiful. Beside her a Xmas tree with little toys containing sweets, which she gave us. Mr. Davis—Ricketts' patron—had brought it—I daresay it was Ricketts' idea. I will keep the little toy she gave me and I daresay she knew this. On a table near were four dolls dressed like

people out of her brother's drawings. Women with loose trousers and boys that looked like women. Ricketts had made them, modelling the faces and sewing the clothes. They must have taken him days. She had all her great lady airs and asked after my work and my health as if they were the most important things in the world to her. "A palmist told me," she said, "that when I was forty-two my life would take a turn for the better and now I shall spend my forty-second year in heaven" and then emphatically "O yes I shall go to heaven. Papists do." When I told her where Mrs. Emery was she said "How fine of her, but a girls' school! why she used to make even me blush!" Then she began telling improper stories and inciting us (there were two men besides myself) to do the like. At moments she shook with laughter. Just before I was going her mother came and saw me to the door. As we were standing at it she said "I do not think she wishes to live—how could she after such agony? She is all I have left now." I lay awake most of the night with a poem in my head. I cannot over-state her strange charms—the pathetic gaiety. It was her brother but her brother was not I think loveable, only astounding and intrepid. She has been ill since June last....

Mabel Beardsley said to me on Sunday "I wonder who will introduce me in heaven. It should be my brother but then they might not appreciate the introduction. They might not have the good taste." She said of her brother "He hated the people who denied the existence of evil, and so being young he filled his pictures with evil. He had a passion for reality." She has the same passion and puts aside any attempt to suggest recovery and yet I have never seen her in low spirits. She talked of a play she wanted to see. "If I could only send my head and my legs," she said, "for they are quite well." Till one questions her she tries to make one forget that she is ill. I always see her alone now. She keeps Sunday afternoon for me. I will send you the little series of poems when they are finished. One or two are I think very good.

They are good letters, informal character sketching of his father's kind, serious and likeable gossip. In the poems reportage becomes drama; her "great lady airs" and improper stories are shaped into "Her Courtesy":

> With the old kindness, the old distinquished grace,
> She lies, her lovely piteous head amid dull red hair
> Propped upon pillows, rouge on the pallor of her face.
> She would not have us sad because she is lying there,
> And when she meets our gaze her eyes are laughter-lit,
> Her speech a wicked tale that we may vie with her,
> Matching our broken-hearted wit against her wit,
> Thinking of saints and of Petronius Arbiter.

They are pictorial poems, finely rendered miniatures, informed, however, with more meaning and feeling than the genre usually carries. Yeats excludes the details — Ricketts, Florence Farr Emery, Mrs. Beardsley — which amplified the scene for Lady Gregory, but which would detract from the poems' concentration upon Mabel, her setting, and the response it elicits. He also excludes aspects of the situation, such as her remark about "my head and my legs," which would be more macabre and self-pitying than the tone of the poems wishes to allow. He emphasizes and develops the dolls; that is, he discovers, in the poems, a meaning only latent in the letters. Ricketts' act of pained solicitude becomes, in "Certain Artists Bring Her Dolls and Drawings," a qualified definition of generosity, and even of heroism:

> Bring where our Beauty lies
> A new modelled doll, or drawing,
> With a friend's or an enemy's
> Features, or maybe showing
> Her features when a tress
> Of dull red hair was flowing
> Over some silken dress
> Cut in the Turkish fashion,
> Or, it may be, like a boy's.
> We have given the world our passion,
> We have naught for death but toys.

The poem is also a recollection of the 'nineties in the shrug towards experience of its final couplet, and in the curious relationships it invokes. Mabel had posed for many of those hermaphrodite, little-boy-girl drawings. She was the model for those images made famous by her brother and which are now copied by their friends in order to comfort her. They are her connection with her lost youth and his lost life as she is losing her own. There is something morbid about the situation—the toys may grow out of incest and are certainly narcissistic—but there is also, in Yeats's rendering, generosity of feeling.

The episode most notably absent from the letters, though probably not invented as Mabel was a sincere Catholic, is the priest's arrival to say mass:

> Because to-day is some religious festival
> They had a priest say Mass, and even the Japanese,
> Heel up and weight on toe, must face the wall

—Pedant in passion, learned in old courtesies,
Vehement and witty she had seemed—; the Venetian lady
Who had seemed to glide to some intrigue in her red shoes,
Her domino, her panniered skirt copied from Longhi;
The meditative critic; all are on their toes,
Even our Beauty with her Turkish trousers on.
Because the priest must have like every dog his day
Or keep us all awake with baying at the moon,
We and our dolls being but the world were best away.

That is not mere anti-clericalism (Irish or *symboliste)* but an assertion both social and eschatological, an alternative way to face last things. Against the priest's grim notions of penance and preparation, the dying lady is gay, "fantastical and wild" (or Wilde). Like the Japanese doll with whom she is conflated—it is her toy and her image—she is a "Pedant in passion, learned in old courtesies,/ Vehement and witty." For someone with enough style, or the right kind of style, penance can be a kind of play. For her visitors, playfulness is a kind of penance, or at least real suffering, "matching our broken-hearted wit against her wit." If style can turn penance into play, it is also true that play, a form of conduct, is a kind of penance. We live, play, always with the knowledge of the finality of death, a finality particularly present, though poignantly muted, in these poems:

She is playing like a child
And penance is the play,
Fantastical and wild
Because the end of day
Shows her that some one soon
Will come from the house, and say—
Though play is but half done—
"Come in and leave the play."

Her courage is pagan as well as playful, associated not with the priest and his baying but with pre-Christian and non-Christian heroes—Grania and Diarmuid, Achilles, Tamburlaine; even the Cardinal mentions not God but Giorgione as he dies. Yeats's self-consciousness, the first-person responses explicit in the letters but dramatically subdued in the poems, now appears as he makes his most ambitiously mythmaking assertion:

When her soul flies to the predestined dancing place
(I have no speech but symbol, the pagan speech I made
Amid the dreams of youth) let her come face to face,

Amid that first astonishment, with Grania's shade,
All but the terrors of the woodland flight forgot
That made her Diarmuid dear, and some old cardinal
Pacing with half-closed eyelids in a sunny spot
Who had murmured of Giorgione at his latest breath—
Aye, and Achilles, Timor, Barbar, Barhaim, all
Who have lived in joy and laughed into the face of Death.

The sequence ends by returning myth to naked experience and assertion to prayer:

Pardon, great enemy,
Without an angry thought
We've carried in our tree,
And here and there have bought
Till all the boughs are gay,
And she may look from the bed
On pretty things that may
Please a fantastic head.
Give her a little grace,
What if a laughing eye
Have looked into your face?
It is about to die.

But it is experience—Mabel's as dying subject, Yeats's as attentive observer—enriched and enobled. Yeats summons his people into significance, realizes them for him and for us, without making them mere counters of the imagination. They retain their historical identity while Yeats discovers their poetic meaning—a meaning that, in these poems, includes the dead brother along with the dying lady. The speech, symbol, and dreams of youth in "Her Courage" recall the young Yeats at Sligo, but they also call up the Rhymers who "unrepenting faced their ends," the "tragic generation" of the *Autobiographies*.

Yeats began recording his memories in 1915, soon after he wrote these poems and before Mabel Beardsley died, and gave them final shape in 1922. "As I have set out to describe nature as I see it," he wrote, "I must not only describe events but those patterns into which they fall, when I am the looker-on." The first draft, now published as *Memoirs*, describes; *Autobiographies* discovers patterns. Although "The Tragic Generation" is not a complete account, it reveals a good deal about Yeats's sense of Aubrey Beardsley, a sense which was already in the letters to Lady Gregory and which had become part of the tact and tactics of the poems. As Aubrey remained the central presence to his dying sister, the dead artist is an important presence in the poems:

> And how should her heart fail her
> Or sickness break her will
> With her dead brother's valour
> For an example still?

He was not loveable, Yeats had written to Lady Gregory, "only astounding and intrepid." The "only" is for emphasis. Yeats admired Mabel's remark about her brother's "passion for reality"; he might have shaped and sharpened it; in *Memoirs* and again in *The Tragic Generation* he remembers saying "'Beardsley, I was defending you last night in the only way in which it is possible to defend you, by saying that all you draw is inspired by rage against iniquity.'" Beardsley was one of Yeats's principal exemplars in the case for intellectual and artistic freedom, the one public issue about which he is always clear-headed and unequivocal. He supported Arthur Symonds' insistence that Beardsley, who had been fired from *The Yellow Book* in the fury of hypocrisy that followed Wilde's trial and condemnation, be appointed art editor of *The Savoy*. He argued that literature should demand the same right as science to explore "all that passes before the mind's eye, and merely because it passes," whether it explore with high moral purpose or "gaily, out of sheer mischief, or that sheer delight in that play of mind." Artists like Beardsley and Baudelaire, he was to write in *A Vision*, exalted "intellectual sincerity to the place in literature which is held by sanctity in theology."

Yeats's defense of Beardsley and his rights as an artist is traditional and admirable. His more personal sense of Beardsley's life and work is idiosyncratic and shrewd. He is careful to dissociate Beardsley from Wilde and claimed, in *The Tragic Generation,* that "he had no sexual abnormality," that, in spite of his occasional misgivings, he neither looked nor behaved a sodomite. Yet Yeats recognizes the perversity and morbidity (as well as the genius) of Beardsley's art and imagination: "I see in his fat women and shadowy, pathetic girls, his horrible children, half child, half embryo, in all the lascivious monstrous imagery of the privately published designs, the phantasms that from the beginning have defied the scourge and the hair shirt." The antithesis of the saint who must exhaust pride in order to achieve humility, Beardsley's "preparation had been the exhaustion of sin in act" in order to achieve "a kind of frozen passion, the virginity of the intellect." He pictures not desire but disillusion, in an increasingly savage satiric art "where his powerful logical intellect eliminated every outline that suggested meditation or even satisfied passion." For Beardsley, in the system of *A Vision*, "entire sensuality is possible" but not romantic love, so he is fascinated by and driven towards evil, taking upon himself "not the consequences but the knowledge of sin" and thereby enabling "persons who had never heard his name to recover innocence." So Bearsley was a "victim"—one of Yeats's special modifications of Catholic theology to account for minds whose particular genius is antithetical to their historical and psychological circumstances. Yeats later decided that Swift, too, was a victim, his era's "poisoned rat in a hole." He justified the apparently odd association of the Anglo-Irish Dean with the English dandy by the willful but plausible assertion that the driven, terrible, and morbid satire of both men "made abstinence easy by making life hateful" and so fed a "hatred of life."

Not all of this, of course, is "in" the poems; but some of it is and the pressure of Yeats's complex awareness of Aubrey Beardsley is behind "Upon a Dying Lady." That pressure may be suggested by two recorded instances of Mabel and Ellen's reaction to Aubrey's illness and death. On the day he died Mabel wrote: "Our dear one passed away this morning very early—He looks so beautiful. He died as a saint. Pray for him and for us—The funeral is tomorrow at nine—We are broken-hearted, I cannot write more—He sent sweet messages to all his friends—He was so full of love and repentance." A few weeks before Ellen had said: "Some two or three weeks before he died, I was just going out when he asked me to put his drawing board, pen and other materials beside his bed. I think he wanted, when he was by himself, to see if he could draw, but he had not the strength. When I came in I found him lying with his face to the wall and he would not speak. After he was dead I found the pen sticking into the floor. I think he must have thrown it away, finding he could not draw."

The Beardsley women constantly recalled Aubrey, dwelling on his artistic and physical martyrdom. As Mabel approached her end, they almost certainly remembered his. It is not accidental that the language and feeling of Mabel's letter—our pain, his repentance—is incorporated into Yeats's poems. It is oddly appropriate that the response of her dolls (his and her images) to the last rites recapitulates his discovery that he can no longer draw, that the most important part of him had already died. After that death, Mabel too became one of the "shadowy, pathetic girls." One act of Yeats's poems is to rescue her from the shadows, to find strength and gaiety, and to revise "pathetic" into pathos. Instead of a monstrous image, she becomes "practically one of us." Yeats has incorporated her into her

brother's generation, turned her sadness into tragedy, triviality into courage, her final loneliness into heroic, or at least intrepid, company. It is
the last and best gift the imagination can give to the dying and the dead,
an especially Yeatsian kind of generosity, precarious and strong-willed
and moving.

A second act of the poems is self-determination, a judgment on some
of his own shadows. In 1904 he had written to AE complaining that "in my
Land of Heart's Desire, and in some of my lyric verse of that time, there is
an exaggeration of sentiment and sentimental beauty.... a region of brood-
ing emotions full of fleshly waters and vapours which kill the spirit and the
will, ecstasy and joy equally." This "region of the shadows" now rouses in
him "a kind of frenzied hatred" much as Beardsley excited in others, "but
he has never the form of decadence that tempted me and so I am not unjust
to him, but I cannot probably be quite just to any poetry that speaks to me
with the sweet insinuating voice of the dwellers in that country of shadows
and hollow images. I have dwelt there too long not to dread all that comes
out of it." Yeats returns to this angry revisionary impulse in the sections of
The Tragic Generation that look back to the turn of the century and
remember Beardsley, lamenting the "slight, sentimental sensuality" he
finds disagreeable in his early verse and in that of the Rhymers. Beardsley's
decadence does not bother him because it does not tempt him; the decadence or effeminacy of the other artists of the Nineties does. If Mabel
Beardsley had not lingered on, the poems would have been published in
Responsibilities (1914), the volume which emphatically declares Yeats's
independence from his late nineteenth-century forebearers and companions. She did not die until 1916; "Upon A Dying Lady" first appeared in
the *Little Review* for August, 1917 and was included in *The Wild Swans at
Coole* (1919). There, a little out of place, they are Yeats's valedictory poetic
celebration of the Nineties and one of his assertions of a new voice. He
pays his tribute and declares his growth, meditates and elevates, incorporates and moves on.

2

Most readers, at least for some moments, have wanted to be beguiled and
bedeviled by Maud Gonne, to believe in her beauty, presence, and force of
personality, to accept as complete Yeats's account of their first meeting and
many of the poems that echo it. After all, he said that that meeting

reverberated through his mind and imagination like the sound of "a Burmese gong, an overpowering tumult that had yet many pleasant secondary notes":

> Presently a hansom drove up to our door at Bedford Park with Miss Maud Gonne, who brought an introduction to my father from old John O'Leary, the Fenian leader. She vexed my father by praise of war, war for its own sake, not as the creator of certain virtues but as if there were some virtue in excitement itself. I supported her against my father, which vexed him the more, though he might have understood that … a man young as I could not have differed from a woman so beautiful and so young. To-day, with her great height and the unchangeable lineaments of her form, she looks the Sibyl I would have had played by Florence Farr, but in that day she seemed a classical impersonation of the Spring, the Virgilian commendation "She walks like a goddess" made for her alone. Her complexion was luminous, like that of apple-blossom through which the light falls, and I remember her standing that first day by a great heap of such blossoms in the window.

> What could have made her peaceful with a mind
> That nobleness made simple as a fire,
> With beauty like a tightened bow, a kind
> That is not natural in an age like this,
> Being high and solitary and most stern?
> Why, what could she have done, being what she is?
> Was there another Troy for her to burn?

> Maud Gonne at Howth station waiting a train,
> Pallas Athene in that straight back and arrogant head:
> All the Olympians, a thing never known again.

Those are stirring lines, but there are several other, less heroic and more revealing views of Maud Gonne, the most insistent note perhaps being the sardonic resignation of a diary entry in 1909: "Today the thought came to me that [Maud Gonne] never really understands my plans, or nature, or ideas. Then came the thought, what matter? How much of the best I have done and still do is but the attempt to explain myself to her? If she understood, I should lack a reason for writing, and one never can have too many reasons for doing what is so laborious."

In her autobiography, *A Servant of the Queen*, Maud Gonne records her view of the same problem: "I never indulged in self-analysis and often used to get impatient with Willie Yeats, who, like all writers, was terribly introspective and tried to make me so. 'I have no time to think of myself,' I told him which was literally true, for, unconsciously perhaps, I had redoubled work to avoid thought."

What there is here, and throughout A *Servant of the Queen,* is a failure of self-consciousness. It is not simply the choice of action over contemplation, but a deficient thoughtfulness — the easy generalization, "all writers"; the willful equation of introspection and self-indulgence; the opposition of "work" and "thought." Dr. Johnson would have said that Maud Gonne was an unideaed person, though it is probably more just to accept her own term, "one-idea'd," that idea being a total and unreflective commitment to Irish independence and a corresponding and undying hatred of England and everything English. It is a reasonable, even noble commitment, and an historically justifiable hatred; she was capable of impressive energy and dedication. It was not her politics that prevented her from understanding Yeats (O'Leary was a more serious nationalist and an astute and sympathetic critic), but her intelligence.

A *Servant of the Queen* is a distressing book. Even though it was published in 1938, well after Maud Gonne's career was over, it reads like a campaign biography, full of the conventionally "heroic" situations and stock responses. The narrative is flat and undifferentiated. Details of vastly different significance are given equal emphasis and color: the dress worn for her debut, the pain of a prisoner in Portland Gaol, the habits of her dog Dagda, O'Leary's force of personality, her pet canary ("Twee-Twee"), famine in the west, securing her inheritance or a revolver or poison, being trailed by spies or betrayed by the I.R.B., the starving Japanese student in Paris who "looked like a sick monkey and, because I like monkeys, we became good friends." Nothing is distinguished from anything else because everything is equally fascinating because it happened to me! The failure to think things through means inconsistency, lack of candor, and some self-deception. Yeats is self-consciously, ironically, and complexly theatrical; Maud Gonne is unreflectively, naively, and self-servingly theatrical. There is a softness and sentimentality about the prose that recalls, treacherously, Gerty MacDowell in *Ulysses.* Her recollection of the Yeats-Gonne tableau of the 1890s would be a bit much, even from a teen-age romantic: "A tall lanky boy with deep-set dark eyes behind glasses, over which a lock of dark hair was constantly falling, to be pushed back impatiently by long sensitive fingers, often stained with paint — dressed in shabby clothes that none noticed...—a tall girl with masses of gold-brown hair and a beauty which made her Paris clothes equally unnoticeable...." When she wrote it Yeats was two years dead, and she was seventy-five.

Her personal, political, and intellectual judgments seem frequently wishful and off-center, partly a consequence of ideology, mostly a result of her complete indifference to history and her highly selective response to ideas. Because of her feelings for Lucien Millevoye, a French journalist, political amateur and right-wing nationalist with whom she had fallen in love in 1885, she assumed that the Boulangists were disciplines of freedom in Europe, natural enemies of England, and dependable allies of Irish revolutionists. She insists that "there is no intolerance or bigotry naturally in Irish people," a judgment not easily sustained by historical analysis, and particularly undercut by her support for Millevoye's virulent attacks on Dreyfus, and an anti-semitism from which she never wholly recovered. She equates Parnell's failure with his repudiation of violence, and unguardedly celebrates Luke Dillon's "heroic attempt to destroy the Welland Canal" in Canada and so stimulate an Anglo-American war. Lady Gregory is dismissed as "a queer little old lady, rather like Queen Victoria," Synge's plays as Anglophile assaults on the Irish peasantry, and *Portrait of the Artist as a Young Man* as the "self-analysis of a somewhat mediocre soul who has failed to see and to understand the beauty it has lived among." Yeats's increasing distance from her own ardent nationalism is blamed on travel: "Miss Horniman brought back Italian plaques to decorate [the Abbey Theater] but Lady Gregory carried off Willie to visit the Italian towns where they were made and Willie's national outlook underwent a complete change. There would be no more poems against English kings' visits." If the tone is Gerty's, the politics approximate those of Joyce's "Citizen," promulgating his nationalism at Barney Kiernan's pub.

Biographers, Johnson tells us, are naturally inclined to perpetrate a wonder. The more so for lovers who are poets, and it is not a surprise that Yeats should create — from his beautiful, limited, arresting, infuriating woman — Cathleen Ni Houlihan, Helen of Troy, Pallas Athene, "a thing never known again." The process of that transformation, from woman to image, biography to myth, is difficult to recapture, but it can tell us something about the quality of Yeats's love and the workings of his imagination.

In the first place, his admiration was never unguarded. From the beginning his letters and diaries show irony, anxiety, and judgment mingling with the enchantment. He senses the willful theatricality: "mixed with this feeling for what is permanent in human life there was something declamatory, Latin in a bad sense, and perhaps even unscrupulous." He worries about "her desire for power, apparently for its own sake," her single-mindedness, restlessness, and incipient fanaticism. He can write with some relaxed irony about himself—"Did I tell you how much I admire Miss Gonne? She will make many converts to her political belief. If she said the world was flat or the moon an old caubeen tossed up into the sky I would be proud to be of her party"—and a more troubled irony about her —"I also knew that vague look in the eyes and had often wondered at its meaning—the wisdom that must surely accompany its symbol, her beauty, or lack of any thought." Furthermore, his feelings were always highly literary. He is ready to fall in love *and* ready to discover and define an emblem, his own Irish epipsyche. Soon after their first meeting he was planning *The Countess Cathleen* where Maud Gonne, in the title role, was to be a symbol of a symbol of Ireland. But the first Maud Gonne section of *Memoirs* begins not with apple blossoms and Virgilian commendations, but with the stark sentence, "I was twenty-three years old when the troubling of my life began." His long account of that troubling includes pity and melancholy, chargrin and fury, as well as passion and devotion.

The account also includes an extended though always implied comparison with Olivia Shakespear, called "Diana Vernon" in *Memoirs* and *Autobiographies,* the other woman in Yeats's early manhood, and a remarkably different influence, gentle, sympathetic, and benign. She was a novelist, widely and intelligently read, and unhappily married when her cousin, Lionel Johnson, introduced her to Yeats in 1894. Photographs confirm Yeats's celebration of her "beauty, dark and still." Their affair was conducted with much hesitation on both sides, and enormous tact on hers, and she may well have rescued Yeats from a nervous breakdown. They lived together in Yeats's apartment in London for a little less than a year in 1896 until a letter from Maud Gonne wholly distracted him once more, and she left, not to visit him for some years. She became a major steadying force in his life and the correspondent to whom he wrote most fully and unguardedly about his work. In "After Long Silence" he poignantly renders one of their later meetings, with its familiar regret for lost youth and search for some compensation in present wisdom, and in "Friends" he aptly thanks her

> because no thought,
> Nor those unpassing cares,
> No, not in these fifteen
> Many-times-troubled years,
> Could ever come between
> Mind and delighted mind.

There are more than a hundred poems plausibly associated with Maud Gonne; in many she is central, in many others marginal or incidental. They can be conveniently and more or less accurately divided into four groups marked by the events of their lives. First, those poems written between their meeting on January 30, 1889, and her marriage to John MacBride in June 1903. Second, up to the critical events of 1916 and 1917 —MacBride's execution, which left her free to remarry; Yeats's proposal; and, once again, her refusal; his proposal to Iseult Gonne and her refusal; his marriage on October 20, 1917, to Georgie Hyde-Lees. The third group was written between 1917 and 1936 or 1937; they are important poems in which Maud Gonne is never central, though often decisive, and always ambiguous. Then there are the recapitulations and valedictions of *Last Poems,* in which she is inevitably included.

The early poems depend upon two poetic conventions — the pre-Raphaelite versions of the Doomed Lover and the Dark Lady—and carry, most notably, Yeats's own longing:

> When you are old and grey and full of sleep,
> And nodding by the fire, take down this book,
> And slowly read, and dream of the soft look
> Your eyes had once, and of their shadows deep;
>
> How many loved your moments of glad grace,
> And loved your beauty with love false or true,
> But one man loved the pilgrim soul in you,
> And loved the sorrows of your changing face;
>
> And bending down beside the glowing bars,
> Murmur, a little sadly, how Love fled
> And paced upon the mountains overhead
> And hid his face amid a crowd of stars.

The feeling is genuine, but not yet attached to a presence that is recognizable, or recognizably Maud Gonne. During these years when Yeats felt he had a chance to win his lady, he cannot realize her in verse. It is only later, when his desire is wholly frustrated, that the poems achieve dramatic substance. Poems conceived in desire and in hopes of its fulfillment are rather bodiless; Maud Gonne only becomes a full sexual presence—a living body—when he has all but despaired of its possession.

Yeat's first play, *The Countess Cathleen,* might seem an exception. He wrote it for Maud Gonne in one of those attempts to become a public writer — "an Irish Victor Hugo," he ruefully recalled — and revised it frequently and extensively, always increasing the role of Aleel, the dreamer and poet, and so increasing the amount of "personal thought and feeling" he mingled with "the beliefs and customs of Christian Ireland." Given several letters written to Lady Gregory about the pain, anxiety, and ill-health Maud Gonne was causing him, it is tempting to see the three principal characters — Aleel, Cathleen, and her foster-mother or nurse Oona — as askew or parodic versions of Yeats, Maud Gonne, and Lady Gregory. Almost fifty years later, in the recollections of "The Circus Animals' Desertion," he seems to see a parallel: Cathleen's soul is pity-crazed as Maud Gonne's is enslaved by hate and fanaticism. He may have felt that way, and many later poems attack her fanaticism and lament her restlessness, but in this play Cathleen is serene and charitable, as Harold Bloom says, rather more like Christ than Maud Gonne.

The true exception is *Cathleen Ni Houlihan,* first performed in 1902 with Maud Gonne in the title role (she did not play the Countess). Michael Gillane bolts his marriage with its comfortable settlement to join the Fenians and help Cathleen drive the strangers from her house and recover her four beautiful fields. After a glimpse of Cathleen, Michael does not hesitate to leave his home and his bride; nationalism is also seduction. The famous last lines

> Did you see an old woman going down the path?
> I did not, but I saw a young girl, and she had the walk of a queen.

were given enormous effect by Maud Gonne's stage presence. She "played very finely," Yeats later recalled, "and her great height made Cathleen seem a divine being fallen into our mortal infirmity." The Virgilian commendation has found its objective, dramatic moment; the goddess, he had come to realize, is political as well as pastoral, a force to be reckoned with as well as admired.

Soon after *Cathleen Ni Houlihan,* in February 1903, Maud Gonne married John MacBride, an Irish nationalist who had fought against the British in the Boer War, and who was looking for work and direction. Yeats received her note as he was about to give a lecture. He managed to get through it, but—"the ears being deafened, the sight of the eyes blind/ With lightning"—he could not remember what he had said. Numerous poems record shock giving way to bitterness and bitterness then softened by continued longing and enormous regret:

> And what of her that took
> All till my youth was gone
> With scarce a pitying look?
> How could I praise that one?

When day begins to break
I count my good and bad,
Being wakeful for her sake.
Remembering what she had,
What eagle look still shows,
While up from my heart's root
So great a sweetness flows
I shake from head to foot.

That sweetness is qualified and ironic, depending as it does upon pain and loss. Even before the marriage, Yeats was cultivating an irony about Maud Gonne; or, rather, the facts of their situation, his dissatisfaction with his dreamy early verse, and his desire to write tougher and more conversational poems led to a fuller and more complex realization of Maud and an ironic awareness of himself and their relationship. As it becomes clear that she will not be won, she becomes a more vivid presence in the poems, and his poetic response becomes more complex. *In The Seven Woods,* published in 1904 and containing poems written before and after her marriage, registers the change. In "The Arrow" and "The Folly of Being Comforted" she begins to appear as a particular, definable historical personage rather than as the abstract Beloved, and his hopeless passion is presented with more irony and less melancholy. "Adam's Curse," the poem that most notably marks Yeats's turn to the dramatic ode and a more colloquial style, begins in the middle of a summer evening's conversation between Yeats, Maud Gonne, and her sister, Kathleen Pilcher. The curse is the difficulty of achieving the appearance of spontaneity in the three parallel labors of writing poetry, being beautiful, and professing love. The poem concludes with a marvellous landscape—a Yeatsian combination of the pre-Raphaelite and the Romantic—and then a thought that undercuts both the landscape and the brave protestations about love, beauty, and verse:

We sat grown quiet at the name of love,
We saw the last embers of daylight die,
And in the trembling blue-green of the sky
A moon, worn as if it had been a shell
Washed by time's waters as they rose and fell
About the stars and broke in days and years.

I had a thought for no one's but your ears:
That you were beautiful, and that I strove

> To love you in the old high way of love;
> That it had all seemed happy, and yet we'd grown
> As weary-hearted as that hollow moon.

Maud Gonne has written about the evening and the poem and its consequences, and her recollection is self-congratulatory and beside the point.
It may be ungenerous to fault her for being Yeats's beloved rather than
his critic, but she misses everything that makes the poem interesting
—its irony, its pathos, its assurance. *Sprezzatura* becomes soap opera in
spite of Yeats's determined efforts to make precisely the opposite transformation. Though Maud Gonne is writing long after the event, she does
not understand what the imagination has done with experience, and she
does not see that with "Adam's Curse" Yeats had become a mature poet. It
is dramatic recreation rather than lyric projection, conversation not croon-
ing; it is ironic not helpless in its frustration; and it demonstrates real
poetic confidence. The new assurance depends upon a lot of experience—
reading, tinkering, living. It also depends upon his increasingly clear ability
to achieve some distance from his subject.

The weary-hearted moon in "Adam's Curse" mimes the defeated
lovers. About ten years later, well after Maud Gonne became Madame
MacBride, Yeats wrote "A Memory of Youth" which returns to a moon-
dominated landscape:

> We sat as silent as a stone,
> We knew, though she'd not said a word,
> That even the best of love must die,
> And had been savagely undone
> Were it not that Love upon the cry
> Of a most ridiculous little bird
> Tore from the clouds his marvellous moon.

But now (1912 looking back on 1902) the moon is marvellous rather than
weary-hearted; it mocks rather than mimes; love asserts itself in spite of
Maud's failure to respond; the cosmos goes on. It is not obliterated as in
"The Sorrow of Love" or sympathetic as in "Adam's Curse." The moon's
detachment from the lover's drama mirrors Yeats's detachment from
Maud Gonne. In the poems of the nineties there was no irony at all.
Around the turn of the century there was considerable irony about the
situation and his role in it. When he wrote "Adam's Curse," Yeats assumed
that "we"—neither of us—shall ever marry—each other or anybody else. "A

Memory of Youth" knows better and the irony of its recollection attaches to Maud Gonne herself, not the situation. The other dominant image of the poem—"We sat as silent as a stone"—is part of the permanent iconography of Maud Gonne, perhaps the central image of her character and their relationship, as revealing as the invocations of goddesses, queens, and apple blossoms. It refers to qualities of her personality both perverse and tragic and to their cost to the poet.

In the summer of 1891, overcome with "an intoxication of pity" for her apparently wasted beauty, Yeats proposed for the first time. They sat in silence until she withdrew her hand from his and said that she could never marry. They spent days together until she returned to France and her underground activities for Millevoye and the Boulangists. Later she wrote a "letter of wild sorrow" and "incoherent grief" reporting the sudden death of a child, whom she said she had adopted three years earlier. The following fall she returned to Ireland on the ship which carried Parnell's body, "in extravagantly deep mourning" for her son, which everyone assumed to be for Parnell. She talked continually of the child's death, asked George Russell about reincarnation, and was told that a recently dead child could be reborn into the same family. Then followed what Richard Ellmann aptly calls "one of the most macabre events in pre-Raphaelite passion." Maud Gonne returned to France and summoned Millevoye to the memorial chapel she had built so that their child's soul might be reconceived. A second daughter, Iseult, was conceived.

After Iseult's birth in 1894, Maud Gonne and Millevoye were estranged and she spent more and more time in Ireland, organizing, protesting, visiting prisoners and graves. Yeats spent as much time as he could with her and one morning awoke from a dream "with the fading vision of her face bending over mine and the knowledge that she had just kissed me." He told her of the dream that morning and she was silent; that evening, however, she said, "'I will tell you now what happened. When I fell asleep last night I saw standing at my bedside a great spirit. He took me to a great throng of spirits, and you were among them. My hand was put into yours and I was told that we were married. After that I remember nothing.' Then and there for the first time with the bodily mouth, she kissed me." She then told Yeats the full story of her affair with Millevoye, the dead child, and the two-year-old daughter. Then, as Yeats recounts in the passage that concludes the first draft of his autobiography, they shared a spiritual marriage and a highly charged symbolic intercourse:

A little later, how many days I do not remember, we were sitting together when she said, "I hear a voice saying, 'You are about to

receive the initiation of the spear.'" We became silent; a double vision
unfolded itself, neither speaking till all was finished. She thought
herself a great stone statue through which passed flame, and I felt
myself becoming flame and mounting up through and looking out of
the eyes of a great stone Minerva. Were the beings which stand behind
human life trying to unite us, or had we brought it by our own dreams?
She was now always very emotional, and would kiss me very tenderly,
but when I spoke of marriage on the eve of her leaving said, "No, it
seems to me impossible." And then, with clenched hands, "I have a
horror and terror of physical love." Lady Gregory was in Venice, but
had come home at once on receiving from me an incoherent letter. She
offered me money to travel, and told me not to leave Maud Gonne till I
had her promise of marriage, but I said, "No, I am too exhausted; I can
do no more."

That stone statue, with its rejection of sexual love that is almost a
rejection of the human, returns again and again when Yeats thinks of
Maud Gone: "Maud Gonne is learning Gaelic. I would sooner see her in
the Gaelic movement than in any Irish movement I can think of. I fear some
new absorption in political opinion. Women, because the main event of
their lives has been a giving of themselves and giving birth, give all to an
opinion as if it were some terrible stone doll."
   It is a political as well as a sexual stone—the body politic as well as her
body—and Yeats insistently, sometimes obsessively, ponders the relationships between nationalism and seduction, sterility and fanaticism, to
explore both the cost and the achievement of personal and political dedication and fixity of purpose. The Kingston Pier tableau of 1889 must have
seemed to him uncanny in its symbolism: the beautiful Maud Gonne in her
mourning, the Uncrowned King in his coffin, both victims of a romantic
love Victorian England and Catholic Ireland considered illicit. She curtly
rejected Parnell because he repudiated violence; his fall from power
marked the end of any real hopes for a legislative and constitutional
settlement of the Irish question. Both of these proud and flamboyant
figures suffered intense personal loss; both experienced political failure;
both turned their character and their experience into a public issue, not
least through the observant imagination of W. B. Yeats.
   The spiritual marriage to the great stone statue in 1897 is probably
the culmination of Yeats's youth, and her actual marriage in 1903 is its end.
In 1900 Maud Gonne was not much interested in marriage to Yeats or to
MacBride; she was in Dublin to organize and lead demonstrations against
the celebration of Queen Victoria's Jubilee. Yeats was overwhelmed by her
energy, exhilaration, and power over crowds. He was also worried about

her and his own responsibility for destruction, injury, and death, and he wonders, watching her lead 40,000 children through the streets of Dublin, "how many of these children will carry bomb or rifle when a little under or a little over thirty?" The woman who has a "horror and terror of physical love" is ecstatic in situations that threaten to explode into violence.

Sixteen years later those boys and girls were around thirty. Home Rule remained frustrated by a recalcitrant House of Lords, British apathy, Ulster resistance, and Irish disorganization. On Easter Monday, 1916, a small group of militant nationalists — led by Thomas Clarke, Padraic Pearse, James Connolly, and Thomas MacDonagh—issued the proclamation of the Provisional Government of the Irish Republic, took over the Post Office and other public buildings, and held out for a week before surrendering. Within a month the British authorities had executed fifteen leaders of the uprising, including John MacBride, and so created the martyrdom that solidified Irish nationalism, precipitated the Anglo-Irish war, and led to the creation of the Irish Free State. Yeats was profoundly disturbed. In May he wrote to Lady Gregory that "The Dublin tragedy has been a great sorrow and anxiety....I am trying to write a poem on the men executed....I had no idea that any public event could so deeply move me— and I am very despondent about the future. At the moment I feel that all the work of years has been overturned, all the bringing together of classes, all the freeing of Irish literature and criticism from politics."

The poem, "Easter, 1916," an ambivalent testimonial to the herosim, despair, and consequences of the Uprising, is not "about" Maud Gonne. It is about national tragedy—politics and redemption—and will be considered in that context. Nevertheless, the third stanza, an apparent digression from the argument of the poem, is organized around that stone. It is a vivid, poignant, and bitter emblem of Maud Gonne, of their relationship, and of what Yeats believes can happen to romantic love, sexual pairing, human affection, and the myriad abundance of life under the pressures of revolutionary politics.

> Hearts with one purpose alone
> Through winter and summer seem
> Enchanted to a stone
> To trouble the living stream.
> The horse that comes from the road,
> The rider, the birds that range
> From cloud to tumbling cloud,
> Minute by minute they change;
> A shadow of cloud on the stream
> Changes minute by minute;

A horse-hoof slides on the brim,
And a horse plashes within it;
The long-legged moor-hens drive,
And hens to moor-cocks call;
Minute by minute they live:
The stone's in the midst of all.

Here, as so often from now on, Maud Gonne is a decisive presence in a poem that is primarily about something else. Yeats's letter to Lady Gregory continues that Maud Gonne had had a vision of the Dublin destruction which he had tried to make light of. "I have sent her the papers every day. I do not yet know what she feels about her husband's death. Her letter was written before she heard of it. Her main thought seems to be "tragic dignity has returned to Ireland.'" The following September Yeats visited her in France, where he completed the poem. Her account is revealing:

> So in 1916, before the magnificent flowering of the seed he had sown with pious exaltation, but left others to water, he stood amazed and abashed. In this mood he came to me in France where I was marooned by the World War. I found his mood hard to understand. The struggle of his mind can be read in his poem on Easter 1916....Standing by the seashore in Normandy in September 1916 he read me that poem; he had worked on it all the night before, and he implored me to forget the stone and the inner fire for the flashing, changing joy of life; but when he found my mind dull with the stone of the fixed idea of getting back to Ireland, kind and helpful as ever, he helped me to overcome political and passport difficulties and we travelled as far as London together. In London we parted; my road led to jail with Constance de Markievicz, and Cathleen Clarke.

There is a striking resemblance between this recollection (written in 1940) and her account of her earlier break with Millevoye (written in 1938): "For a long while I did not speak. I gazed at those cruel snow mountains which were turning my heart into stone in spite of the scent of the flowers and the hum of the wild bees around us, whispering of life.... Millevoye died when I, with Constance Markiewicz and Tom Clarke's widow, was a prisoner in Holloway Prison, accused of taking part in a German plot and grieving that the charge was false." For Maud Gonne love gives way to politics, human connection to jail, the stream to a stone. When Yeats conjoins personal feelings and public events, the result is characteristically complex and ambivalent, a study of the costs as well as the achievement of nationalist dedication and fixity of purpose. He admires and authenticates the heroism, but longs for the brimming stream of life that she repudiates. For Maud "tragic dignity" is not an insight but a weapon. She rejects the personal and the natural for a starkly simplified apprehension of the public—an apprehension that may lead to valid action but which ends in embittered solitude. Yeats was always aware of that possibility. As early as 1899 he had worried about her "life of hatred" and her "war of phantasy and of a blinded idealism against eternal law." Now he was shocked by her "joyous and self forgetting condition of political hate the like of which I have not yet encountered." Later, in a more relaxed and senatorial mood, he wrote that Ezra Pound "has most of Maud Gonne's opinions (political and economic) about the world in general, being what Lewis calls 'the revolutionary simpleton.' The chief difference is that he hates Palgrave's *Golden Treasury* as she does the Free State Government, and thinks even worse of its editor than she does of President Cosgrave." The figure of Maud Gonne is as much warning and monitor as muse and phoenix.

Still, the celebrations are glorious, and many of Yeats's poems in *The Green Helmet* (1910), *Responsibilities* (1914), and *The Wild Swans at Coole* (1914), are vigorously mythologizing. The mythmaking is double: a celebration of her beauty and power and his increasing skill. The poems are developments of the earlier Dark Lady-Doomed Lover tropes, but now there are notes of finality and pride—pride in pain overcome and beauty rendered. Maud Gonne becomes more of a presence as Yeats becomes more resigned to and ironic about his role as failed lover, and as he becomes more confident in his powers as a poet.

Maud Gonne's view of her role in all of this is predictably clear-cut. First, both he and the world were lucky she kept refusing him, so he would write about her instead. Second, "my real use to Willie was, I kept him in close touch with the people." That view seems confirmed by Yeat's frequent remarks that in all his joining and organizing "there was much patriotism and more desire for a fair woman," that throughout the endless meetings he watched her "as though I were a hunter taking captive some beautiful wild creature." But Maud Gonne as Yeats's common touch needs some thinking about. Her own relationship to the people is not wholly clear. O'Leary was gently but persistently skeptical, thinking her "but a beautiful woman seeking excitement." "'She is no disciple of mine.'" Yeats remembers him saying about a demonstration, "'she went there to show off her new bonnets.'" Sarah Purser (not an unbiased witness) told him that "'Maud Gonne talks politics in Paris, and literature to you, and at the

Horse Show she would talk of a clinking brood mare.'" Sean O'Casey, the only writer of the Literary Renaissance with real working-class credentials, felt that her knowledge of the people was scanty, willful, and manipulative, that they concerned her "only when they issued from their places headed by a green flag.... Here she sat now, silent, stony; waiting her turn to say more bitter words. ... There she sits stonily silent, once a sibyl of patriotism from whom no oracle ever came; now silent and aged; her deep-set eyes now sad, agleam with disappointment; never quite at ease with the crowd, whose cheers she loved; the colonel's daughter still." That is too harsh (O'Casey was writing about her opposition to *The Plough and the Stars*), but it is fair to say that she was more interested in the crowd than the people, action more than democracy. She was certainly a check on Yeats's estrangement and snobbery; but she was more emphatically an idea of fulfillment through action, an indictment of his sense of himself as dreamy and indecisive, a major force in his life-long imaginative struggle with the tensions between action and contemplation:

> She lived in storm and strife
> Her soul had such desire
> For what proud death may bring
> That it could not endure
> The common good of life,
> But lived as 'twere a king
> That packed his marriage day
> With banneret and pennon,
> Trumpet and kettledrum,
> And the outrageous cannon
> To bundle time away
> That the night come.

Maud Gonne does not mediate between Yeats and the people, but she often comes to stand for the nation—an idealized literary National Being which he wishes to create. A journal entry for May 1910 reveals the process:

> Les Mouettes, Colleville, Normandy. Yesterday afternoon, there being much wind and rain, we all stayed indoors—... and Maud Gonne and I got into the old argument about *Sinn Féin* and its attack on Synge, and the general circumstances that surrounded the first split in the Theatre. I notice that this old quarrel is the one difference about which she feels strongly. I for this very reason let myself get drawn into it

again and again, thinking to convince her at last that apart from wrongs and rights impossible to settle so long after, it was fundamental. I could not have done otherwise. My whole movement, my integrity as a man of letters, were alike involved. Thinking of her, as I do, as in a sense Ireland, a summing up in one mind of what is best in the romantic political Ireland of my youth and of the youth of others for some years yet, I must see to it that I close the Synge essay with a statement of national literature as I would re-create it, and of its purpose. It is useless to attack if one does not create.

The journal goes on for several pages of notes which are to become *J. M. Synge and the Ireland of his Time* (1911), an appreciation of his dead friend, meditation upon the creative process, and lecture about national literature. Yeats argues not primarily to explain himself to her, which he has long known not to work very well, but to transform her into an apt emblem for Romantic Ireland. Her actual presence and their specific quarrel becomes an idealized Ireland and a very ambitious public argument about politics, literature, and national identity "as I would re-create it." Personal relations become "my whole movement, my integrity as a man of letters." The rainy day gives way to "the Synge essay," a particular piece of writing which addresses fundamental questions. Maud Gonne is, all at once, antagonist, occasion, and audience. She stands for everything he has to combat, and everything he wishes to accomplish.

From 1917 on she is more often antagonist, or nemesis. In "A Prayer for My Daughter," published in the same volume as "Easter, 1916" though written three years later, Maud Gonne defines what Anne Butler should not be and what he has lost; she embodies a hatred and fanaticism that has preempted domesticity and perverted sexuality. In "The Tower" (1925) she is the woman lost, and the memory of losing can lead to the precarious balance between sanity and irrationality, the curse and triumph of the heightened imagination which that poem confronts. In "Among School Children" (1926) the vivid apprehensions of Maud Gonne—living child, Ledaean body, gaunt old woman—can occur only in fragments, which sets the terms of the quest for unity which the poem undertakes. In "A Dialogue of Self and Soul" (1927), a bitter pride has finally overcome remembered passion and beauty.

> I am content to live it all again
> And yet again, if it be life to pitch
> Into the frog-spawn of a blind man's ditch,
> A blind man battering blind men;

Or into that most fecund ditch of all,
The folly that man does
Or must suffer, if he woos
A proud woman not kindred of his soul.

The judgment is harshest, the ironic distance from her beauty and his passion most complete, in these four poems. They are among Yeats's most affirmative. Since he is not a poet of easy or consistent optimism, the conjunction is deeply intentional. Affirmation requires achieved repudiation.

3

Yeats's first recollection of meeting Lady Gregory sets the terms for his many subsequent invocations: "A few days afterwards a new friend, Lady Gregory, called and invited me to stay at Coole, and even before I arrived began collecting for me stories of faery belief.... I found at last what I had been seeking always, a life of order and of labour, where all outward things were the image of an inward life.... here many generations, and no uncultivated generation, had left the images of their service in furniture, in statuary, in pictures, and in the outline of wood and of field."

He shapes and amplifies that memory in *Dramatis Personae*—"Lady Gregory, in her life much artifice, in her nature much pride, was born to see the glory of the world in a peasant mirror," rigidifies it in *A Vision*—"The code must rule, and because that code cannot be an intellectual choice, it is always a tradition bound up with family, or office, or trade, always a part of history," and celebrates it in a dozen poems:

Augusta Gregory seated at her great ormolu table,
Her eightieth winter approaching: "Yesterday he threatened my life.
I told him that nightly from six to seven I sat at this table,
The blinds drawn up."

Mancini's portrait of Augusta Gregory,
"Greatest since Rembrandt," according to John Synge;
A great ebullient portrait certainly;
But where is the brush that could show anything
Of all that pride and that humility?
And I am in despair that time may bring
Approved patterns of women or of men
But not that selfsame excellence again.

On his first trip to Galway in 1897 Yeats found much of the Anglo-Irish past he was determined to discover and later to mythologize, an extraordinary (because fruitful) union of Big House and Cottage, the ancient Irish tradition and the Protestant Ascendancy establishment. Lady Gregory, born Isabella Augusta Persse, was the youngest daughter and thirteenth child of Dudley Persse, whose ancestors had come into Ireland during the seventeenth century, probably as part of the Cromwellian settlement of English families on Irish land. Family history represents class history. One ancestor, as Attorney General, prosecuted the patriot Robert Emmet; another gave birth to Standish Hayes O'Grady, one of the first native collectors of Irish folklore. Some Persses, including Augusta's mother and sister, exercised their Protestant zeal by proselytising poor Catholics, some of whom would "turn" for soup or subsistence employment. Others, including some brothers, were wild squireens, shooting, riding, and intimidating the countryside, like characters (as Yeats says), in Barrington's *Memoirs* of eighteenth-century flamboyance. The first Persse of whom there is written record, like Swift an Anglican Ascendancy Dean, built the family mansion, Roxborough, which was occupied by the I.R.A. during the Troubles of 1922, then burned to the ground. Lady Gregory had three dominant memories of growing up in that house. The adults were stern Protestants and unbending supporters of English hegemony in Ireland. The "strict Orangism of the drawing-room," was countered by the influence of her nurse, Mary Sheridan, a nationalist who remembered the cheers when the French landed at Killala in 1798, a Gaelic speaker, a Catholic, and a compendium of fairy tales and folklore. The nationalist impulse was furthered by patriotic pamphlets secretly brought and by an instinctive and abiding love of the Irish countryside which nurtured, over the years, a profound love of country.

In 1880 Augusta Persse married Sir William Gregory and so became part of a different Anglo-Ireland — the public world of service, achievement, culture and travel. Sir William was educated at Harrow and Oxford, twice served as member of Parliament for Dublin, and was a considerable success as Governor of Ceylon. He had his reckless moments as well, was a combatant in what may have been the last duel fought on English soil, won and lost a great deal of money on horse racing, and had finally to sell the outlying parts of Coole Park, the family estate, in order to pay his debts. This meant that he could no longer live off his rents; it also made him realize the wretched position of the Irish tenant. Originally a Conservative, he joined the Liberal party in 1865, was a friend and admirer of Daniel O'Connell, and supported agrarian reform and Catholic emancipation. He was an active and influential trustee of the National Gallery until his death in 1892.

Family history and connections imply a strong character, even a formidable one. She was a woman of personal dignity, determined will, and real capacity for work—"one must work or die or one's mind must"—who could demand as much of others as she did of herself. "The only wrong act that matters," she told Yeats, "is not doing one's best work." Consequently, in the widow's black she wore for forty years, she sometimes seemed austere and distant. J. B. Yeats writes of her "touch me not" attitude, her appearance of being "infernally haughty to lesser mortals"; but the same letter goes on to defend her disinterestedness and to admire her achievements. The chilly manner comes less from a sense of superiority than from a reserve, a shyness that bothered her as a girl and stayed with her through a long public career. If she seemed to some the Grande Dame, she was also capable of impressive self-effacement. The several journals reveal an ego always giving way to what is loved—family, Coole—and what is worked for — the Abbey, Ireland. She was a superb organizer and manager, but her assertiveness was rarely self-serving, a fact Yeats shapes into hyperbole, as he remembers an old peasant saying "'She has been like a serving-maid among us. She is plain and simple, like the Mother of God, and that was the greatest lady that ever lived.'" The most balanced judgment about Lady Gregory's will and sense of self is her own, written May 1918, in the full pain of her only son's early death:

What has been expelled from my life?

Interest in politics except as they affect Ireland. I think any sort of personal ambition. I have done some good work that the children may be proud of—Robert was. I would be glad to do more, because it is rather sad giving up creating—but not, I think, for praise. I have had enough.

Since Robert's death I do not covet money. I wished to leave him better off. I think the children [her grandchildren] will have enough for freedom from anxiety. I should like a little more to spend on woods and keep garden better, but if the sale of books goes on, I shall have that. Desire for Society went with Hugh's [Hugh Lane, her nephew] death, it could never be as pleasant as those Lindsay house visits.

I passionately wish for the children's love and their happiness. For the return of Hugh's pictures [from England to Ireland]. For the government of Ireland in the hands of Ireland; for the rebuilding to begin. For the increased worthiness of the Abbey until we hand it over. With all the anguish of Robert's death I have lost my one great fear of losing his affection. Now there is nothing that could hurt me so much to dread.

"Politics except as they affect Ireland" includes a great deal of politics, and Lady Gregory's are important, not least of all for what they will tell us about Yeats's. From Roxborough she inherited the politics of her class — Ascendancy in history, Unionist in assumption, aristocratic in tone and outlook. If she never exactly repudiated this position, it is because she was not given to irrevocable breaks with the past; but she thoroughly revised it in the course of her involvement with Ireland's turbulent modern history. Her love of people and place and the influence of Mary Sheridan challenged and chastened the narrow, Anglo-Irish Protestant gentryism while she was still a girl. Her marriage to William Gregory and the travel, reading, and conversation that accompanied it further enlarged and liberalized her views. She developed a steady resistance to unjust authority and an admiration for strong men, and in twentieth-century Ireland most of the strong people were nationalists. Her experience in the world also fostered her innate sense of restraint and decency; her response to the Easter Uprising, recorded in her journal, is a model of open-minded intelligence and good will. Isolated in Galway, cut off from knowledge and understanding of the events in Dublin, her husband dead and her son away in the Royal Flying Corps, she begins with Orwellian attempts to sift through rumors, exaggerations, and lies. Sickened by the bloodshed and destruction, she refuses to blame the rebels, whom she carefully calls "the disturbers," though she thinks them misguided. In the absence of letters and newspapers she reads through Shelley's political prose, and observes that "one begins to distinguish between the leaders who had some ideal, and the village tyrants." Her mourning for the dead rebels she knew — Pearse, Plunkett, MacDonagh, the Abbey actor Sean Connolly — is genuine, and without hysteria or blame. In the midst of another conflict she wrote, "we are back to the old story — English interests must have ours sacrificed to them. One hates one's own bitterness of feeling as much as the injustice itself." There is no denying the nationalist impulse of her work, or of her repeated assertion that the chief purpose of the Movement was "to bring dignity to Ireland." Dignity means self-respect, and it depends, in her view, upon both political and intellectual freedom, and serious artistic purpose, great effort and continuing judgment. The Theater should be devoted, she says in a late letter, to "art and a thinking Democracy."

So she becomes, in the course of a long and busy life, a "Republican without malice"; that phrase suggests the balance, but not the depth of her political feelings. "It did shake the nerves," she wrote in 1922 about the possibility of a terrorist attack on Coole, "yet at the worst moment I felt it was right, somehow. I should know what others had suffered in like cases, and that I might be glad later to have known it." She prays "for peace and 'the coming of Thy Kingdom' — in Coole — in Kiltartan — in Ireland. One measure of her achievement is the authenticity with which she is able to make those terms synonymous. Shortly before her death she thinks about her grandson's coming of age and contrasts it to her son's "with the gathering of cousins and the big feast and dance for the tenants—Coole no longer ours. But the days of landed property have passed. It is better so. Yet I wish some one of our blood would after my death care enough for what has been a home for so long, to keep it open." Such feelings require historical and political imagination as well as generosity of spirit. Like Thomas Hardy, with whom she had a good deal in common, Lady Gregory in her long maturity is liberal about the political issues, stoical about present conditions, and powerfully conservative about place, people, and the past. In a country struggling to free itself from foreign dominion, to declare and define a new national consciousness, that conservatism can be revolutionary.

Lady Gregory's admirers have maintained that Yeats does not do her justice. He never gives her work the full tribute which he said he intended and which it deserved. He is too inclined to see her writing as the occasion for or complement to his own and does not sufficiently acknowledge the genuine, creative help she gave him. He writes of their mutual surprise at the manifestation of her genius with guarded though unmistakeable condescension. He is, such critics say, the chief instrument in a "conspiracy of denigration and banishment" against her, as in his failure to include her among the potential members of "an autonomous committee of men of letters" he proposed to the Royal Irish Academy in 1926. There is some truth to these charges, though they are often overstated, and they obscure the real importance of Yeats and Lady Gregory to each other. It is true that he honors patriotism and determination, her existence as a cultural force, more fully than he does her achievement as a writer. He elaborately praises particular works, but does not give an adequate idea of the extent of her creative and intellectual achievement: eighteen volumes in the *Coole Edition,* including translation (the prose epics, the Kiltartan books, Molière), plays (at least thirty, about a dozen of which seem permanent), folklore and history (family, Coole, the Abbey, the Western Counties— necessary to any comprehensive account of modern Ireland). He sees her too often as manager and too little as mythmaker — maker of national ideals and identities—perhaps because her mythmaking was more objective than his own, more rooted in observed Irish reality.

The point about their collaboration is that they really did collaborate. "I hardly know how much of the play is my work," he wrote about *A Pot of Broth,* "for Lady Gregory helped me as she has helped in every play of mine where there is dialect, and sometimes where there is not." "If their style has merit now," he said of his early stories in 1925, "that merit is mainly hers." She understands the people, and dialect, and the play as action better than he does. He does not have Synge's gift—a sense of the people and of native language—and depends upon her for his approximations of both. For her part, Lady Gregory is not as bold or imaginative about themes and construction, has not his lyric genius, and learns from him about taking risks. Her careful and settled judgment about his influence seems right:

> If I had not met Yeats I believe I should still have become a writer, because my energy was turning to that side, and I had got a certain training in the editing of the *Autobiography* and the *Letter Box*. But I might never have found opportunity or freedom; I might have become a writer of middle articles in literary papers, or one of those "dull people who edit books" I was once in the early days of our acquaintance rather hurt by hearing him speak of. He is a severe critic of himself and others. He was slow in coming to believe I had any gift for writing, and he would not encourage me to it, thinking he made better use of my folk-lore gatherings than I could do. It was only when I had read him one day in London my chapter the "Death of Cuchulain" that he came to look on me as a fellow writer. From that time I read him each story or chapter as it was finished, and even when he did not criticise, the feeling that I was putting it to the test of his criticism was my greatest help, and I was glad when his prefaces to those first two books gave them his sanction and benediction.

His opinion of her work is, for the most part, just and generous, animated by understanding and sincere admiration. Even in the Nobel Prize speech where, it is true, he once talks as if her plays were an adjunct of his own and returns to the idea that "her genius must have seemed miraculous to herself," he admires her leadership and her language, her discovery "in that speech of theirs our most powerful dramatic instrument." After all, it is his occasion, and the fact that he chose to speak about Lady Gregory's and Synge's plays rather than his poetry is a significant tribute. He worked hard writing articles, founding societies, giving lectures to create an audience for their work, including hers, and his letters are full of praise. Where he seems guarded or even patronizing, her own comments support most of his judgments, as indeed she was a little surprised by the full flowering of her talent.

Yeats's letters to Lady Gregory are rather like those to a favorite aunt —open, honest, respectful, newsy, but not intimate. He writes about most of his central concerns—Maud Gonne and later George Hyde-Lees and then marriage and the experiences that led to *A Vision;* literary politics and literary journalism; folklore and the occult; a few national events, most notably the Easter Uprising; his finances, health, battles and successes—but he writes in a slightly detached way, a little on the surface. He is more likely to write about his chances of getting something published than about the writing itself, and about revision rather than creation. He needs support and advice, is grateful for hers, and trusts her judgment. She is a friend and a manager, not a muse. The letters say little about his deepest personal life, or about the workings of his imagination, its despair, excitement, or fulfillment. The omissions are appropriate. Lady Gregory was not his beloved or his daimon and both she and the poet had a considerable reserve, even with old and close friends (he begins his letters "My Dear Lady Gregory" or "Dear Friend" and signs them "Yours always, W. B. Yeats"). She matters to him greatly, but in a different way from Maud Gonne or Olivia Shakespear. She is important as a partner and guide, and (with occasional hesitations) as a writer and a creative force. She is also important as an emblem—a definition of the possibilities of Anglo-Ireland —and as a presence — a fully rendered life in his consciousness. Yeats discovers the emblem in his journals and creates the life in his poems.

The first aspect of that discovery is a sense of place and privilege, of having inherited the earth: "Lady Gregory is planting trees; for a year they have taken up much of her time. Her grandson will be fifty years old before they can be cut. We artists, do not we also plant trees and it is only after some fifty years that we are of much value? Every day I notice some new analogy between the long-established life of the well-born and the artists' life. We come from the permanent things and create them, and instead of old blood we have old emotions and we carry in our heads always that form of society aristocracies create now and again for some brief moment at Urbino or Versailles."

Yeats's task is to redeem the feeling from snobbery, to give it imaginative and historical weight so that it becomes a pattern of excellence rather than an expression of class privilege. He is most likely to fail when he is most angry and alienated, when Coole and its mistress are simply used as counters to attack bourgeoise Ireland (the tree-planting passage comes from *Estrangement,* a diary Yeats kept in 1909 to record his disillusion); he is most likely to succeed when he celebrates a world that he knows is doomed and passing. A week after Lady Gregory's death he wrote to Olivia Shakespear, saying that he could not write of it, trying instead to describe the pleasant gardens of his new house: "but as I write the words I know that I am heartbroken for Coole and its great woods. A queer Dublin sculptor dressed like a workman and in filthy clothes...came the day after Lady Gregory's death 'to pay his respects.' He walked from room to room and then stood where hang the mezzotints and egnravings of those under or with whom the Gregorys have served, Fox, Burke and so on, and after standing silent said 'All the nobility of earth.' I felt he did not mean it for that room alone but for lost tradition. How much of my own verse has not been but the repetition of those words."

Yeats was often estranged; Lady Gregory was not. Aristocratic in heritage and manner, she loved and was loved by the people of Galway, two qualities of life Yeats admired and envied. He also admired her strength and self-possession, her deliberate isolation "from all contagious opinion of poorer minds." Though rather too much has been made of the image of Lady Gregory as nurse and manager of an indolent Yeats, tortured and nearly paralyzed by sexual frustration and intellectual indecision, he did need her care in the nineties, and he continued to respect and often to emulate her determined sense of purpose and of self. "I have lost one who has been to me for nearly forty years my strength and my conscience," he wrote two weeks after her death; much earlier, when she was seriously ill, he wrote in his diary that "she has been to me mother, friend, sister and brother. I cannot realize the world without her — she brought to my wavering thoughts steadfast nobility. All the day the thought of losing her is like a conflagration in the rafters. Friendship is all the house I have."

These are the feelings—snobbery, yearning, affection, need, admiration — that Yeats transforms into some of his strongest poetry. In the journals there is sometimes a straining after meaning and weightiness, the will doing the work of the imagination, as Yeats is discovering Coole and organizing himself. In the best poems the image, her presence, is achieved, and Lady Gregory's life is rendered into public significance, as poetry mythologizes what prose defined and evaluated. "I cannot realize the world without her" implies realizing the world—making it real—with her. As so often in Yeats's poetry, making the world means making a self.

From the beginning, there is a sense of doom. Yeats's first poem about the building itself, "Upon a House Shaken by the Land Agitation," is written in response to the Land Act of 1909, which compelled large landholders to sell portions of their estates to the peasantry. Though the questions are rhetorical, the mood conditional, and the tone quietly triumphant, the poem does glimpse the ruin to come, an intuition which chastens the celebration of class interest. The implied loss makes the poem not really about land reform and economics, but about tradition and value, the ways in which place, through time and with luck and leadership, can become speech. Certain kinds of life, usually gifted and precarious, directly become culture:

> How should the world be luckier if this house,
> Where passion and precision have been one
> Time out of mind, became too runious
> To breed the lidless eye that loves the sun?
> And the sweet laughing eagle thoughts that grow
> Where wings have memory of wings, and all
> That comes of the best knit to the best? Although
> Mean roof-trees were the sturdier for its fall,
> How should their luck run high enough to reach
> The gifts that govern men, and after these
> To gradual Time's last gift, a written speech
> Wrought of high laughter, loveliness and ease?

The other Lady Gregory poems of Yeats's early maturity are either affectionately grateful or angrily assertive. "Friends" (1911) is Maud Gonne's poem, but it does contain a wholly sincere tribute to Lady Gregory's strength and understanding which "So changed me that I live/ Labouring in ecstasy." "To a Friend Whose Work Has Come to Nothing" (1913) is written in the bitter mood of *Estrangement:* "One must agree with the clown or be silent, for he has in him the strength and confidence of the multitudes." In it Yeats adopts the role he admired in Ben Jonson and, later, Edmund Burke—unpropertied but proud advisor to the aristocracy, and satirist of their enemies:

> Now all the truth is out,
> Be secret and take defeat
> From any brazen throat,
> For how can you compete,
> Being honor bred, with one
> Who, were it proved he lies,
> Were neither shamed in his own
> Nor in his neighbours' eyes?
> Bred to a harder thing
> Than Triumph, turn away
> And like a laughing string
> Whereon mad fingers play
> Amid a place of stone,
> Be secret and exult,
> Because of all things known
> That is most difficult.

The definition of political lying is acute and tonic; the discipline of the difficult is admirable and the advice curiously powerful. Still, as the strained repetition of "bred" and the uneasiness and inappropriateness of the concluding simile suggest, it was not a role Yeats could easily assume, at least not yet.

He is more assured in less social poems, like "The Wild Swans at Coole," written "in a mood of intense depression" during the Fall of 1916. The autumnal beauty, "brimming water," and "nine-and-fifty swans" of the lake at Coole Park antithetically define his own fatigued, passion-spent condition. He had once again proposed to Maud Gonne, and she again refused; it is not so much the refusal as his own inability to feel it that he now laments. The mysterious beauty and continuity in nature of the swans may suggest immortality; they certainly insist upon his own mortality, where awakening implies death. It is an unusual poem for the mature Yeats, fairly complex in its emotion, but simply organized, directly stated, and readily available. While the language and landscape are different from Hardy's ("Neutral Tones," for example, another pond poem), it has a similar immediacy and impact:

> Unwearied still, lover by lover,
> They paddle in the cold
> Companionable streams or climb the air;
> Their hearts have not grown old;
> Passion or conquest, wander where they will,
> Attend upon them still.
>
> But now they drift on the still water,
> Mysterious, beautiful;
> Among what rushes will they build,
> By what lake's edge or pool
> Delight men's eyes when I awake some day
> To find they have flown away?

Between 1916 and 1918 Yeats's and Lady Gregory's lives changed radically. The Easter Uprising and its tragic consequences drew on her stoicism and balance and deepened her nationalism. It demanded that Yeats reevaluate his politics, his assumptions about the quality of Irish life and the poet as a national figure, and that he modify the stance and the tone he had adopted in *Estrangement* and *Responsibilities*. The Rising also led, through a series of missteps, to his marriage. MacBride's execution left Maud Gonne free to remarry; Yeats again proposed and she again declined; he then proposed to Iseult who politely dissembled and declined.

In October 1917, his mind "unhinged by strain" he married Bertha
Georgiana Hyde-Lees (George), step-daughter of Olivia Shakespear's
brother, and wrote to Lady Gregory that "from being more miserable than
I ever remember being since Maud Gonne's marriage I became extremely
happy. That sense of happiness has lasted ever since." (Lady Gregory
replied: "It is really an ease to my mind your going into good hands.")
Marriage gave him the sense of comfort and potential family that he had
long wished for; it soon gave him a new sense of purpose as his wife's
automatic writing began the experiences that led to *A Vision*. It also gave
him a sense of place and history, of rootedness, as he brought his bride to
Thoor Ballylee, the tower and cottages which had been part of the Gregory
estate since 1783, and which Robert Gregory suggested that Yeats pur-
chase from The Congested Districts Board which had acquired the property for redistribution. It became his most personal emblem with intricate
and wide-ranging associations, both literary (Milton, Shelley, Villiers de
L'Isle-Adam) and historical (it was a Norman or Burke tower constructed
as a defense against invasions). It also represented a renewed commitment to Ireland, not quite to Sligo where he had been born, but close
enough, and removed from Dublin where he felt so embattled and
embittered.

   Then, on January 23, 1918, Robert Gregory, serving in the Royal
Flying Corps, was shot down over northern Italy. For Lady Gregory the
loss was incalcuable, her only child and the virtual end of her hopes of
keeping Coole in the family, and her restrained account of his death and
her response to it is very moving. Yeats grieved for the dead hero and his
stricken mother, pondered what the loss meant for her, for him, and for
Ireland, and wrote four poems of consolation and exploration. The first,
"Shepherd and Goatherd" (March 1918), "a pastoral, modelled on what
Virgil wrote for some friend of his and on what Spenser wrote of Sidney," is
more admirable in its impulses than secure in its achievement, partly
because of the difficulty of the genre in a twentieth-century setting, partly
because its chief ideas—Gregory's character and Yeats's occult beliefs—do
not conjoin well with each other, or with the classical models. Still,
"Shepherd and Goatherd" attempts something fine—a poem of genuine
consolation. The two speakers are Coole's tenants and antithetical figures
—Youth and Age, Valley and Mountain, social and visionary understanding of the event—who together summarize Gregory's talents and achieve
harmony by facing loss and giving comfort.

   Like "Shepherd and Goatherd" and the traditional elegy, "In Memory of Major Robert Gregory" (June 1918), aims to be a poem of lament
and consolation—sorrow for the hero's death and commemoration of his

enduring values—but it becomes as well a poem of deprivation. It is one of Yeats's most carefully crafted poems, perhaps the first in which he seems absolutely in control of his structure, the range of his voice, his movement through a complex experience. The first two stanzas establish the social and domestic situation, Yeats and his bride "almost settled" in their new home, entitled to anticipate warm celebration with old friends. Instead of conviviality and consummation, there is silence, as the most likely guests are all dead, present only in his fitful and somber thoughts (the key rhyme words—bed, dead, head—contain the situation). Stanzas III to V recall three friends who collectively define Robert Gregory, who are partial fulfillments of what he might have wholly embodied. Lionel Johnson, learned and courteous, was alienated from ordinary mankind and doomed to failure in an impossible quest for sanctity. John Synge discovered himself in the West of Ireland, but early death cheated him, and Yeats, of the wild and passionate celebrations he had earned. Synge, who "dying chose the living world for text," reminds Yeats of his own morbidity: living, newly married and settled, he cannot keep his thoughts away from the dead. George Pollexfen, like Gregory a skilled horseman, declined into stolid middle age, growing "sluggish and contemplative," which Gregory will never do, and Yeats worries he already has.

In the sixth stanza the three old friends recede into static recollection as the realization of Gregory's death, which has been accumulating force even though it has not been mentioned, makes all memory impossible:

> They were my close companions many a year,
> A portion of my mind and life, as it were,
> And now their breathless faces seem to look
> Out of some old picture book;
> I am accustomed to their lack of breath,
> But not that my dear friend's dear son,
> Our Sidney and our perfect man,
> Could share in that discourtesy of death.

It is a moment of remarkable restraint and power. Gregory is not mentioned, his death not faced, until halfway through his elegy. The eulogy—"*Our* Sidney..."—is both extravagant and limited, thus plausible. Death is a discourtesy to a man brave enough not to be afraid of it, who, alive, had made courtesy a discipline and a mode of communal harmony. The poem is a courtesy to "my dear friend" who "writes me grief-stricken but courageous letters."

In stanza VII Yeats looks outside the tower — "for all things the delighted eye now sees/ Were loved by him" — and discovers a landscape that recalls Gregory's painting and Synge's prose, a landscape that he is in the process of making Yeatsian. But the last line — "He might have been your heartiest welcomer" — contains no consolation; the tower remains bleak and silent; what "might have been" never will. The next three stanzas parallel stanzas III and V and summarize Gregory's accomplishments, his completion of the lives of Johnson, Synge, and Pollexfen as soldier, scholar, horseman, artist, Renaissance man of taste and culture who unifies action and contemplation. In the most moving lines of the poem Yeats claims a perfected society of artists properly located in the western counties; again the praise is muted and made plausible — "We dreamed" — by making the community small and the action conditional.

> We dreamed that a great painter had been born
> To cold Clare rock and Galway rock and thorn,
> To that stern colour and that delicate line
> That are our secret discipline
> Wherein the gazing heart doubles her might.
> Soldier, scholar, horseman, he,
> And yet he had the intensity
> To have published all to be a world's delight.

"Secret discipline" reminds us of the political context of this personal poem. In 1918, in the West of Ireland, the phrase would have been most readily associated with the secret discipline of Michael Collins' Volunteers, the military arm of Sinn Fein, fiercely opposed to the idea of English conscription of Irishmen during the Great War. The "our" defines a class contrast and suggests the moral and political complexities of an Anglo-Irishman serving in the Royal Air Force, a problem Yeats mutes here but fully, and grimly, faces in the last Robert Gregory poem. The eleventh stanza summarizes Gregory's career through a vivid metaphor which has been variously read:

> Some burn damp faggots, others may consume
> The entire combustible world in one small room
> As though dried straw, and if we turn about
> The bare chimney is gone black out
> Because the work had finished in that flare.
> Soldier, scholar, horseman, he,
> As 'twere all life's epitome.
> What made us dream that he could comb grey hair?

Is Yeats cannily admiring the slow fire of sustained accomplishment and implicitly criticizing Gregory's self-destructive energy? Is he self-contemptuously comparing his own damp life to Gregory's bright death? Is he arguing that the only escape from the toil of artistic subjectivity is early death? While the answers have depended upon the prose passages brought to bear on the lines, the stanza itself seems clear about Gregory and ambiguous about Yeats. Gregory's heroic fire is necessarily self-consuming; his life was extraordinarily full through inescapably short; no amount of tender memory can erase the fact of his death. The poet remembers, meditates, and suffers. He is neither ruefully admitting nor slyly claiming slow burning as his condition of life; the image's point in the poem is that it is not Gregory's.

The last stanza recapitulates the poem, reveals its structure, and returns to the opening scene, Yeats and his wife alone in the tower that is not yet a home. But the windy quarrels that are blown up by the intellectual combat of a coherent community, and softened by conviviality, have become the bitter wind of an alien and diminished world:

> I had thought, seeing how bitter is that wind
> That shakes the shutter, to have brought to mind
> All those that manhood tried, or childhood loved
> Or boyish intellect approved,
> With some appropriate commentary on each;
> Until imagination brought
> A fitter welcome; but a thought
> Of that late death took all my heart for speech.

Neither memory nor imagination has brought welcome; both have been overcome by the full recognition of Gregory's death. What should have been domestic joy and social coherence has become human silence inside the tower and natural assault without. It is a painful and complex experience and Yeats moves through it with great self-control. The poet's movement of mind is carried by the dramatic structure and by his shifts of tone, from chatty and convivial, to formal and elegiac, to the final silence. The poem's social situation, its implied audience and relation to that audience, first widens, then contracts. It begins with Yeats and his wife, then includes the company of dead friends, and then the larger audience of sympathetic readers-as-guests. Mrs. Yeats is the listener within the poem, but Lady Gregory is surely an implied auditor; in the sixth and eighth stanzas—"He might have been your heartiest welcomer," "We dreamed ... ," — the audience includes those who knew and loved Gregory and those capable of appreciation and mourning. After the conflagration of the eleventh stanza, which marks the moment in the poem when Gregory dies, and the wind of the twelfth, which suggests the consequences of that death for his society, the poet is virtually alone, talking to himself and lapsing into silent grief. The expansion and contraction dramatizes the way in which a wishful feeling of community between the living and the dead is overcome by discontinuity when the fact of death is fully faced.

"In Memory of Major Robert Gregory" achieves "the grave distinction of ... imagination" that Yeats admired in Gregory's painting. It is a model of Yeats's mythmaking. Friends define Robert Gregory; Gregory includes friends. People remain people, historical identities, at the same time that they become emblems and values. Gregory is dead, Yeats lonely and silent, but intensity, grace and courage remain to chasten and sustain a diminished world. The mythmaker exercises his privilege and the praise may seem overabundant, a little out of touch with the real Gregory, the Anglo-Irish gentry as they actually lived, and the facts of Irish life in 1918. The last two Gregory poems are more carefully qualified; they face the fact of Gregory's death from distinctly Yeatsian perspectives; they are explorations of the personal and political significance of the event rather than poems of consolation.

"An Irish Airman Foresees His Death" elaborates an idea that seems to have thrust itself upon Yeats when he wrote his first public tribute, a prose "Note of Appreciation" in *The Observer* for February 17, 1918. "I hope you thought my little essay on Robert was right," he wrote to Lady Gregory, "I tried to imagine to myself those who knew his pictures a little and what they thought and to write so as to settle and define their admiration." The first paragraph does just that. The second, which Yeats does not mention to Lady Gregory and which cannot have been part of her understanding of her son, begins with Gregory's versatility, and quickly turns to one of Yeats's central preoccupations, the relationship between action and contemplation, the burdens of subjectivity:

> Though he often seemed led away from his work by some other gift, his attitude to life and art never lost intensity — he was never the amateur. I have noticed that men whose lives are to be an evergrowing absorption in subjective beauty ... seek through some lesser gift, or through mere excitement, to strengthen that self which unites them to ordinary men. It is as though they hesitated before they plunged into the abyss. Major Gregory told Mr. Bernard Shaw, who visited him in France, that the months since he joined the Army had been the happiest of his life. I think they brought him peace of mind, an escape from that shrinking, which I sometimes saw upon his face, before the

growing absorption of his dream, the loneliness of his dream, as from his constant struggle to resist those other gifts that brought him ease and friendship. Leading his squadron in France or in Italy, mind and hand were at one, will and desire.

The poem renders that moment of hesitation, sees the death as a willed refusal to plunge "into the abyss" of the self, an impulse that is no less suicidal for being ecstatic:

> I know that I shall meet my fate
> Somewhere among the clouds above;
> Those that I fight I do not hate,
> Those that I guard I do not love;
> My country is Kiltartan Cross,
> My countrymen Kiltartan's poor,
> No likely end could bring them loss
> Or leave them happier than before.
> Nor law, nor duty bade me fight,
> Nor public men, nor cheering crowds,
> A lonely impulse of delight
> Drove to this tumult in the clouds;
> I balanced all, brought all to mind,
> The years to come seemed waste of breath,
> A waste of breath the years behind
> In balance with this life, this death.

"My country is Kiltartan Cross." "In Memory of Major Robert Gregory" accepts service to English military power with only a glance at its complexities; in "An Irish Airman" it is irrelevant; in "Reprisals," which Yeats wrote in late 1920 and withheld from publication so as not to offend Lady Gregory, it is culpable:

> Some nineteen German planes, they say,
> You had brought down before you died.
> We called it a good death. Today
> Can ghost or man be satisfied?
> Although your last exciting year
> Outweighed all other years, you said,
> Though battle joy may be so dear
> A memory, even to the dead,
> It chases other thought away,
> Yet rise from your Italian tomb

Flit to Kiltartan cross and stay
Till certain second thoughts have come
Upon the cause you served, that we
Imagined such a fine affair:
Half-drunk or whole-mad soldiery
Are murdering your tenants there.
Men that revere your father yet
Are shot at on the open plain.
Where may new-married women sit
And suckle children now? Armed men
May murder them in passing by
Nor law nor parliment take heed.
Then close your ears with dust and lie
Among the other cheated dead.

In this last and astonishingly bitter poem, written during the terror-ridden months of the Anglo-Irish war, Gregory is not a Renaissance or legendary hero (Sidney, Cuchulain), but a historical victim (Swift, Parnell) betrayed alike by English bad faith and rapacity and Irish madness and bestiality. Neither Yeats nor Lady Gregory knew that he had been shot down in error by an Italian pilot.

In April 1927 Lady Gregory sold Coole to the Irish Land Commission and Department of Forestry. Daniel Harris has described the significance of that decision: "Although she occupied the house until she died in 1932, her familial guilt was great: she considered her act the destruction of a fine tradition and the betrayal of her grandson's birthright. She had signed away the principal symbol of the literary renaissance; decreased participation in Abbey affairs, the loss of close friends, recurrent cancer, and intermittent broodings on death made the sale a personal and historical crisis." Her journals sound weary and defeated, at moments almost pathetic. The day after learning of her decision to lease Coole, Yeats decided to give up Thoor Ballylee. He wrote two important poems about the estate, its mistress, its history, and personal and national significance, "Coole Park, 1929," and "Coole Park and Ballylee, 1931." They make a better tribute than *Dramatis Personae* or "The Irish Dramatic Movement," richer, fuller, more intimate, and more balanced. In these poems Yeats achieves his role. He can affirm the Anglo-Irish aristocracy without false notes because the central fact of his affirmation is its transcience; the aristocracy of which Lady Gregory is the ideal exemplar is passing, perhaps has passed, into history and myth. In his own old age Yeats is imaginatively most confident when most embattled, when he articulates a sense of well-being that can only be fleeting, or indulges a youth he no longer has, or celebrates a dying society from which he did not quite come. "Coole Park, 1929" was completed at Coole in 1928 and published as a preface to Lady Gregory's *Coole,* one last "sanction and benediction" of her work. It begins randomly, a meditation in search of a unifying subject, which it finds at the close of the first stanza, as the swallows flight is metamorphosed into the vague but resonant glory given birth by the Gregory estate:

> I meditate upon a swallow's flight,
> Upon an aged woman and her house,
> A sycamore and lime-tree lost in night
> Although that western cloud is luminous,
> Great works constructed there in nature's spite
> For scholars and for poets after us,
> Thoughts long knitted into a single thought,
> A dance-like glory that those walls begot.

The next two stanzas define and develop the achievements in literature, art, and politics fostered by Coole and focused by Lady Gregory, whose "powerful character" forms a "compass point" around which service and genius swirl. In the last stanza Yeats finally makes good his claim (at the end of *The Trembling of the Veil,* not quite realized in any of the prose) to have "written ... that young men, to whom recent events are often more obscure than those long past, may learn what debts they owe and to what creditor":

> Here, traveller, scholar, poet, take your stand
> When all those rooms and passages are gone,
> When nettles wave upon a shapeless mound
> And saplings root among the broken stone,
> And dedicate—eyes bent upon the ground,
> Back turned upon the brightness of the sun
> And all the sensuality of the shade—
> A moment's memory to that laurelled head.

"When she died the great house died too," Yeats was shortly to write to Mario Rossi, a mutual friend and recent visitor. "Coole Park, 1929" anticipates the event of 1932. It places Lady Gregory in the landscape and architecture which she loved and which situated her most notable achievements. With great feeling and tact it readies the poet for her death and faces the loss to come. It also insists upon continuity and permanence. The letter to Rossi continues that "the heirlooms and pictures go to Celbridge — Vanessa's house," Swift's Vanessa, thus linking Coole once more with the Anglo-Irish heritage Yeats admired. The poem, as it moves from swallow's flight to compass point to laurelled head, establishes the same correspondence and maintains that Lady Gregory is one of the authentic heroes of that doomed but invaluable culture the poet struggles to keep alive.

"Coole Park and Ballylee, 1931" is a complex and difficult poem. The territory has been expanded to include Yeats's tower, and the poem begins with a highly personal, symbolic landscape. His mind moves from lonely tower to the "cellar" of Raftery — blind, itinerant, Gaelic poet discovered while collecting folklore in the nineties and celebrated in the early stories and, more recently, "The Tower"—to Coole demesne, and so includes most of the Irish cultural history Yeats cares about. Even symbolic landscapes can be jointly held, and this one recalls both Yeats's description of Coole in *Autobiographies* and Lady Gregory's dream of Roxborough and Coole while under anasthesia for a cancer operation in 1926:

> Under my window-ledge the waters race,
> Otters below and moor-hens on the top.
> Run for a mile undimmed in Heaven's face
> Then darkening through "dark" Raftery's "cellar" drop,
> Run underground, rise in a rocky place
> In Coole demesne, and there to finish up
> Spread to a lake and drop into a hole.
> What's water but the generated soul?

The concluding question may depend upon Yeats's reading of Porphyry and Shelley, but the force of the image is local and natural: Coole is his vale of soul-making, the active stream its fitting emblem. The next two stanzas discover the poem's second emblem, the "mounting swan ... arrogantly pure," which, Yeats wrote his wife, is "a symbol of inspiration, I think," but which is also decidely "like the soul." Recollection becomes intensely present; temporal distinctions vanish; the swan is glorious, but fleeting and vulnerable, as feelings of loss and fury confuse the discovery of meaning and the assertion of permanence or transcendence. In the fourth stanza the "dry sticks" of Coole in winter have become Lady Gregory's cane, as the poem moves indoors to face decrepit age and vanishing culture:

Sound of stick upon the floor, a sound
From somebody that toils from chair to chair;
Beloved books that famous hands have bound,
Old marble heads, old pictures everywhere;
Great rooms where travelled men and children found
Content or joy; a last inheritor
Where none has reigned that lacked a name and fame
Or out of folly into folly came.

The penultimate stanza bitterly compares Lady Gregory's rootedness (the poetic realization of "planting trees") with the situation of the poet in the modern world, "all that great glory spent," who can merely "shift about" as "fashion or mere fantasy decrees." The famous last stanza is not a summary of Romanticism or a vision of historical cycles, but a deeply pained rendering of the total loss contained in the sale of Coole and the imminent death of Lady Gregory. Yeats has discovered that swan and water need to be completed by a third emblem, Pegasus without a rider. Blind Raftery is joined by blind Milton and Homer; the swan no longer mounts; the racing water is directionless and darkened. A friend is dying, an achievement frustrated and ignored, a tradition ended:

We were the last romantics—chose for theme
Traditional sanctity and loveliness;
Whatever's written in what poets name
The book of the people; whatever most can bless
The mind of man or elevate a rhyme;
But all is changed, that high horse riderless,
Though mounted in that saddle Homer rode
Where the swan drifts upon a darkening flood.

But the tone is not apocalyptic or defeated, and Thomas Whitaker's fine reading of the end of this poem, and this era, is still persuasive:

It seems a vision not of the cycles of history but of a radical fall. Yet winter does lead to spring, a riderless horse may be ridden, a drifting swan may mount. Even in despair the emblems cannot deny the force of life that produces a continual dialogue between Yeats and the temporal world. Indeed, in this final stanza the meditation itself rises to great lyricism as it claims its impossibility. No more than Lycidas does this swan of a past era float upon his watery bier unwept. Song mourning the lack of song belies itself. Yeats, who knew that no battle has ever been finally lost, knew also that tradition may live in the lament for its passing.

Except for the brief valedictions of "Beautiful Lofty Things" and "The Municipal Gallery Revisited," these are the last poems about Lady Gregory and her estate. But there is more to say. The full significance of Lady Gregory's presence in Yeats's consciousness is revealed by her absence from his life. Most of the published letters referring to her death are to Olivia Shakespear. Several move directly from sad thoughts about Lady Gregory to excited reports of Yeats's new political activities: "April, 1933: I have been in a dream finishing a poem, the first I have done for perhaps a year. I have written nothing in verse since Lady Gregory's death.... I have endless occupation always, which in some way feeds my verse when the moment comes. At the moment I am trying in association with [an] ex-cabinet minister, an eminent lawyer, and a philosopher, to work out a social theory which can be used against Communism in Ireland — what looks like emerging is Fascism modified by religion."

The loss of Lady Gregory and what she represented did not cause Yeats's involvement with fascism; but it is one of several reasons for the expression and endorsement, during 1933–34, of reactionary and totalitarian impulses. Lady Gregory was unique and inimitable: conservative by heritage and temperament yet drawn to revolutionary nationalism; an enthusiastic admirer of strong men who loved the people and knew how powerless they were; an aristocrat by birth and marriage whose sense of responsibility always overcame her sense of privilege. Even her language, as Daniel Harris has pointed out, has political significance: "a Protestant aristocrat consciously writing *of* and *for* Catholic audiences, [she] used 'Kiltartan' to achieve an important private reconciliation with the peasantry she loved and, thus, to alleviate the historical guilt which haunted enlightened members of her class." Her politics are the politics of reconciliation among the aristocratic Ireland or her youth and marriage, the romantic Ireland she struggled to bring into being, and the republican Ireland which grew around her. Her achievement is to effect personally and provisionally that reconciliation, to make family, Coole, Abbey, and nation coalesce without being wishful, cynical, or superficial.

With Yeats, in the three or four years that followed her death, the terms are all askew and reconciliation impossible. He is a middle-class poet who occasionally adopts an aristocratic pose, and then undercuts or explodes it by ruthless or mocking judgment of himself and his country. He is removed from the middle class by choice, what little was left of the aristocracy by birth, and the peasantry by history, temperament, and language, an anti-clerical conservative in a country where the conservatives are Catholic. He wanted to play Jonson to her Countess of Bedford, to make Coole his Penshurst; he is inescapably more like Edmund Burke in old age, mythologizing an aristocracy which he can never join, thirsting for power he no longer has, desperately celebrating an order he sees crumbling, and violently attacking its enemies, who seem to be everywhere. The plunge into alienation, rage, and authoritarianism is expressed politically by Yeats's brief, dismal support for General O'Duffy and his Blueshirts, Ireland's abortive but scary Fascist movement. It is expressed imaginatively in *On the Boiler* and its strident, foolish poems, in the ranting prologue to *The Death of Cuchulain*, the sense of doom in "The Black Tower," and the arrogant assertions of "Under Ben Bulben." Coole became his emblem of a moribund culture and a lost aristocratic order; while Lady Gregory was alive his sense of apocalypse is chastened; after she passes, that sense is sharpened, as in the powerful nihilism of his penultimate play, *Purgatory*.

Lady Gregory was not only a model but a monitor, one of the few people who could admonish the poet with confidence. She criticized his removal to France after the Easter Uprising and his stay in Oxford during the Troubles of 1920. She always supported Yeats in their joint battles for intellectual freedom and artistic integrity, but she cautioned him about the "bitterness of feeling" she occasionally found in herself, often in him, and hated. Now he feeds upon it:

> Come, fix upon me that accusing eye.
> I thirst for accusation. All that was sung,
> All that was said in Ireland is a lie
> Bred out of the contagion of the throng,
> Saving the rhyme rats hear before they die.

Those feelings are outside her pattern, her sense of appropriate response to Irish life. So were the Blueshirts and the writing done in the mood which Yeats's support engendered. He missed her awareness, and he missed her.

4

Anglo-Ireland and Celtic Ireland
1865–1913

W hen John Eglinton reviewed *Reveries over Childhood and Youth* in 1927, he found "a sublimation of the old Ascendancy feeling," a sense of stability and of "possessing the earth" that attaches to privileged leisure even without inherited wealth: "The Yeats family, members of a little patriarchal community in the enchanting county of Sligo, were...born into a natural sense of aristocracy, and the poet, though his father was an impoverished artist, acquired a strong feeling of superiority—which has not been altogether serviceable to him as a national poet—to all phases of human activity except 'the arts.'" There is a personal edge to the observation, and "impoverished" is a little mean; nevertheless, it is an acute response to the first installment of Yeats's autobiography, and it is necessary to understand the geographical, ancestral and historical components of "the old Ascendancy feeling."

The ancestral background, like that of almost all the great Anglo-Irish, is the respectable middle-class family of merchants and rectors. Yeats's steadfast interest in his heritage, and his frequent invocation of it, must have been prompted initially by his pride in ancestors who "bore a part in Irish history," and in "all that joins my life to those who had power in Ireland." His "delight in passionate men" and "reckless Ireland," and his attribution of passion and audacity to his forebears, is only partly made up, only partly an antidote to his youthful timidity. By his own, his father's, and others' accounts, his maternal grandfather, that "silent and fierce old man," William Pollexfen, was indeed the type of violent and romantic Irishman, indifferent to popular opinion yet respected, even loved, for his pride, his "sense of decorum and order," his instinctive consciousness of a position and a legend. He is the first of a large gallery of "indomitable Irishry" that later included the Wilde family, Lady Gregory's famous "seven brothers", Mrs. French of "The Tower," and the "bitter and violent men" of "Meditations in Time of Civil War"—all heroes capable of coming "proud, open-eyed and laughing to the tomb."

In 1863, the year after J. B. Yeats's father died, he inherited some property in Kildare and its income, and married Susan, the eldest, pretty, and much-sought-after Pollexfen daughter. He later recalled that she accepted him because he was there often and the family helped. In many ways the marriage seems a representative, and melancholy, nineteenth-century arrangement: active, buoyant husband and passive, receding wife. Oliver Elton remembers Mrs. Yeats as "a silent, flitting figure ... from the fairy shores of Sligo" whose husband thought her "the right kind of mother for a poet and dreamer." Her health was poor: a cataract in one eye soon after marriage, a stroke in 1886 or '87, and another the following year from which she never recovered, living out her quiet life mostly in one room, feeding the birds at her window and never admitting that she was an invalid. The emotional burden of precarious finances fell largely on her; she was never really happy away from Sligo and spent as much time there as she could while her husband was in London or Dublin. She was not comfortable with artists and intellectuals and seems never to have gone to an exhibition of JBY's paintings or to have entered his studio. There was often real tension between them (JBY later said that he "would advise women not to marry either a poet or an artist. It is too dangerous, though like most dangerous things, it is enticing.") Neither her husband nor her children, who recall so much with such animation, say a great deal about her, and biographers have had to struggle for their portraits. Ten years after her death, JBY wrote two sympathetic and cheerful essays about American feminism, and it is difficult not to feel some uneasiness about his happy endorsement of lives and styles so different from those his wife and, later, his daughters, were able to maintain.

Yet perhaps their uncharacteristic reticence is a kind of tribute. Jack Yeats wrote nothing about his mother's death in 1900, but his sketchbooks cease altogether for six months and do not return to their usual vigor and abundance until the following year. *Reveries* attests to the feelings for Sligo that she created in her children. The few times JBY does mention his wife, it is not only with affection, but with a sort of wondrous respect for the richness of her inner life, her natural kinship with the people of Sligo, and the sympathy behind her apparent reserve. Genial agnostic in so many matters, he always believes in the sanctity and permanence of marriage, and in the personal growth achieved through a solid one. When he was ill in New York in 1919, and again just before he died, he dreamed of her repeatedly.

Susan (indirectly) and her brother George (explicitly) form the center of both father and son's idea of the Pollexfens, their transformation of them from a family into an image and a lesson. The stern and somber Pollexfens define JBY's freedom; but they have a force and presence that he lacks, envies, and—along with his son—meditates upon. The two families become emblems for his mental and social universe, the terms of an unsystematic and shifting dialectic that shapes his perceptions. On the one hand, Yeatses, Dublin, the world and (later) Joyce; on the other, Pollexfens, their in-laws the Middletons, Sligo and Synge. His world values pleasure and growth; theirs order, duty, and direction. His occupies itself with ideas, opinions, and play; theirs is preoccupied by possessions, convictions, and industry. His thrives on art and intellect; theirs depends on nature and instinct. He sets a tone of gregarious amiability, they of silent and solitary strength. His characteristic accomplishment is one of range and intensity; theirs of depth and permanence. The one has to struggle to transcend a too-diffused identity; the other to escape from a too-narrow identity. JBY remembers saying, when he first realized that W.B. was a poet, "Behold I have given a tongue to the sea cliffs," and he believes that his sons evolve from both worlds, but that the crucial strain in William comes from the critical and communicative Yeatses, in Jack from the instinctive Pollexfens, the voice and the sea-cliffs themselves, epitomized in his two talented sons.

Along with such strong family feeling, Yeats grew up with a complex sense of various national identities. For JBY, his family, and others like them, there were actually four Irelands—and a man had to sort out his connections, commitments, and interpretations. There were the Ulster Presbyterians, northern Irishmen of Scots origin whom the Yeatses found stiff and narrow in religion, embattled and determined in loyalty to England and in fearful contempt for Catholic nationalism, commercial in outlook and ethics. There were the southern Unionists, more relaxed and urbane than their northern counterparts, but still Anglicized in culture and politics, displaced Englishmen without the characteristic British virtues. Like other nineteenth-century Irishmen, JBY sees the "pure Irish," the bulk of the southern population, in religious rather than ethnic terms; for him they are Catholics more than they are Celts. He compares them, almost always favorably, to the Protestants of Belfast, Dublin, London, and New York. It is an affectionate and generous portrait, and in ways a patronizing one.

The particular slant of the family's view of Belfast or Sligo, Dublin or London most depends upon their class and its history. "Anglo-Irish" is a term of convenience, abuse, pride, and confusion. It has been used to attack all Irish Protestants and to praise them or apologize for them, as an emblem of confiscation and oppression, and as one definition of modern Irish nationalism. The religious origins of the Anglo-Irish are characteristically Anglican and Huguenot rather than Catholic, like most Southerners, or Presbyterian, like most Ulstermen. Their political and cultural origins are British rather than Gaelic or Scots, which means that they share both the burden of English hegemony in Ireland and the strain of not being quite at home in either country. It is a long and grim history of dominion, going back to the twelfth century, firmly and widely established with the Cromwellian plantations, fixed by the defeat of the loyalist, Catholic forces at the Battle of the Boyne, and codified under the treaty of Limerick.

During the eighteenth century the Ascendancy — the Protestant minority—controlled four fifths of the property and all the conventional political and economic power. It was, according to Edmund Burke, one of its brilliant and disgruntled sons, "a complete system...a machine of wise and elaborate contrivance, and as well fitted for the oppression, impoverishment, and degredation of a people, and the debasement, in them, of human nature itself, as ever proceeded from the perverted ingenuity of man." In spite of selfishness, indifference and failure, however, the achievements of eighteenth-century Anglo-Ireland are real and impressive. They did articulate and organize the first effective modern sense of Irish nationalism. Berkeley's *Querist,* Molyneux's *The Case of Ireland,* and Swift's *Drapier's Letters* come from the Protestant minority, as do Emmet, Tone, Grattan, and, by extension, the United Irishmen, the Great Parliament of 1782–1800, and one major impetus towards Irish independence. They steadily lessened the restrictions and disabilities imposed on Catholics. The Anglo-Irish leadership came not from the Big Houses of powerful landlords but from the professional middle class. They were born in Ireland and for the most part educated there rather than England. They made Dublin one of the most important and lovely eighteenth-century capitals and they virtually created modern Irish culture.

It is an ambiguous and embittering history but not an altogether shameful one. It creates a strong family and class sense, a feeling for a tradition to be upheld and a position to be maintained. It leads to the pervasive yearning of the Anglo-Irish artist and intellectual to achieve some kind of unity out of the experience of so many Irelands, a yearning Yeats characteristically expresses by first reducing the four Irelands to two: "Preserve that which is living and help the two Irelands, Gaelic Ireland and Anglo-Ireland, so to unite that neither shall shed its pride." The quest was never easy and the alternatives often bewildering. "It was not that I do not love order," he recalled his struggle to write a coherent Irish novel, "or that

I lack capacity for it, but that—and not in the arts and in thought only—I outrun my strength. It is not so much that I choose too many elements, as that the possible unities themselves seem without number, like those angels that...dance spurred and booted upon the head of a needle." Much of the drama of Yeats is that of a great talent and agile mind seeking order but finding antinomies, attempting resolution but being thrown into doubts and confusion. So he becomes a man of many masks and sometimes of mere contradictions; he is supple and resourceful, and makes conflicting statements, including many about England and Ireland, nationalism and the Ascendancy world, forms of national identity. The quest for "the possible unities" among these several and opposed Irelands is often thwarted, and the most sustained note is a pained ambivalence, as in this paragraph from "A General Introduction for my Work," a selfconsciously valedictory essay of 1937:

> The "Irishry" have preserved their ancient "deposit" through wars which, during the sixteenth and seventeenth centuries, became wars of extermination; no people, Lecky said at the opening of his *Ireland in the Eighteenth Century*, have undergone greater persecution, nor did that persecution altogether cease up to our own day. No people hate as we do in whom that past is always alive, there are moments when hatred poisons my life and I accuse myself of effeminacy because I have not given it adequate expression. It is not enough to have put it into the mouth of a rambling peasant poet. Then I remind myself that though mine is the first English marriage I know of in the direct line, all my family names are English, and that I owe my soul to Shakespeare, to Spenser and to Blake, perhaps to William Morris, and to the English language in which I think, speak, and write, that everything I love has come to me through English; my hatred tortures me with love, my love with hate.... This is Irish hatred and solitude, the hatred of human life that made Swift write *Gulliver* and the epitaph upon his tomb, that can still make us wag between extremes and doubt our sanity.

Since Yeats drags all of his experience with him, dates are a little arbitrary, even misleading. Nevertheless, it is possible to discern five phases, and a rough chronology, in his engagements with and programs for Anglo-Ireland and Celtic Ireland. Between 1885 and 1903 he is the leading figure of the Celtic Revival, committed to Irish independence, boldly confronting Unionist prejudice and cosmopolitan culture in the name of a native literary movement. From 1903 to 1916 he is most typically disillusioned and estranged; he recognizes the points of tension between the two Irelands and he has to face the disparity between the ideal nation prophesied by The Revival and the state as it was actually emerging. Between 1916 and 1922 he is often detached, ambivalent, and confused, admiring and authenticating nationalist determination and heroism but pondering as well its personal and public cost. For about ten years thereafter he is a public man, though not always a smiling one, coming to grips with the difference between his new, largely conservative ideas and his old belief in romantic Ireland, trying to bring Anglo-Ireland "back into the tapestry" of national life and to forge a new synthesis. He never ceased to struggle, sometimes to scream, and his last years (1932–39) alternate between reactionary rage and attempts at reintegration.

2

Yeats's first program, a plan for himself and for Ireland, has been variously named, usually depending upon the amount of experience referred to and the range of feeling about that experience. *The Celtic Twilight* is the title of a book he published in 1893 and the expression of an attitude—pastoral, atavistic, pre-Raphaelite—towards Ireland and its literature. *The Literary Revival* means the work of a group of Anglo-Irish writers—Yeats, Lady Gregory, Douglas Hyde, Synge, George Russell (AE), Standish O'Grady, George Moore—between 1885 and 1910. The broadest term is *The Irish Renaissance* which refers to several forms of a cultural nationalism that has its roots in the eighteenth century, and began to be an important force during the middle of the nineteenth, when Thomas Davis founded *The Nation* as a vehicle for patriotic writing and for "Irish" or "native" definitions of national consciousness. The writers of *The Nation* formed the Young Ireland movement which created an image, "the real Ireland," and attempted to define an essence and express an idiom, the "true Irish note, racy of the soil," as their motto proclaimed. By the end of the century, the two most formidable instruments of cultural nationalism, in addition to the literary movement, were the Gaelic League and the Gaelic Athletic Association. The League, which was founded by Douglas Hyde in 1893, aimed to revivify Gaelic and make it the national language, to preserve the ancient literature written in it, and to foster new writing. The Association, founded by Michael Cusack (Joyce's "Citizen" in *Ulysses*) in 1884, aggressively fostered Irish games, local patriotism, and — finally — militant nationalism. Members of these two groups had important differences, especially about direct political allegiance and activity, but they agreed in their firm commitments to an independent nation, a native culture, and a hostility to English power and influence.

Yeats's involvement in this revived and expanding cultural nationalism began in 1885 when, as a young poet imitating Spenser and Shelley and more aware of family and class than of any national consciousness, he met John O'Leary and decided that he must become an Irish poet. O'Leary's nationalism — his dedication, and self-sacrifice authenticated by years of work, jail, and exile—was unquestioned and unquestionable. But it was a critical nationalism informed by O'Leary's acute and sympathetic literary sense and by a firm belief that the two were related. "There is no great literature without nationality," he taught his young men, "no great nationality without literature." In 1888 O'Leary and his sister Ellen brought out a small collection of poetry which they called *Poems and Ballads of Young Ireland.* The title claims an association with Davis and his movement, but it also implies a difference, for the young poets (Hyde, Todhunter, Rolleston, Katherine Tynan, Yeats and others) are a new generation with different ideas about literature and nationalism. They are less overtly nationalistic, far less rhetorical, and much more interested in technique and craftsmanship, with the effort, as Yeats put it, "to get a style." The conflict over the primacy of literature or politics, and about the possible relationships between them, had begun. Yeats did not originate the idea of Irish Literary Societies; they had been around, struggling, since 1880; but he revitalized and reshaped them (the most notable were the Irish Literary Society in London and the National Literary Society in Dublin), under O'Leary's aegis and partly for his own ends, beginning in 1891 in the midst of the fierce controversy over Parnell's leadership of the Irish party. Yeats's account, given many years later as he accepted the Nobel Prize, would have been accepted by most of his co-workers:

> The modern literature of Ireland, and indeed all that stir of thought which prepared for the Anglo-Irish war, began when Parnell fell from power in 1891. A disillusioned and embittered Ireland turned from parliamentary politics; an event was conceived; and the race began, as I think, to be troubled by that event's long gestation. Dr. Hyde founded the Gaelic League, which was for many years to substitute for political argument a Gaelic grammar, and for political meetings village gatherings, where songs were sung and stories told in the Gaelic language. Meanwhile I had begun a movement in English, in the language in which modern Ireland thinks and does its business; founded certain societies where clerks, working men, men of all classes, could study the Irish poets, novelists and historians who had written in English,

and as much of Gaelic literature as had been translated into English. But the great mass of our people, accustomed to interminable political speeches, read little, and so from the very start we felt that we must have a theatre of our own. The theatres of Dublin had nothing about them that we could call our own. They were empty buildings hired by the English travelling companies, and we wanted Irish plays and Irish players. When we thought of these plays we thought of everything that was romantic and poetical, because the nationalism we had called up —the nationalism every generation had called up in moments of discouragement—was romantic and poetical.

Parnell's fall did not create a lasting political vacuum. It was soon filled, as Yeats worried it would be while watching Maud Gonne lead demonstrations, by young men and women willing to carry bombs and rifles. It marked instead the end of any real hope for a non-violent solution to the Irish Question and the end of the political supremacy of the class to which Yeats and Parnell belonged. From Yeats's point of view, The Chief's catastrophe and death created something more important than a vacuum. It created an audience—people only interested in speeches did start reading histories, fables, poems, and stories—and it created a myth—the great man and heroic nationalist tragically brought down and basely betrayed.

While engaged in these strenuous efforts, Yeats published a poem he called "Apologia addressed to Ireland in the coming days," which begins

> Know, that I would accounted be
> True brother of a company
> That sang, to sweeten Ireland's wrong,
> Ballad and story, rann and song;
> Nor be I any less of them,
> Because the red-rose bordered hem
> Of her, whose history began
> Before God made the angelic clan,
> Trails all about the written page.

A poem of self-definition, it is, as the title, syntax, and deflecting irony of the last line indicate, a bit anxious. A belief in "the angelic clan," the true Irish race, is not inevitably or even naturally linked to a belief in the occult and its symbol, the rose. The "company" of patriotic poets would include Young Ireland, but Yeats was already determined that his movement would have different aims and assumptions, and it was soon clear that the leaders of the Literary Revival had not the same experience or interests as

Davis and his followers. One of Yeats's achievements during these hectic and important years of building is to bring together his idea of the Celt and his belief in the occult, and to transform what might well have been a coterie into something like a national movement.

Celticism involves a belief in racial consciousness and imagination, and in the natural (and pastoral) superiority of the Irish countryman to the more familiar (and Anglicized) products of modern civilization. Studying the Celt means tapping folklore, mythology, and legend. Yeats, an amateur folklorist who did not know Gaelic, nevertheless responded deeply to the written and spoken literature. It provided an access to the Irish past and a sense of identity with the oral culture of Sligo and the western counties. It portrayed an ideal rural society where peasant and gentry were united by interest, instinct, and passion, a literary version of his father's whimsically ideal society of poor country gentlemen. In "The Celtic Element in Literature," an important essay of 1897, he revised "a little" Renan's and Arnold's definitions, emphasizing the unself-conscious belief in a nature that is always animate, magic, a religious sense, and the visionary. The essential Celtic element, he says, is wild, ecstatic, passionate as well as melancholy and, sometimes, embittered. The old tales, whether written or spoken, grown from an ancient tradition, rich in symbolism, that will feed the modern imagination in its reaction against eighteenth-century rationalism and nineteenth-century materialism.

At the same time Yeats was an avid pupil at Madame Blavatsky's London Theosophical Lodge and a member of the Hermetic Students of the Golden Dawn. He most simply connects the occult and theosophy with Celticism by asserting what was basically true, that country people also believe in magic and that "all folk literature, and all literature that keeps the folk tradition, delights in unbounded and immortal things."

Occult doctrine fosters a belief in the existence and the recoverability of an ancestral past and a national being that can be intuited and expressed by the imagination. Furthermore, turn-of-the-century occultism held a messianic belief in the coming of an apocalypse, a new revolutionary epoch and a new leader. It was not difficult to relate that conviction to the hopes of an oppressed people, the existence of an underground tradition, or the fall of one national leader and potential arrival of another. If imaginative writers could be fully in touch with the deepest, most secret elements of their culture, they could perhaps become prophets and create the sacred book to capture the spirit of Ireland and announce the new Messiah. The writer who would be both patriotic and creative attends not to the details of politics or the facts of history, but to spiritual essences of the race through which it may rediscover itself and claim its rightful place among nations.

3

Yeats was 20 when he met O'Leary in 1885 and 26 when Parnell fell from power. During those years he faced a difficult task—how to get on, how to survive on talent and ambition without a university education, or marketable training, or family income. What could be gotten from literary journalism and odd jobs for publishers, and at what cost to that talent? Yeats soon transformed this genuine but familiar task into an enormous and unconventional undertaking—to reform the literature of his country, to revise its literary history, and, no less than Stephen Dedalus, to create its consciousness—"a new region for the mind to wander in," a recreation of "the imaginative tradition of Ireland." He needed an income, was determined to form a style, wanted to discover an audience and start a movement. Between 1886 and 1903 he talked with and wrote to other young writers, advising and encouraging, directed literary societies as a way to discover new writers and more readers, and wrote over a hundred essays and reviews seeking to create a substantial and well informed audience for his and their work. His literary journalism is rarely just hack work or the puffing of friends, though there is some of both, but an effort to capture and educate a public. His lack of Gaelic poses a problem. He admits that lack, occasionally laments it, and celebrates Douglas Hyde's Gaelic and Lady Gregory's Kiltartin, but insists that a writer has to work in the language with which he is born.

As a nationalist, poet, and publicist, Yeats needs to link patriotic acts with a native literary tradition. He acknowledges the oppression of the Irish, but in a way that sublimates politics into spiritual history, that includes nationalism rather than capitulates to it. In spite of the genuine wish for poet and people to be one, politics yields to personal vision and symbolic expression. He revises O'Leary's dictum about literature and nationality in order to say that any true literature written by an Irishman (in Gaelic or English) will be national, and any national literature will be nationalistic, will teach Irishmen to love and hate, admire and understand. When pressed for a definition, he says that a national literature is "the work of writers who are moulded by influences that are moulding their country, and who write out of so deep a life that they are accepted there in the end," which puts the burden of acceptance on the people, not the poet. He urges young writers that, in addition to being in touch with national feeling and history, they must study the masters of world literature, and find themselves by studying their own models and perfecting their own craft. AE, like several others, suffered and profited from Yeat's criticism and, sometimes grudgingly, benefited from his example. He later wrote that Yeats was "the pivot around which Irish literature turned from instinctive to conscious art ... the first artist in Irish literature," so that "after his verse began to find readers, there came a shrivelling of the resounding and empty rhetoric in which so many had been content to express themselves."

JBY worried about his son's journalism, that all the criticism and propaganda would be preemptive and perhaps corrupting, and urged him to undertake fiction instead. Yeats certainly tried, and between 1887 and 1900 completed one novel, *John Sherman,* abandoned another, *The Speckled Bird,* and wrote twenty short stories, most of which appeared in *The Secret Rose* in 1897, and were later included in *Mythologies,* along with *The Celtic Twilight* and *Per Amica Silentia Lunae. John Sherman* is a more or less realistic novella organized around the choices faced by its protagonist and imagined by its author: London and Sligo, worldly success and provincial contentment, restless ambition and sense of place. The stories are shadowy, lyrical, and symbolical, not "mere phantasies," Yeats wrote to Olivia Shakespear, "but the signatures—I use a medium's term—of things invisible and ideas." The heroes, Red Hanrahan and others, are outcasts, exiles, wanderers, beggars, and mystics, usually victims of the violence inflicted on the visionary by the orthodox and materialists. *The Speckled Bird* alternates the modes, being realistic in its sense of character and "folk" in setting, but also concerned with visionary otherness and victimage, and reaching flights of lyrical prose. Yeats struggled for four years ("I could neither write nor cease to write") and abandoned it in confusion and frustration. As it turned out, he was also abandoning prose fiction. In writing it—and fighting it—he had discovered themes, worked through difficulties and preoccupations, and determined the range and limitations of his talents. By the turn of the century he knew that his strength was in poems and plays, that in them he could best express himself and both represent and further the national literary movement.

His first important poem, "The Wanderings of Oisin," had been written in 1886 and '87 and was published in January 1889. Ten years later Yeats moved it to the back of his *Poems,* thinking that it received too large a share of his critics attention simply because it came first. He did not anticipate one consequence of the move, that the poem would henceforth be seen as a kind of appendix to his continually growing *Collected Poems.* Though "The Wanderings of Oisin" is neither an afterthought nor juvenilia, it is a young man's poem and Yeats put all of his young self into it. "When I had finished it," he wrote to Katherine Tynan about Part II, "I ... could hardly read, so collapsed I was. My voice quite broken. It really was a kind of vision. It beset me day and night." The poem itself and Yeats's commentary in letters, essays, and other poems—abundant and unusually direct and consistent for him—makes clear how central it is to his career. Centrality, however, is not coherence. The parts do not completely fit together; critics have had some difficulty treating it as a whole and finished work, and so have differed in interpretation and evaluation.

One problem is the extent to which the poem—a narrative of the life of a legendary Irish hero—is autobiographical. Richard Ellmann was the first critic to see the poem as directly personal, arguing that the three islands visited by Oisin represent three stages of growth — childhood, maturity, old age — and more particularly Yeats's happy youth at Sligo, embattled years in London, and days of reverie at Howth—a reading which seems fruitful only if it remains a loose association and is not pressed into an allegorical representation. The poem does have autobiographical impulses: the erotic yearning and anxiety, the envious regard for the man of action, the premature identification with old age and fatigue. They are all over the surface of the poem and remain important Yeats themes, but they are not what the poem is about, or what it allegorizes or symbolizes. Readings which attempt to tease out a *bildungsroman* (most notably the claim that the dusky demon of Book II is either "orgasm incarnate" or John Butler Yeats) seem far-fetched or reductive.

A second problem is that "Oisin" reveals as fully as any Yeats poem his remarkable receptivity to multiple and diverse literary influences. It is impossible not to notice them and difficult to chart them with precision. His choice of subject is important. At this crucial point, soon after meeting O'Leary, while beginning to work for and organize an Irish movement, he chooses a hero and tale from his country's legendary past. That choice is a political act and the poem is a statement; it is also, of course, personal, and his revisions of the legendary material reveal subtle but telling choices. The narrative is based upon an eighteenth-century Irish poem attributed to Michael Comyn which Yeats found translated in the *Transactions of the Ossianic Society;* so he is reshaping a translation of a version of an oral tale. He changed the substance of the narrative (three journeys instead of two) as well as the order and relationship between the episodes. His treatment of one scene indicates the difference from Comyn. Early in the poem, as Oisin and Niamh journey to the first island, they see a tableau upon the waters:

> now a hornless deer
> Passed by us, chased by a phantom hound
> All pearly white, save one red ear;
> And now a lady rode like the wind

With an apple of gold in her tossing hand;
And a beautiful young man followed behind
With quenchless gaze and fluttering hair.

A similar scene appears in Comyn, but only once and it seems mostly decorative. In Yeats, the endless chase appears three times, once in each book as the lovers approach a new island. The scene takes on added weight until, in Book III, Niamh is no longer able to distract Oisin from its significance. He now knows what she has wanted to keep from him, "the immortal desire of Immortals," the defeat of fulfillment by endless longing, the fact that his quest will never be achieved because the essence of human experience is desire, not its realization. It is a *fin-de-siècle* version of a romantic variation on a Johnsonian theme, crucial to Yeats and imposed upon his source. Comyn's scene is static and simply an object of perception; Yeats's scene, like Keats's urn, is an event for the imagination to penetrate and attempt to animate. So the Irish merges with the Romantic tradition, which enriches the poem and nicely confuses the attribution of sources and echoes. Shelley, too, and his questers are a potent force behind the idea of Yeats's poem; and there are times when Yeats's voice seems shaped and informed by the voices of Morris (Book I), Spenser (Book II), and Tennyson (Book III). Such a profusion of ancestors, important but not fully incorporated into the imagination of the poet or the movement of the poem, is a little unsettling.

The allegory is a further problem. "Oisin" is decidedly allegorical, but it is not a direct, consistent, pictorial allegory where all the pieces fit into a scheme that can be unlocked with a single interpretive key. It is more symbolical than allegorical or, as Yeats put it in "Symbolism in Painting," "allegory and symbolism melt into one another." The melting, however, is subtle, a little secretive, and even precious. Yeats's letter to Katherine Tynan continues: "In the second part of 'Oisin' under disguise of symbolism I have said several things to which I only have the key. The romance is for my readers. They must not even know there is a symbol anywhere. They will not find out. If they did, it would spoil the art. Yet the whole poem is full of symbols—if it be full of aught but clouds." We are entitled to wonder if there has ever been a serious reader of Yeats wholly content with the romance, unaware of symbols, not wanting to find out. The poem, like the letter, is a bit teasing, obvious in places, obscure in others, a romance most of the way, but also a confession and a meditation. It is an important part of Yeats's canon, but its experience is not wholly absorbed, some of its issues not completely resolved, and some of its language rather strained, as when Oscar asks Niamh, panting from exertion and desire, "'Were there no better than my son/ That you through all that foam should run?'" It is a fascinating and imperfect poem, intriguing partly because of the imperfections. It reveals more imaginative energy and psychic investment than the text can quite contain or manage, and energy and investment spill over in confusing but marvellous ways. "Perhaps," Yeats wrote, "only shadows have got themselves on to paper. And I am like the people who dream some wonderful thing and get up in the middle of the night and write it and find next day only scribbling on the paper."

The main line of the narrative is reasonably clear. A few months after the first letter Yeats wrote again to Katherine Tynan, both complaining and hinting, "'Oisin' needs an interpreter. There are three incompatible things which man is always seeking — infinite feeling, infinite battle, infinite repose — hence the three islands." Forty-five years later, remembering his response to the Victorian myth of progress — a "satisfaction in certain public disasters," an "ecstasy at the contemplation of ruin," and a preoccupation with a "myth that was itself a reply to a myth"—he charts Oisin's journey in amplified but similar terms:

> He rides across the sea with a spirit, he passes phantoms, a boy following a girl, a hound chasing a hare, emblematical of eternal pursuit, he comes to an island of choral dancing, leaves that after many years, passes the phantoms once again, comes to an island of endless battle for an object never achieved, leaves that after many years, passes the phantoms once again, comes to an island of sleep, leaves that and comes to Ireland, to Saint Patrick and old age. I did not pick these images because of any theory, but because I found them impressive, yet all the while abstractions haunted me.

Those abstractions, the basis of his countering myth, were rooted, Yeats later decided, in cyclical theories of history: "the choral song, a life lived in common, a futile battle, then thought for its own sake, the last island, Vico's circle and mine, and then the circle joined." In "Oisin" the circles exist as story rather than theory — Yeats had read little historiography in 1888 — but they do give shape to the poem and to its view of human experience. The narrative present forms one circle as the poem begins and ends with, and intermittently returns to, Oisin's debate with Patrick after he has returned to ordinary life in a much diminished world. That dialogue contains a more fully realized circle, Oisin's account of his three journeys, each lasting one hundred years, to the islands of the Otherworld. Niamh, who has fallen in love with Oisin and claimed him from the fellowship of his warriors, first takes her mortal lover to Tir-nan-Oge, the country of her father Aengus, Celtic god of Love and Beauty, the island of eternal dancing and infinite feeling. There Oisin experiences a century of loving, hunting, and companionship, what Yeats would later call "sensual music." It is a world of endless desire and fulfillment, an image of the natural world freed from mortality and pain.

But Oisin cannot escape the osprey nor express the boundless joy of the immortals. He can only sing of human joy and when he does the Immortals weep, snatch his harp and hurl it away; as Michael Sidnell has said, he is a poet with a theme, while they have "no poetry, merely rhythm." After his first century of what Patrick sternly calls "dalliance with a demon thing," Oisin discovers a piece of wood from the broken lance of a warrior, remembers the Fenian battles, weeps, and, in spite of Niamh's murmuring anxiety, leaves the magical island while its ageless natives join in a chorus of lamentation.

The second voyage, to the "Isle of Many Fears," is the most obscure, as Yeats knew. Symbolism does not quite melt into allegory; rather, a highly symbolical landscape and architecture seems to demand an allegorical interpretation yet resist coherent formulations. The island is urban-aquatic (a sort of nightmare Venice) as "dark towers/ Rose in the darkness," suggesting both Yeats's and Blake's sense of London. "Dark statues" rise above "dark thrones." Two aged and impotent eagles — "earless, nerveless, blind," apt representatives of a decaying Empire and a moribund cultural imperialism — stand guard over a pale lady whom Oisin must liberate by repeated battle with the "dusky demon … hung with slime." They fight at the bottom of a "high dome,/ Windowless, pillarless, multitudinous home" of shadowy faces merging into one another, and giving the sense of both nameless enemies and ancestral imperatives. The demon has been variously interpreted (JBY, sexual anxiety, insufficient rendering of the Gaelic original), most invitingly by Sidnell who sees him as the figure of the critic-scholar.

> beyond on a dim plain
> A little runnel made a bubbling strain,
> And on the runnel's stony and bare edge
> A dusky demon dry as a withered sedge
> Swayed, crooning to himself an unknown tongue:
> In a sad revelry he sang and swung
> Bacchant and mournful, passing to and fro
> His hand along the runnel's side, as though
> The flowers still grew there.

More particularly, this tired and mournful demon could be an oblique caricature of Edward Dowden with his Unionist bias, Trinity College security and smugness, and condescending hostility towards Irish literature and the young movement. The identification is made either problematic or piquant by Dowden's unreserved admiration for the poem and another professor, Robert Atkinson, who had testified that "all folklore was at bottom abominable," may be the more likely candidate. No particular association is necessary, as the demon is something more threatening than an enemy, the poet's double, the pedant who "arose/ Barking," an anti-self that must be confronted by the active imagination. For a hundred years Oisin fights the shape-changing demon for a full day, then rests and feasts for three, ministered to by his otherworldly mistress and his never wholly liberated or repatriated muse. Whatever allegorical particularity one finds, it seems clear that Oisin's second voyage dramatizes struggle, the illusion of choice and victory, continual triumph which is also continual frustration, the muddled middle age of responsibilities, "theatre business, management of men." It is also clear that Oisin is more warrior than poet. Frustrating as the second voyage is, this is still the Otherworld and Oisin can escape precisely those aspects of self-consciousness that so burden the poet. But not quite forever, as, after a century, a beech-bough surfaces on the waves reminding Oisin of his father and his mortal companions. He and Niamh leave the Island of Victories and the demon whose "monotone,/ Surly and distant, mixed inseparably/ Into the clangour of the wind and sea."

The isle of repose or sleep, thought or dreams, forgetfulness or immortal longing (the poem itself and Yeats's commentary wish to allow all the alternatives) is populated by "a monstrous slumbering folk" with feathered ears, birds' claws, and beards grown so long that owls nest in them. These titans may seem inescapably quaint, but they are not caricatures. They are aged but not dessicated beings — no Gerontions — whose faces, "alive with such beauty" as man has never seen, are animated by their reveries. They are recalling, longing for the heroism, magnitude, and grace which the poem associates with the legendary past of the Red Branch cycle of tales. After one strenuous attempt to arouse them, Oisin succumbs to the power of "the bell-branch, sleep's forebearer" and begins his own reverie ennobled by the objects of its desire. But it cannot last any longer than the first two voyages. At the beginning of this journey Niamh has murmured that they go to "the Island of forgetfulness" since the islands of Dancing and Victories "'Are empty of all power.' And which of these.'" Oisin asks, "'Is the Island of Content?' 'None know' she said," and he now discovers that there is no such island. At the end of this century a starling sings and awakens Oisin, recalling to him the Fenians setting out on an adventure. His horse appears unsummoned, for it knows that Oisin is again feeling "the ancient sadness of man,/ And that I would leave the Immortals, their dimness, their dews dropping sleep" as well as the stricken Niamh.

Oisin's return to Ireland and mortality (the terms are synonymous) is marked by two moments the intensity of which is suggested by Yeats's return to them in much later poems. Oisin's first sense of the natural world is "an odour of new-mown hay" which causes him to weep in ecstasy and which becomes, in "Vacillation" (a poem of 1932 which made Yeats think again about "The Wanderings of Oisin") a cause of and justification for joy and equanimity in the face of loss. The second moment is tragic. Oisin has been less than a day in an Ireland which he finds Christianized, repressed, and feeble. He tries to rouse his countrymen with scorn and Fenian warcries only to be told that "'The Fenians a long time are dead.'" "Lonely and longing for Niamh," He is about to return to the Otherworld when he sees two weak old men carrying "a sack full of sand," their burden of life and time. Like Parnell in a bitter epigram of 1937 ("Parnell came down the road, he said to a cheering man:/ 'Ireland shall get her freedom and you still break stone.'"), this uncrowned king stoops in contempt and flings their load ahead. Then the girth of his saddle snaps, he touches the ground, and like Tennyson's Lady, the curse comes upon him:

> And my years three hundred fell on me, and I rose, and
> walked on the earth,
>
> A creeping old man, full of sleep, with the spittle on his beard
> never dry.

Decrepit in body, enraged by his churchy country, and taunted by Patrick

> But kneel and wear out the flags and pray for your soul that
> is lost
>
> Through the demon of love of its youth and its godless and
> passionate age.

Oisin makes the last choice available to him, a choice that is defiant, stoical, and romantic:

I will go to Caoilte, and Conan, and Bran, Sceolan, Lomair,
And dwell in the house of the Fenians, be they in flames or
    at feast.

"The Wanderings of Oisin" is a poem about three hundred years of
quest and its inevitable conclusion in heroic defeat. It is predominantly a
poem of antithesis, of choice: Oisin and Patrick, Pagan and Christian,
Warrior and Saint, this world and the next, language and life, self and
shadow. "I keep saying," Yeats wrote to Olivia Shakespear in 1932 as he
was correcting page proof and thinking especially about "Vacillation,"
"what man is this who in the course of two or three weeks...says the same
thing in so many different ways. My first denunciation of old age I made in
The Wanderings of Usheen...before I was twenty and the same denunciation comes in the last pages of the book. The swordsman throughout
repudiates the saint, but not without vacillation. Is that perhaps the sole
theme — Usheen and Patrick — 'so get you gone Von Hugel though with
blessings on your head?'"

The antithesis of the narrative frame, Oisin's debate with Patrick, is
the conflict between Pagan and Christian Ireland and between the two
conceptions of a world out of time, one an infinite extension of sensual
pleasure, the other a stern religious idealism. "When Oisin is speaking with
Saint Patrick of the friends and the life he has outlived," Yeats wrote in
1904, "he can but cry out constantly against a religion that has no meaning
for him." While Oisin's and the poem's view of a pale and repressive
Christianity has had some help from Swinburne, it is more in touch with
and dependent upon the sense of cultural diffusion that was to become one
of the themes of modern Irish literature. There is a further tension between
mortal life and immortality no matter how conceived. On his journeys to
the Otherworld Osin constantly feels the pull from his life with the Fenians
and concludes each book by a return to their company. This nostalgia for
reality is complicated as Oisin the actor — virile and invincible — merges
with Oisin the teller — aged and overcome. As a wandering hero he longs
for mortality, though he feels the countering desire for life eternally in
Niamh's arms. As a fallen mortal and narrator he has only Patrick's stern
vision and a tragically diminished country. The poem insists on the comparison between actor and teller, gratification and duty, heroic quest and
defeated wisdom, and so dramatizes tensions that were to preoccupy Yeats
for the rest of his life: dreams and responsibilities, youth and age, innocence and knowledge, sensuousness and aceticism, the infinitude of desire
and its constantly changing objects, the overriding importance of energy
and will.

"The Wanderings of Oisin" also introduces questions about the relationship between language and life, symbolist creation and circumstantial reality. In his first speech Oisin asserts that

> the tale, though words be lighter than air,
> Must live to be old like the wandering moon.

and Niamh, like Desdemona, says that

> 'I loved no man, though much besought,
> Until the Danaan poets brought
> Rhyme that rhymed upon Oisin's name.'

They seem to claim, or want to claim, the triumph of imagination over reality, words over life. It is a hope Yeats explores in "The Circus Animals' Desertion," which is, among other things, his last look at this poem:

> What can I but enumerate old themes?
> First that sea-rider Oisin led by the nose
> Through three enchanted islands, allegorical dreams,
> Vain gaiety, vain battle, vain repose,
> Themes of the embittered heart, or so it seems,
> That might adorn old songs or courtly shows;

He then seems to refer the impulse of the poem to his own sexual frustration while writing it:

> But what cared I that set him on to ride,
> I, starved for the bosom of his faery bride?

But the next two stanzas assert that embittered life leads to an enchanting dream, a poem or play, a realized vision, which then claims "all my thought and love." The last stanza proudly claims that "Those masterful images because complete/ Grew in pure mind," but instantly recognizes that they begin in that very reality that poems seek to order if not quite defeat, that the imaginative ladders must begin "In the foul rag-and-bone shop of the heart." As Oisin must find his reality in the decrepitude and loneliness that awaits him, the poem must find its interpreters, and the poet his complex relationship to life. Secret meanings and sensuous escape, as seductive and compelling as they are, will not suffice. Oisin and his creator must lie down in the same place, though it took a lifetime of his own loving, battle, and reverie for the poet to be sure.

From his twentieth year until his death, Yeats always wrote verse, or tried to, no matter how busy and preoccupied he was. The poems eventually published as *Crossways* were written while he was at work on "Oisin" and first published in the same year. Those that became *The Rose* were composed between 1889 and 1892 and appeared in 1893. *The Wind Among the Reeds* was written 1892–93 and published in 1899. They were much changed for subsequent editions, and the revisions are a study and a controversy in themselves; nevertheless, the poems as printed in *Collected Poems* do fairly represent his early work, written during his twenties and early thirties, between "Oisin" and his first full immersion in the Irish Literary Theater.

They are poems of the period, that is, late Romantic, indebted to Spenser, Shelley and Blake as modified by the pre-Raphaelites and Morris, and influenced by Yeats's friends in the Rhymers Club, the lessons he learned from them and the debates he had with them. Arthur Symons had introduced him to French Symbolist theory and Lionel Johnson, to whom *The Rose* is dedicated, had tried to convince him of the necessary separation of art from life, and of the decided superiority of art. At the same time they are distinctly personal poems in matter and manner (both get called "the Celtic Twilight"), evocations of moods rather than representations of subjects or explorations of themes; but there are still some recognizeable experiences that Yeats draws on: his intense and frustrated love for Maud Gonne and his liberating but impermanent affair with Olivia Shakespear; Irish stories, landscapes and feelings; the Otherworld; occult ritual, wisdom, and magic. There are also attempts, not wholly successful, to join all four sets of experience into a coherent view of the world and the place of the young poet in it.

The poems are evocative and purposefully vague. It is not unjust to Yeats's intention or to his accomplishment to call them dreamy. The action is remote, the feeling often dim, and the coloring pale. There is the occasionally strained diction that marks early Yeats as clearly as the young Keats. The attitude is typically lonely, wistful, bemused, yearning and hesitant.

The three volumes are less rich and intriguing than "The Wanderings of Oisin" and, in spite of high claims for them, less satisfying than his later poetry. But they contain some important attempts and some genuine achievements: ballads that treat Irish life with vigor and wit; lyrics that convey his sense of the mystery and the pain of experience; dramatic monologues that anticipate later, more successful plays and odes; dream or occult poems that adequately reflect his investment in both; and, most successfully, a commingling of the Irish tradition and personal emotion as in the haunting "Who Goes with Fergus":

> And no more turn aside and brood
> Upon love's bitter mystery;
> For Fergus rules the brazen cars,
> And rules the shadows of the wood,
> And the white breast of the dim sea
> And all dishevelled wandering stars.

or "The Song of Wandering Aengus," one of the few Yeats poems that really is a song:

> Though I am old with wandering
> Through hollow lands and hilly lands,
> I will find out where she has gone,
> And kiss her lips and take her hands;
> And walk among long dappled grass,
> And pluck till time and times are done
> The silver apples of the moon,
> The golden apples of the sun.

As early as 1888, when Yeats was already correcting and revising, he worried "that it is almost all a flight into Fairyland from the real world, and a summons to that flight ... that it is not the poetry of insight and knowledge, but of longing and complaint — the cry of the heart against necessity. I hope some day to alter that and write poetry of insight and knowledge." By the turn of the century he was writing to Lady Gregory and AE about his dissatisfaction with his "dreamy" early poems, and his determination to write tougher, "colder," more "masculine" verse, poetry "with more salt in it." He was also trying to become a playwright. *The Countess Cathleen,* with its dreamy poet, pacific nationalism, and Celtic Twilight diction, was part of his reputation. *Cathleen Ni Houlihan,* with its more realistic social situation, brisker language, and stern, demanding nationalism was in his head. He was necessarily becoming a public man and a fighter. His style, and his life, and his relationship to his country were about to change in more decisive ways than he could have anticipated.

4

As a founder of the Irish Literary Theater, President of the National Dramatic Society, and Manager or Director of the Abbey, Yeats was frequently involved in controversies. They swirled around many issues, but the fundamental disagreement was over whether Irish literature, especially drama, should be a vehicle for nationalist opinion or for the unrestricted expression of personal experience and vision. On that issue he always knew where he stood, and fought with skill and determination, even, though he liked to deny it, with joy. For an enthusiast and publicist it is better to be attacked than ignored. The attack was most heated early in 1907 when nationalist and Catholic opinion joined in a sustained assault on Synge's *Playboy of the Western World* which was thought an impious and subversive attack on the Irish character. A small and well organized group attempted, for a week, to keep the players from being heard; rioting followed and the police were called; later, there were similar disturbances in England and America when the *Playboy* was taken on tour. Yeats wrote letters and essays, organized meetings, conducted debates—persuading and hectoring—and his and Lady Gregory's intransigent and successful defense of the *Playboy* and the rights of the Theater is one of their real contributions to modern Irish culture.

At the same time they were engaged on another front. Sir Hugh Lane, Lady Gregory's nephew, an adventurous and skilled collector of modern art, had offered to give his collection of French impressionist paintings to Dublin if the Municipal Corporation built a suitable gallery. Opponents argued that the paintings had no real value, that Lane and his friends were pushy dilettantes trying to impose their decadent tastes on an innocent populace, that a gallery would be a waste of money. Lane, furious, agreed to leave the collection to London; later he changed his mind and his will leaving them once more to Dublin; but the codicil was unsigned when he went down with the *Lusitania* in 1915; a prolonged battle over possession was finally ended in 1959 by a compromise agreement through which the paintings are shared by London and Dublin. Chief spokesman for the opposition was William Martin Murphy, wealthy businessman and powerful publisher of *The Evening Herald* and *The Irish Independent*. He had already attacked Yeats and the Theater; he had been a principal supporter of Tim Healy in the overthrow of Parnell; he was later to organize and direct the infamous Dublin Lock-out of 1913, when Irish employers attempted to break Jim Larkin's Irish Transport and General Worker's Union. Yeats engaged Murphy on all fronts, political, aesthetic, and humanitarian. Murphy became the most complete embodiment of what Yeats saw as a new and hostile force in Irish life: philistine, rapacious, ruthless; a new Catholic middle class replacing the alliance between the Anglo-Irish gentry and the country people represented by Parnell; both receptive to clerical pressure and able to manipulate religious sentiment for its own ends. Much of Yeats's writing from 1903 onward is an extended argument with this force and a cry of rage against its increasing dominance. His frustration was augmented and sharpened by his own relationship to Maud Gonne—her marriage and its difficulties leading to separation; MacBride's execution making her a widow; his proposals and her refusals. That is not a political problem, but, because of her situation and personality and because she represented so much of Ireland to Yeats, it affected his feelings about public life. One decisive moment in the evolution of his public character occurred in 1905 when she appeared at an Abbey premiere and some followers of MacBride hissed.

Yeats wrote a great deal of critical and controversialist prose between the turn of the century and the Easter Uprising. Most of it has been collected as *The Irish Dramatic Movement* in *Explorations, The Cutting of an Agate* in *Essays and Introductions,* and *Estrangement* and *The Death of Synge* in *Autobiographies*. It reflects his partcipation in battles difficult to win, the burden of those passing issues, the disappearance of saints and heroes; and it reveals important shifts in tone and attitude. He begins with genuinely nationalistic feeling and intellectual excitement. He is part of a movement which is finding an audience. There are friends and helpers everywhere. This is the right moment and we are in touch with the spirit of our time and place. If there is an ironic or cautionary note ("I am perhaps writing an epitaph, and epitaphs should be written in a genial spirit"), it is relaxed and affectionate. Soon, however, there is sharp criticism: an Abbey performance is "the worst I ever saw"; "the pulpit and newspaper are but voices of the mob"; "there is nothing so passionate as a vested interest disguised as an intellectual conviction." An essay of 1903 begins with two stark sentences: "I think the theatre must be reformed in its plays, its speaking, its acting and its scenery. That is to say, I think there is nothing good about it at present."

Behind that criticism is a strong sense of personal determination: "I answer to those who say that Ireland cannot afford this [artistic] freedom because of her political circumstances, that if Ireland cannot afford it, Ireland cannot have a literature." Irony gives way to outright alienation: "The soul of Ireland has become a vapour and her body a stone." This new, embittered attitude and harsh tone is partly caused by fatigue, impatience, and frustration, an angry awareness of lost time and talent, energy and productivity confessed in an essay of 1905: "I have had very little to say this year in *Samhain,* and I have said it badly.... I am busy with a practical project which needs the saying of many things from time to time, and it is better to say them carelessly and harshly than to take time from my poetry. One casts something away every year, and I shall, I think, have to cast away the hope of ever having a prose style that amounts to anything."

The tone hardened into an attitude in two poems of 1908–9:

> The fascination of what's difficult
> Had dried the sap out of my veins, and rent
> Spontaneous joy and natural content
> Out of my heart....
>
> My curse on plays
> That have to be set up in fifty ways,
> On the day's war with every knave and dolt,
> Theatre business, management of men.
>
> All things can tempt me from this craft of verse:
> One time it was a woman's face, or worse—
> The seeming needs of my fool driven land.

This impatience is accompanied by an increasingly open and aggressive class sense, acknowledging or endorsing the Anglo-Irish middle class from which he came and the gentry which he admired and now started to emulate. The sense of class had always been with Yeats, though during the building years it had been surpressed or sublimated. In 1895 he had written to Katherine Tynan that he was sending Irish books out on crusades and evangels to "Lady Gore-Booth's" and other "Unionist household[s]," adding, "these people are much better educated than our own people, and have a better instinct for excellence." The pronouns are instructive. The Yeatses were in fact closer to "these people," descendants of the Ascendancy, than to the Catholic nationalists and Gaelic Leaguers the young poet was trying to cultivate and claim as "our own." At the turn of the century he was still arguing that "a writer or public man of the upper classes is useless to this country till he had done something that separates him from his class," a sentiment he codifies in the unlovely slogan he suggests to potential converts from "University or Castle": "Now you must be baptized of the gutter." As the movement becomes dominated by Lady Gregory, Yeats and Synge (who reflect a broad range of Anglo-Irish success and position), and as the new middle class becomes dominated and represented by the Healys and Murphys, his class sense becomes less cushioned. He had confidently hoped that the true poet would be a nationalist by following his own instincts; he is now likely to argue that it is the obligation of the people to accept and honor the poet. While he once claimed that the Irish people would develop into an ideal audience, he now writes that it requires an elite—educated, privileged, leisured—to understand and foster art, that only a "few scattered people...have the right to call themselves the Irish race." Metaphors based on class permeate his understanding and analysis of individual character and artistic excellence, as in the passage on Lady Gregory's trees, with its conclusion in wistful alienation.

The desire "to create an intellectual aristocracy, a leisured class—to set apart and above all others, a number of men and women who are not very well pleased with one another or the world they have to live in" has literary as well as political impetus. Yeats's sense of class is fed and heightened by his consistent, sometimes violent, opposition to realism, naturalism, popular literature, propaganda, and the mass audience, an antipathy that gets increasingly aggressive the longer he works with the Abbey Theatre. He associates "the literature of suggestion" with traditional culture and with "leisure, wealth, privilege ... a soil for the most living," and "the literature of logic, the most powerful and the most empty" with argument, democracy, and mass education. The fullest expression of the opposition is *The Cutting of an Agate,* a series of theater essays written between 1902 and 1912. Yeats asserts that, with the help of Ezra Pound and the Noh plays, "I have invented a form of drama, distinguished, indirect, and symbolic, and having no need of mob or Press to pay its way — an aristocratic form" committed to "that high breeding of poetical style where there is nothing ostentatious, nothing crude, no breath of parvenu or journalist." Politics, literary theory, and the very difficult practice of writing and producing plays come together and result in a characteristic and willful set of antinomies. On the one hand realism, journalism, politics; "mathematicians, theologians, lawyers, men of science of various kinds"; the world of character and doctrine; "professors, schoolmasters, letter-writing priests and the authors of manuals"; Ireland as it seems to be developing. On the other hand passion, intensity, reverie; "that tragic ecstasy which is the best that art—perhaps that life—can give"; the world of personality and feeling; imaginative energy; "abundant, resonant, beautiful, laughing, living speech"; the ideal Ireland of his youth and his hopes. It is, throughout, a renewed choice of the lamp: "The end of art is the ecstasy awakened by the presence before an ever-changing mind of what is permanent in the world, or by the rousing of that mind itself into the very delicate and fastidious mood habitual with it when it is seeking those permanent and recurring things." And the representative figure is Synge, his tragic life, his intense art, and the resonant myth Yeats is already creating out of both:

> The strength that made him delight in setting the hard virtues by the soft, the bitter by the sweet, salt by mercury, the stone by the elixir, gave him a hunger for harsh facts, for ugly surprising things, for all that defies our hope.

> He was a solitary, undemonstrative man, never asking pity, nor complaining, nor seeking sympathy but in this book's [*Deirdre*] momentary cries: all folded up in brooding intellect, knowing nothing of new books and newspapers, reading the great masters alone; and he was but the more hated because he gave his country what it needed, an unmoved mind where there is a perpetual Last Day, a trumpeting, a coming up to judgement.

The passages and the essays that contain them are acute tributes and fine celebrations. They are also, as Yeats's notes make clear, the creation of an ideal audience and nation: "I always rouse myself to work by imagining an Ireland as much a unity in thought and feeling as ancient Greece and Rome and Egypt.... We three [Synge, Lady Gregory, Yeats] have conceived an Ireland that will remain imaginary more powerfully than we have conceived ourselves." The imagining becomes more and more desperate until, by 1914, there is a radical disjunction:

> All this day I'd looked in the face
> What I had hoped 'twould be
> To write for my own race
> And the reality.

> Maybe a twelvemonth since
> Suddenly I began,
> In scorn of this audience,
> Imagining a man,

> A man who does not exist,
> A man who is but a dream;
> And cried, 'Before I am old
> I shall have written him one
> Poem maybe as cold
> And passionate as the dawn.'

There are moments when Yeats's scorn and celebration are animated by mere snobbery ("Synge who was proud and lonely, almost as proud of his old blood as of his genius"), and moments when he slyly combines snobbery and integrity, as in the insistence that Synge and Lady Gregory "are the strongest souls I have every known," retaining "the self-possession of their intellects" by isolating themselves "from all contagious opinion of poorer minds." Neither friend would have accepted that explanation of their genius, but they did recognize that Yeats, whatever the excesses of condescension or ravages of estrangement, was fighting real battles, that he had to fight them with the weapons available, and that the most fundamental issues were crucial. He remains fierce about intellectual freedom and artistic integrity: "We have to write or find plays that will make the theatre a place of intellectual excitement," he wrote in 1903, "a place where the mind goes to be liberated. ... We must learn that beauty and truth are always justified of themselves, and that their creation is a greater service to our country than writing that compromises either in the seeming service of a cause." He works on two plays that dramatize that conviction. Seanchan of *The King's Threshold* and Cuchulain of *On Baile's Strand,* poet and warrior, are betrayed and destroyed by "ordinary" politics — manipulative, prudential, dishonest — in the persons of their kings, Guaire and Conchubar, and by the worldly, grubby blandishments and misunderstandings of their societies. Both heroes revolt against constituted authority and diminished expectations, but at the same time both are conservatives, seeing themselves as links with a more heroic past as well as a more ennobling vision. In each play Yeats draws on Irish legend, but takes his doomed protagonist's ideology from his idea of Synge, from Shelley, and from the recently discovered Nietzsche:

> Seanchan.
>> What was it that the poets promised you,
>> If it was not their sorrow? ...
>
>> And I would have all know that when all falls
>> In ruin, poetry calls out in joy,
>> Being the scattering hand, the bursting pod,
>> The victim's joy among the holy flame,
>> God's laughter at the shattering of the world.
>
> Oldest Pupil.
>> Not what it leaves behind it in the light
>> But what it carries with it to the dark

> Exalts the soul; nor song nor trumpet-blast
> Can call up races from the worsening world
> To mend the wrong and mar the solitude
> Of the great shade we follow to the tomb.

He is equally determined, though more reticent, about the necessities of his imagination and its development. He can be ungenerous in his scorn and inaccurate in his analysis, but he is right to stick by the dictates of his conscience and the imperatives of his imagination. And he knows, in the ways most important to him, what is happening. "I thought myself loving neither vice nor virtue," he writes at the close of *Estrangement,* recalling both Seanchan and his friends of the Rhymers club, "but virtue has come upon me and given me a nation instead of a home. Has it left me any lyrical faculty? Whatever happens I must go on that there may be a man behind the lines already written; I cast the die long ago and must be true to the cast."

During this period Yeats published *In The Seven Woods* (1904), *The Green Helmet and Other Poems* (1910), and *Responsibilities* (1914). The volumes include poems to and about Lady Gregory and Maud Gonne, lyrical and dramatic poems, the important, transitional "Adam's Curse," and some verses and epigrams from public life. *Responsibilities,* the most complete expression of his current feelings about Ireland, begins "Pardon, old fathers, if you still remain/ Somewhere in ear-shot for the story's end." The story is his own and the poem reflects his sense of having come to the end of something, his new interest in family history (he was at work on *Reveries over Childhood and Youth*), and his search for the "tradition of myself." It is not an altogether successful *apologia,* marred by simple snobbery ("Merchant and scholar who have left me blood/ That has not passed through any huckster's loin" does not establish the difference between old merchant and new Murphy) and embarrassing to Yeats as an early version had his ancestors fighting on the wrong side at the Battle of the Boyne, and his revisionist revision is a little strained. The poem only comes to life at the end, and it is not family or self, but Maud Gonne, that animates it:

> Pardon that for a barren passion's sake,
> Although I have come close on forty-nine,
> I have no child, I have nothing but a book,
> Nothing but that to prove your blood and mine.

Regret yields to anger in the five public poems which first appeared in the *Irish Times*, then in the aptly titled *Poems Written in Discouragement*. Yeats's note establishes the relationship between the poems and the battles over Parnell, *The Playboy*, and Lane's paintings: "These controversies, political, literary, and artistic, have showed that neither religion nor politics can of itself create minds with enough receptivity to become wise, or just and generous enough to make a nation." Irish piety, he argues, is separated from life and obsessed by a narrow sense of duty, while Irish politics can only tolerate conventional, doctrinaire opinion. "Against all this we have but a few educated men and the remnants of an old traditional culture among the poor." Ireland is now dominated by "our new middle class" which continually demonstrates "how base at moments of excitement are minds without culture."

Ezra Pound, who had been living with Yeats and acting as his secretary, caught the impulse and reviewed the volume in a way Yeats must have appreciated: "There is a new robustness; there is the tooth of satire which is in Mr. Yeats's case, too good a tooth to keep hidden.... There are a lot of fools to be killed and Mr. Yeats is an exultant slaughtermaster." "Exultant" comes from Yeats, the advice he gives Lady Gregory — "Be secret and exult" — in one of the poems, "To a Friend Whose Work Has Come to Nothing," a fine attack on Murphy and less assured recommendation to her. In fact only one of the poems successfully shows the tooth of satire. "To a Wealthy Man" sets Duke Ercole, Guidobaldo, and Cosimo against the stingy and prudent middle class, but cannot quite rise out of the snobbish posing that George Moore pilloried in *Vale*. Yeats may have rid himself of Shelley's Italian light, but he has not absorbed Castiglione's *noblesse* and cannot make it a plausible force in contemporary cultural politics. "Paudeen" begins in indignation, but quickly turns to anxious apology and a Christian humility it is difficult to imagine Yeats really feeling in 1913. "To a Shade" is more controlled, imagining that the ghost of the Chief has returned to Dublin to discover that "they are at their old tricks yet," that another aristocratic and magnanimous nationalist, Hugh Lane

> has been driven from the place,
> And insult heaped upon him for his pains,
> And for his open-handedness, disgrace;
> Your enemy, an old foul mouth, had set
> The pack upon him.

That mouth, O'Brien nicely observes, is a "collective orifice" of the old Sullivan gang, "the tongue of Healy and the teeth of Murphy," a Swiftian embodiment of Yeats's animus. In the last stanza, Yeats plays the Oldest Pupil to Parnell's Seanchan and quietly returns the "unquiet wanderer" to the safety of his grave in Glasnevin cemetary. It is more defeated than exultant, however, Yeats's equivalent to "Ivy Day in the Committee Room," one of several moments when his use of the myth of Parnell, his betrayers and paltry successors is similar to Joyce's.

The most powerful presence in these bitter poems is John O'Leary, and his poem, "September, 1913," is the one triumph that merits Pound's praise, the first of Yeats's poems that proves what he much later wrote, that "indignation is a kind of joy." The poem goes back to Yeats's recollection that "when O'Leary died I could not bring myself to go to his funeral," because he would there find men and women who could not understand the old Fenian and were likely to betray his memory. "Power passed to small shopkeepers, to clerks, to that very class who had seemed to John O'Leary so ready to bend to the power of others, to men who had risen above the traditions of the countryman, without learning those of cultivated life or even educating themselves, and who, because of their poverty, their ignorance, their superstitious piety, are much subject to all kinds of fear." There is some sympathy for the clerks, or Paudeens, in that essay of 1907; by 1913 it has vanished, and the poem begins with a furiously sarcastic question:

> What need you, being come to sense,
> But fumble in a greasy till
> And add the halfpence to the pence
> And prayer to shivering prayer, until
> You have dried the marrow from the bone?

turns to mean parody

> For men were born to pray and save

and establishes its absolute, estranged refrain:

> Romantic Ireland's dead and gone,
> It's with O'Leary in the grave.

The second stanza invokes but does not name other heroes, Irish soldiers driven into exile and European armies when the victorious British passed confiscatory and oppressive laws after the battle of the Boyne.

The next stanza names the heroes, establishes a type of self-sacrificing bravery antithetical to Paudeen and Biddy, dogmatic church and greasy till, the modern Ireland of prudential morality and timid behavior.

Their magnanimity is then linked with Parnell's leadership, and the renunciation of Parnell because of his affair with Kitty O'Shea is seen as a continuation of the Irish habit of betraying its leaders. The rhyme (gave/grave) punctuates the poem's conclusion that true nationalism will lead to exile and solitude, pain and death:

> Yet could we turn the years again,
> And call those exiles as they were
> In all their loneliness and pain,
> You'd cry, 'Some woman's yellow hair
> Has maddened every mother's son':
> They weighed so lightly what they gave.
> But let them be, they're dead and gone,
> They're with O'Leary in the grave.

"September, 1913" makes two angry assertions, the obvious one that romantic Ireland's dead and gone, the less obvious one that romantic and heroic Ireland was never what "you" thought it was. For romantic Ireland is associated not with O'Connell or Davis, not even with Cathleen and Cuchulain, and certainly not with Healy and Murphy, but with O'Leary, Parnell, Emmet, Fitzgerald, Tone — all Anglo-Irish Protestants, two from the aristocracy and two from the landed gentry. It is a politically "metaphysical" poem in Dr. Johnson's terms: a violent yoking together of apparent opposites, and the violence is a political act. It is unfair and tactless but, like Keats's street brawl, its energy is fine. It accurately compresses Yeats's sense of Ireland in 1913. It reveals a move he is going to make over and over in the years to come as he substitutes Anglo-Irish and aristocratic for popular and Catholic heroes, willfully defines the Irish national tradition, and hurls the new definition into the teeth of modern Ireland.

In 1910, while working on "Synge and the Ireland of his Time," and so thinking about poetry and politics, Yeats wrote in his journal that "literature discovers; it can never repeat. It is the attempt to repeat an emotion because it has been found effective which has made all provincially political literature ... so superficial. Literature is inspired by the vision also of the naked truth, but she clothes herself before she walks out onto the roads." Two or three years later he was not so sure about the clothing. "A Coat" has to do with his determination not to repeat himself, to drive towards new discoveries, with his dissatisfaction with his early style, and with his proud contempt for those imitators who are part of the price of leading a movement. It also reflects his new sense of the national being and the estranged and combative mood with which he confronts it. The poem concludes *Responsibilities,* and this portion of his life:

> I made my song a coat
> Covered with embroideries
> Out of old mythologies
> From heel to throat;
> But the fools caught it,
> Wore it in the world's eyes
> As though they'd wrought it.
> Song, let them take it,
> For there's more enterprise
> In walking naked.

5

Politics and Public Life
1913 — 1939

omantic Ireland's dead and gone sounds old-fashioned now, Yeats wrote in July, 1916. "It seemed true in 1913, but I did not foresee 1916. The late Dublin Rebellion, whatever one can say of its wisdom, will long be remembered for its heroism. 'They weighed so lightly what they gave,' and gave too in some cases without hope of success." That double qualification—the authentic heroism demands that he revise his recent, dismissive judgments; but he remains uncertain about its wisdom — reveals Yeats's mixed response to the Easter Uprising, a problem for him and for his friends and readers. Immediately after the rebellion and executions he wrote to Lady Gregory about his agitation ("I had no idea that any public event could so deeply move me") and about a poem he was trying to write "on the men executed—'terrible beauty has been born again.'" Maud Gonne thought the poem was inadequate; others felt that it conceded too much to revolutionary enthusiasm. In fact, "Easter, 1916" is not equivocation but ambivalence, a crucial distinction in poetic as well as political discourse. It begins with a recollection and evocation of the grey world of Dublin before the Rising, the repeated "polite meaningless words" emphasizing the banality of ordinary discourse in a society held together by surface conventions and camaraderie, as is most society, most of the time. The second stanza catalogues the martyrs—"that woman," "this man," "this other"—but does not name them, which has the effect of both generalization and tact. Unnamed heroes approximate the epic as ordinary lives become heroic. At the same time, the poet is reticent; he can only name the martyrs—"I write it out in verse"—at the close of the last stanza, when the poem, by the balance and depth of its feeling, has earned the right to participate in this history.

The third stanza, only apparently a digression, sets fixity of purpose against the marvelously attractive, myriad abundance of ordinary life; but now that life is seen as natural rather than social, animated rather than ancient, grey, and inert. Setting the stone, an image at once personal and political, "in the midst of" and against the stream which it blocks and alters, the lines explore the achievement and the cost of revolutionary dedication. The final stanza begins with the poem's only flat assertion — "Too long a sacrifice/ Can make a stone of the heart" — and then poses a series of unanswerable questions. Will there ever be sacrifice enough? Is death merely the coming of night (a sentimental evasion instantly caught and rejected)? Was that death needless? Might England, after the Great War, have kept its promise and granted Home Rule without violence? Most painfully, in words which echo both Pearse's invocation of Colmcille — "If I die it shall be for the excess of love I bear the Gael" — and that "delirium of the brave" ruefully admired in "September, 1913,"

> And what if excess of love
> Bewildered them till they died?

Now able to confront but not answer those questions, to authenticate the self-sacrificing heroism and still worry about the consequences and grieve over the stone, the poem reaches its strong, ringing conclusion:

> I write it out in verse —
> MacDonagh and MacBride
> And Connolly and Pearse
> Now and in time to be,
> Wherever green is worn,
> Are changed, changed utterly:
> A terrible beauty is born.

In this grave, balanced, deeply felt poem, Yeats has done three difficult and admirable things. He has seen a national event as tragedy, tragedy in the classical, redemptive mode. The poem is organized around theater metaphors — motley becomes green, MacBride "has resigned his part/ In the casual comedy" — in order to assert that at certain moments of intense crisis, national life achieves the richness and terror of great drama. Catharsis may occur, though rarely, for those who participate in and meditate upon the pity and fear of heightened human action. He has recovered meaning for the word "green," no small accomplishment in a literary culture that so much abused it and for a poet so self-conscious about that abuse. There is a Gresham's Law of language, too, bad use driving out good and turning nice little words into harlots and pimps; so it is exhilirating to see a poet engaged in an act of rehabilitation. He has embodied his own powerful and mixed feelings and made them part of the public domain. In this poem Yeats achieves what Eliot claimed Arnold did not, an ability to penetrate beneath the superficial squalor and ugliness of life and see something of the horror and the glory.

"Easter, 1916" is, however, an exception. In the years following the Uprising, Yeats most often seems uncertain or indifferent or wishful about issues of national identity and possibility. He wrote the poem immediately, but withheld it from publication until 1920. He does not make a consistent or coherent political commitment until 1922 when he returns to Dublin, buys a Georgian house, and becomes a Senator of the newly created Free State. Meanwhile, while Europe and Ireland are falling apart, Yeats is consolidating his past, temporarily pulling away from the nation and its tumult, and moving on to new explorations and achievements. The Uprising did change his life, but not at first in political ways. The execution of Major MacBride left Maud Gonne free to remarry; Yeats proposed and was rejected; he then proposed to Iseult Gonne, who declined. Then, on October 20, 1917, he married Georgie Hyde-Lees, a friend of Ezra Pound and Olivia Shakespear whom he had known since 1911. She shared his interest in the occult and in 1914 had been encouraged to join the Golden Dawn by Yeats, who acted as her Hierens or sponsor. Shortly after their marriage, in an attempt to distract him from thoughts about Iseult, Mrs. Yeats tried automatic writing with the now-famous results. Within a month Yeats had transformed her fragmentary notations into the first outline of *A Vision,* giving focus and definition to years of occult study, and establishing the preoccupations that were to be the center of his life for the next six years. Marriage also had conventional consequences. Anne Butler Yeats was born in 1919, Michael in 1921, liberating him from the disconnected middle age he had lamented in *Responsibilities,* and fostering his family and clan feeling. He and his wife decided to restore the Tower at Thoor Ballylee and live there summers. *A Vision* names, classifies, and so orders experience. The tower is a physical embodiment of the same impulse, another world of his own making, and Yeats plans renovations, arranges furniture, and envisions a new life.

At the same time, as Lady Gregory tartly noted, he is much out of Ireland, wintering in Oxford, lecturing in America, and worrying that life at home during The Troubles would be "blood and misery":

> If that comes we may abandon Ballylee to the owls and the rats, and England too (where passions will rise and I shall find myself with no answer), and live in some far land. Should England and Ireland be

divided beyond all hope of remedy, what else could one do for the children's sake, or one's own work? I could not bring them to Ireland where they would inherit bitterness, nor leave them in England where, being Irish by tradition, and by family and fame, they would be in an unnatural condition of mind and grow, as so many Irishmen who live here do, sour and argumentative.

The major texts of the period show the same impulses to consolidate, to pull away, and to move on. In 1919 the Cuala Press published "If I Were Four-and-Twenty," which begins with one of Yeats's most confident, even self-congratulatory proclamations:

> One day when I was twenty-three or twenty-four this sentence seemed to form in my head, without my willing it, much as sentences form when we are half-asleep: 'Hammer your thoughts into unity.' For days I could think of nothing else, and for years I tested all I did by that sentence. I had three interests: interest in a form of literature, in a form of philosophy, and a belief in nationality. None of these seemed to have anything to do with the other, but gradually my love of literature and my belief in nationality came together. Then for years I said to myself that these two had nothing to do with my form of philosophy, but that I had only to be sincere and to keep from constraining one by the other and they would become one interest. Now all three are, I think, one, or rather all three are a discrete expression of a single conviction. I think that each has behind it my whole character and has gained thereby a certain newness — for is not every man's character peculiar to himself? — and that I have become a cultivated man.

Yet the body of the essay is about the lack of national culture, unity, character. Writing during the Anglo-Irish war, Yeats posits his newly found sense of personal integration, traditional social coherence, and "family struggle ... family strength" as a counter against national disintegration. The irony of its conclusion does not quite cover a distancing sense of superiority: " ... if I were not four-and-fifty, with no settled habit but the writing of verse, rheumatic, indolent, discouraged, and about to move to the Far East, I would begin another epoch by recommending to the Nation a new doctrine, that of unity of being." Similarly, he began *The Trembling of the Veil* just before his marriage in an attempt, he wrote John Quinn, to "lay many ghosts, or rather I will purify my own imagination by setting the past in order." But he extensively revised it between 1919 and 1922, eliminating some embarrassing confessions, and suffusing it, as Ellmann notes, "with the serenity of a man who has achieved Unity of Being." In

both cases there is a striking disjunction between the harmony and purposefulness Yeats feels and the confused and terror-stricken nation
he addresses.

He writes a good many poems of place, possession, and progeny—all
particular in scene and personal in reference. "The Wild Swans at Coole,"
written shortly before his marriage, captures his feelings of increasing age
and lost passion, and establishes Coole and its desmene as one of his few
available poetic locations. "In Memory of Major Robert Gregory" declares, through its mourning, his increasingly firm allegiance to the
Anglo-Irish tradition. "A Prayer on Going into My House," written to
commemorate the move to Thoor Ballylee, begins seriously, turns aggressive, and concludes comically, a parody of the new property owner's
nervous anger:

> and should some limb of the Devil
> Destroy the view by cutting down an ash
> That shades the road, or setting up a cottage
> Planned in a government office, shorten his life,
> Manacle his soul upon the Red Sea bottom.

Another memorial, "To Be Carved on a Stone at Thoor Ballylee," shows
anger becoming anxiety, and a not quite consumated wish that creative
effort can overcome both:

> I, the poet William Yeats,
> With old mill boards and sea-green slates,
> And smithy work from the Gort forge,
> Restored this tower for my wife George;
> And may these characters remain
> When all is ruin once again.

"A Prayer for My Daughter" richly elaborates and fully embodies a parallel wish, that the individual soul, properly rooted and raised, can
recover innocence in the face of a disintegrating world. In the poems, as in
the prose, Yeats asserts or creates a harmony he can envision privately, but
not socially or politically. Even the plays on Irish subjects—*At the Hawk's
Well* and *The Only Jealousy of Emer,* the third and fourth of the Cuchulain cycle, and *The Dreaming of the Bones,* where a young revolutionary
soldier meets the shades of Diarmuid and Dervorgilla—are more personal
than national in their myth making. They are shaped by Yeats's modifica-

tions of the theories of the Noh drama introduced to him by Ezra Pound, by the developing theories of *A Vision,* and by his desire to create a new and "aristocratic" form of drama, which would combine music, mask, dance, and verse in a highly stylized and unapologetically symbolic representation of moments of intensity. They are concerned with heroism and suffering, defeat and reconciliation, but as qualities of the individual imagination rather than of the national being. They are sexually charged as Yeats explores, once again, the risks and terrors of devotion to the quest and submission to the muse. *The Dreaming of the Bones* contains one of Yeats's rare moments of political sentimentality as he has his young man, escaped from the Post Office and searching for refuge in the West, declare that "no man of us but hated/ To fire at soldiers who but did their duty/ And were not of our race." It is a generous sentiment and in tune with one of Yeats's themes, the burdens of revolutionary dedication, but not with the historical realities of 1919, when the play was written, or 1916, when it is set.

Two poems explicitly and emphatically reject political commitment. "On Being Asked for a War Poem" is an evasively playful response to World War I. "The Leaders of the Crowd" is a much angrier comment on Irish politics, always closer to Yeats than European, and a fierce insistence on his own right to detachment. "The Second Coming" is one of Yeats's most famous poems and one of the most fully representative of his mature writing. It was written in January 1919, begins in a mood similar to "The Leaders of the Crowd" and is placed soon after it in *Michael Robartes and the Dancer,* the volume characterized most notably by Yeats's exhortations to various women to avoid hatred and abstraction, advice parallel to his own impulse to withdraw. The vocabulary is specialized and could only be Yeats, but the first stanza reflects a public condition and embodies a perception common to Lady Gregory and many Irishmen and Europeans at this time. The solitude of students of the imagination has become the powerlessness and drift of good people in bad times, while the leaders remain frenzied:

> Turning and turning in the widening gyre
> The falcon cannot hear the falconer;
> Things fall apart; the centre cannot hold;
> Mere anarchy is loosed upon the world,
> The blood-dimmed tide is loosed, and everywhere
> The ceremony of innocence is drowned;
> The best lack all conviction, while the worst
> Are full of passionate intensity.

"Gyre" comes from *A Vision,* the spiralling cone of historical process, but also appropriate to the falcon's flight. The falcon was originally a hawk, probably changed to remove the particular symbolic associations of Yeats's hawks. Mere anarchy and its emblem, the blood-dimmed tide, are glossed by the storm and murderous sea of the next poem in the volume, "A Prayer for My Daughter," as is the ceremony of innocence. What is one to do when all control seems spent, when willfulness, chaos, and destructiveness flood unchecked?

The drafts indicate the political sources of the poem: the collapse of the Russian front to the Germans in 1917, the Bolshevik revolution, Lenin's surrender of territory at the Treaty of Brest-Litovsk, concern for the fate of the Russian Royal family, the troubles in Ireland which were increasing in violence and bloodthirstiness as the poem was written. A cancelled line, "And there's no Burke to cry aloud no Pitt," laments the absence of traditional, counter-revolutionary forces to stem the rising tide of barbarism. It suggests that the tension of the poem is ideological as well as dramatic. Its political occasion is a conservative reaction to Socialist revolution in Europe and terrorism in Ireland. Its chief literary sources are Shelley — "Ozymandias" for the beast, "Prometheus Unbound" for the political condition—and Blake—"The First Book of Urizen" for the "stony sleep" and second birth. But Shelley and Blake side with the revolutionaries and celebrate the apocalypse. Yeats's apocalypse is to be terrifying and ironic, an instructive and unsettling revision of romantic optimism; as Harold Bloom says, he appropriates for the Right some crucial insights of the Left.

In the second stanza, description gives way to prophecy, or rather to a stammering prophecy of a prophecy:

> Surely some revelation is at hand;
> Surely the Second Coming is at hand.
> The Second Coming!

Prophecy immediately becomes a vision welling up from the *Spiritus Mundi,* Yeats's storehouse of archetypal images. It has the widest possible resonance as Yeats conflates Christ's prediction of His rebirth, the beast of the Apocalypse in Revelations, Ozymandias, and Urizen, the Egyptian sphinx, and the personal demons recalled in *The Trembling of the Veil* and, later, in the "Introduction" to *The Resurrection:* "I began to imagine, as always at my left side just out of the range of the sight, a brazen winged beast that I associated with laughing, ecstatic destruction." The social and political falcon has its nightmare recapitulation in the sinister birds of prey that circle around *their* center:

> Hardly are those words out
> When a vast image out of *Spiritus Mundi*
> Troubles my sight: somewhere in the sands of the desert
> A shape with lion body and the head of a man,
> A gaze blank and pitiless as the sun,
> Is moving its slow thighs, while all about it
> Reel shadows of the indignant desert birds.

The poem concludes with an assertion that the poet has put on knowledge if not power (Yeats's predictions always contain the prophet), a dramatization of his belief that the end of one age "always receives the revelation of the character of the next age," and an incomplete and ironic prophecy of that annunciation through another figure of multiple resonance:

> The darkness drops again; but now I know
> That twenty centuries of stony sleep
> Were vexed to nightmare by a rocking cradle,
> And what rough beast, its hour come round at last,
> Slouches towards Bethlehem to be born?

The relationship is parallel and sequential. As the rocking cradle of Christ vexed the Greek and Roman era and turned it into a nightmare, so the slouching beast—apt emblem—announces the end of ours and, vague and terrifying, prefigures the dispensation to come.

It is a remarkable poem. Examinations of its impetus and sources, cruxes and rhetoric cannot quite account for its power. Stallworthy's study of the drafts shows Yeats steadily widening its scope, focus, and purpose while at the same time intensifying its power. The detachment of these years becomes a prophetic, nightmarish involvement in the conditions of modern life. It is an involvement that depends upon both subjectivity and complicity. Yeats is compelled by the images of destruction; he does not admire, but he does will the beast. Apocalyptic poems like "The Second Coming," as Whitaker has finely said, "render and judge an evil that can be fully known only by one who has conversed with an interior Lucifer." Solitude, quietism, and retreat become a kind of exultation, not a perverse delight in chaos, but in the power of confronting immense, destructive forces. The shifting perspective of the poem compresses four thousand years of association into twenty-two lines and mirrors the shifting dialogue with history that Yeats was developing in *A Vision*. History is an apprehension of the past, an accounting for the present, and a prediction of the future. It is also drama—a full, nervous (for all its rhetorical control, the voice of the poem is right on the edge of hysteria), highly personal encounter with the center that refuses to hold, the blood-dimmed tide, the fiercely implacable sphinx, and the sinister, slouching beast. As Ireland merges with Europe, politics become vision, and Yeats discovers a subject that comprehends both. By making the issues and terms personal, subjective, eclectic, he makes his work more rather than less politically and historically relevant.

The poems of this period most fully engaged in public life are very different. "Easter, 1916" is sober, balanced, reconciliatory. "The Second Coming" is personal, prophetic, intuitive. "Nineteen Hundred and Nineteen," written in that year and first called "Thoughts Upon the Present State of the World," is aggressive, feverish, and violent. It enriches and complicates "The Leaders of the Crowd" and reflects the feelings expressed in a contemporaneous essay, "A People's Theatre: A Letter to Lady Gregory." That theater is now seen with contempt rather than solidarity or affection, and the essay vents Yeats's general distrust of the mob and particular hostility towards its leaders: "I have Ireland especially in mind, for I want to make, or to help some man some day to make, a feeling of exclusiveness, a bond among chosen spirits, a mystery almost for leisured and lettered people. Ireland has suffered more than England from democracy, for since the Wild Geese fled who might have grown to be leaders in manners and in taste, she has had but political leaders." He sharpens his familiar distinction between old aristocracies, "when the great personified spiritual power," and the present state, "when the great are but the rich," and unabashedly asserts his intention "to create for myself an unpopular theatre and an audience like a secret society where admission is by favour and never to many." The poem begins with some of the same distinctions and a similar lament for the past and contempt for the present, especially for its political self-deception:

> Many ingenious lovely things are gone
> That seemed sheer miracle to the multitude,
> Protected from the circle of the moon
> That pitches common things about. There stood
> Amid the ornamental bronze and stone
> An ancient image made of olive wood—

And gone are Phidias' famous ivories
And all the golden grasshoppers and bees.

We too had many pretty toys when young:
A law indifferent to blame or praise,
To bribe or threat; habits that made old wrong
Melt down, as it were wax in the sun's rays;
Public opinion ripening for so long
We thought it would outlive all future days.
O what fine thought we had because we thought
That the worst rogues and rascals had died out.

"Public opinion" reflects both Yeats's reading of W. E. H. Lecky, the conservative Anglo-Irish historian who would have been appalled by the events that began in 1916, and his recollection of blandly optimistic "no more war" conversations before 1914. The poem then plunges into the present, combines his knowledge of atrocities in Galway with his sense that political hatred taps dark psychic forces, and recognizes that even the solitary are complicit:

Now days are dragon-ridden, the nightmare
Rides upon sleep: a drunken soldiery
Can leave the mother, murdered at her door,
To crawl in her own blood, and go scot-free;
The night can sweat with terror as before
We pieced our thoughts into philosophy,
And planned to bring the world under a rule,
Who are but weasels fighting in a hole.

The next two stanzas define the situation of the poem:

He who can read the signs nor sink unmanned
Into the half-deceit of some intoxicant
From shallow wits; who knows no work can stand,
Whether health, wealth or peace of mind were spent
On master-work of intellect or hand,
No honour leave its mighty monument,
Has but one comfort left: all triumph would
But break upon his ghostly solitude.

But is there any comfort to be found?
Man is in love and loves what vanishes,

> What more is there to say? That country round
> None dared admit, if such a thought were his,
> Incendiary or bigot could be found
> To burn that stump on the Acropolis,
> Or break in bits the famous ivories
> Or traffic in the grasshoppers or bees.

Yeats is beginning to make "break" his particular verb, a process completed in "Byzantium." In the first quoted stanza it means both "intrude" and "break up," and solitude seems slightly less powerless than worldly triumph. But the stoic comfort is soon taken away as the speaker sees that *ubi sunt* is too easy, a dodge. There is more to say, and it is grim. Past and present, lost Athens and ravaged Ireland, merge into one vision of destructiveness, evasion, and corruption. The poet no less than the rogues, rascals, and weasels is responsible for the present traffic.

The second section of "Nineteen Hundred and Nineteen," like the final stanza of "The Second Coming," swings into an enlarged, panoramic vision. For a moment history is joined to aesthetics as Loie Fuller's choreography figures the largest movements of time that the mind can comprehend. But for *this* year there is little solace in the perception of patterns which are instantly overwhelmed by barbarous noise:

> When Loie Fuller's Chinese dancers enwound
> A shining web, a floating ribbon of cloth,
> It seemed that a dragon of air
> Had fallen among dancers, had whirled them round
> Or hurried them off on its own furious path;
> So the Platonic Year
> Whirls out new right and wrong,
> Whirls in the old instead;
> All men are dancers and their tread
> Goes to the barbarous clangour of a gong.

The third poem develops the ideas of solitude and adversity and dramatizes the urgent need to consolidate, to find a center that will hold, and to create some distance between the self and the chaos that surrounds it. The rhythms are more relaxed and declarative as the poet attempts to achieve that distance by stoically facing the destruction rather than avoiding it through nostalgic contemplation of the lovely things that have vanished:

> Some moralist or mythological poet
> Compares the solitary soul to a swan;
> I am satisfied with that,
> Satisfied if a troubled mirror show it,
> Before that brief gleam of its life be gone,
> An image of its state;
> The wings half spread for flight,
> The breast thrust out in pride
> Whether to play, or to ride
> Those winds that clamour of approaching night.

Shelley, Spenser, and Coole provide the swan, contemporary history the troubled mirror that defines it. In its brief moment of anticipatory strength and pride the swan/soul can choose; it can play with or ride out those winds rather than being ridden by the nightmare. The winds clamour of apocalypse throughout the poem: they pitch common things about and ride the days; they whirl out the new and whirl in the old; they are soon to become the "winds of winter" and the "levelling wind" that herald the end of an era and a political philosophy; they finally become the wild "labyrinth of the wind" with which the poem concludes; they immediately become the private, meditative labyrinth of the individual mind, the inescapable isolation of consciousness that torments Yeats as it does Eliot:

> A man in his own secret meditation
> Is lost amid the labyrinth that he has made
> In art or politics;
> Some Platonist affirms that in the station
> Where we should cast off body and trade
> The ancient habit sticks,
> And that if our works could
> But vanish with our breath
> That were a lucky death,
> For triumph can but mar our solitude.

Even solitary pride is a trap; triumph mars rather than breaks; the body cannot be transcended and the achievements of mind are transitory; the self, whether acknowledging complicity or escaping into meditation, is wholly vulnerable; so

> The swan has leaped into the desolate heaven:
> That image can bring wildness, bring a rage
> To end all things, to end

What my laborious life imagined, even
The half-imagined, the half-written page;
O but we dreamed to mend
Whatever mischief seemed
To afflict mankind, but now
That winds of winter blow
Learn that we were crack-pated when we dreamed.

Riding and playing lead to vertigo, to a consuming and masochistic rage for destruction, and end even to what has not yet been created. It is a crisis of imagination and poetic vocation that mirrors Ireland's crisis and returns the poem from dreams (peace, solitude, public harmony and personal productivity) to nightmare. In the next two sections, straight-forward and embittered, the swan becomes the weasel, and, the hopes of solitude defeated, the poet develops the implications of his situation, replacing nostalgia and stoicism with mockery of "the great," "the wise," and "the good" who have all been blasted by the wind.

Mock mockers after that
That would not lift a hand maybe
To help good, wise or great
To bar that foul storm out, for we
Traffic in mockery.

That is an oblique comment on the sentiment of "On Being Asked for a War Poem" or the "mocking tale" of "Easter, 1916," which had seemed, at first, the apt response to the leaders of the rebellion. But this poem discovers no terrible beauty. An early version has "Mock poets after that," and poets who "traffic in mockery" are more deeply complicit than the incendaries and bigots of the first section. They are punished, at least this one is, by an overwhelming, horrifying vision of violence, lust, and emptiness:

Violence upon the roads: violence of horses;
Some few have handsome riders, are garlanded
On delicate sensitive ear or tossing mane,
But wearied running round and round in their courses
All break and vanish, and evil gathers head:
Herodias' daughters have returned again,
A sudden blast of dusty wind and after

Thunder of feet, tumult of images,
Their purpose in the labyrinth of the wind;
And should some crazy hand dare touch a daughter
All turn with amorous cries, or angry cries,
According to the wind, for all are blind.
But now wind drops, dust settles; thereupon
There lurches past, his great eyes without thought
Under the shadow of stupid straw-pale locks,
That insolent friend Robert Artisson
To whom the love-lorn Lady Kyteler brought
Bronzed peacock feathers, red combs of her cocks.

It is an extraordinary pair of sentences. The actual violence in Galway is metamorphosed—through Yeats's reading and folklore collecting, and his thinking and imagining—into an apprehension of the total condition of contemporary life. The horses, he says in a note, come from apparitions reported by countrypeople: "I have assumed...that these horsemen, now that the times worsen, give way to worse." They give way to the daughters of Herodias—emblems of blind passion, willful destruction, and labyrinthine purposelessness — whom his note associates with the Sidhe, "also Gaelic for wind." Loie Fuller's dance "breaks" into wild destructiveness. The image includes Irish politics as well as folklore; Yeats had already, especially in "September, 1913" ("You'd cry, 'Some woman's yellow hair/ Has maddened every mother's son'") equated sexual hysteria with political vengeance, and one of the canceled ideas of this poem is that armies and explosions exist because "women love shows." When the wind finally drops and the dust settles, the culminating image, cousin to the beast of "The Second Coming," lurches past. Robert Artisson, "an evil spirit much run after in Kilkenny at the start of the fourteenth century," may seem an odd figure with which to conclude a poem on "The Present State of the World." He is, however, an exact representation of the condition of "Nineteen Hundren and Nineteen": an incubus lusted after by Dame Kyteler, perched on her sleeping form, mindless and predatory: "nightmare/ Rides upon sleep." To this vacuous fiend, in this ghastly and powerful coda, she brings peacock feathers and cock's combs, perverse annunciation of the modern apocalypse. At the beginning of "Dove or Swan," Yeats wrote: "A civilisation is a struggle to keep self-control, and in this it is like some great tragic person, some Niobe who must display an almost superhuman will or the cry will not touch our sympathy. The loss of control over thought comes towards the end; first a sinking in upon the moral being, then the last surrender, the irrational cry, revelation — the scream of Juno's peacock."

He had complained in "A People's Theatre" that there are no great tragic persons. There are certainly none in the poem. The struggle to read the signs of self and history leads to traffic in violence and mockery, lust and emptiness. The courage of the poem is to face its perceptions; Yeats's achievement is to survive them, to push on to new and major accomplishments in the presence of large difficulties.

2

The Tower, which includes "Nineteen Hundred and Nineteen," was published in 1928, and *The Winding Stair* in 1932. They are probably Yeats's two most impressive collections, the volumes that establish his position among modern poets. Together they illustrate a characteristically Yeatsian paradox. By the mid-twenties he was clearly and firmly established. Married and the father of two healthy children, he had returned to Ireland, established his family in Merrion Square, and purchased and refurbished Thoor Ballylee. He had just completed the first version of *A Vision,* with its sweeping theories of history and psychology and its highly personal eschatology. He was at last financially secure and internationally famous with honorary degrees from Trinity College and Queens University, and the Nobel Prize in 1923. He was an Irish public figure and Free State senator. Yet *The Tower* is a bleak and bitter volume. He was then extremely ill, in 1927 from lung congestion, and in 1928–29 from Malta fever. Yet *The Winding Stair* is intensely affirmative and energetic. It is customary to attribute the change of atmosphere to his poor health, to say that as death moved perceptibly closer, Yeats's mind turned towards life, that the mood of his poems, and their images of life and blood, operate as a kind of self-administered transfusion. This is no doubt true enough. It is easier to contemplate eternity, even to long for it as "Sailing to Byzantium" seems to do, from a respectful distance. Life, even if you feel old and infirm, is sweeter after you have come close to losing it. Some of the poems of *The Winding Stair*—"A Dialogue of Self and Soul," "Vacillation," "A Woman Young and Old"—do answer earlier poems like "Sailing to Byzantium" and "A Man Young and Old" which had reviled life if they did not quite reject it. Some letters confirm the impression. He wrote about the lung congestion: "Three days ago I spat a little red and that roused me to defy George and begin to work....How strange is the subconscious gaiety that leaps up before danger or difficulty. I have not had a moment's depression

—that gaiety is outside one's control, a something given by nature." He said that "Self and Soul" was a "choice of rebirth rather than deliverance from birth," and later wondered if that choice was not "perhaps the sole theme" of his poetry.

Nevertheless, illness does not fully or adequately explain the difference between these two volumes. In 1928 he wrote to both Lady Gregory and Olivia Shakespear that he was "astonished" by the bitterness of *The Tower* and longed to "live out of Ireland" so that he might overcome it. By 1930 he was writing chipper letters about the "scheme of intellectual nationalisms" he was developing for his country. The negative mood of *The Tower* and the positive mood of *The Winding Stair* reflect his involvement with the Free State, first isolation and frustration, then energy and hope. One is always more sanguine when one has a program. Yeats's first program had been the Literary Renaissance and all its related activities. By the 1920s, however, the language movement and the Gaelic League seemed objectionable or irrelevant. The Renaissance was spent, Synge dead, Lady Gregory aged and infirm, and Yeats interested in other matters. The heroic period, Gaelic myth and legend, and the Folk seemed increasingly inadequate as national mythologies. Politics were no better. From the Rising in 1916 until the election of deValera in 1932, Irish public life was in a constant state of crisis. A series of military crises — the Rebellion, the executions, the Black and Tan Terror, the Anglo-Irish war and the Civil War — were followed by political and constitutional crises that always threatened to return to warfare, as the Free State government, after the bitterly debated Treaty of 1922, struggled to demonstrate that it could in fact govern and restore the country to some semblance of law, order, and democratic process. The tension between republican and conservative forces that follows a revolution was doubly complicated because there were more deeply conservative impulses in Irish life than in most post-revolutionary societies, and because the need to master the forces of revolution, to consolidate and govern, was intensified by the existence of so much opposition and such strong animosity. Irishmen had to make a clear and fundamental choice: whether to support Cosgrave and the ministers of the new government that had negotiated and reluctantly accepted the Treaty, or deValera and his followers who rejected the Treaty and would not participate in parliamentary government.

Yeats thought the choice was inevitable, and he consistently supported Cosgrave and the government which had appointed him Senator. But it was also a complicated choice. The most powerful conservative force in the country and behind the government was the Church; but Yeats remained opposed to clerical power, even to clerical authority; so he became an anti-clerical conservative, while the Church dominated any conservative alliance. Furthermore, the government was committed not only to the Treaty and to order, but to electoral politics. DeValera and the anti-treaty forces chose, for the moment, to remain outside electoral politics. Yeats does not express indignation over their withdrawal. He is committed to building on the Treaty and to law and order, but not to democratic process. In letters and in an interview with *The Irish Times* in 1924, he praises "Paul Claudel and Mussolini — A New School of Thought," "authoritative government," "a nation controlled by highly trained intellects," "Autocracy," and "a return to conservative politics as elsewhere in Europe, or at least to a substitution of the historical sense for logic. The return will be painful and perhaps violent, but many educated men talk of it and must soon work for it and perhaps riot for it." He celebrated Kevin O'Higgins, the minister he most admired, as the Irish Mussolini, seeing only the ruthless determination and energy, not O'Higgins's belief in democracy. So his political position is anmalous, idiosyncratic, and isolated; his political rhetoric is likely to be aggressive, cranky, and tactless. He began his Senate career with three brisk sentences: "I think we should put aside once and for all all diplomacy in dealing with the people of the country. We have been diplomatized for a generation. Let us stop it." His final speech, five and a half years later, begins: "I think we should not loose sight of the simple fact that it is more desireable and more important to have able men in this House than to get representative men into this House." The thrust is not on *able* men, but on the implied contradiction between able and representative men.

He was often very angry. Ireland was at last independent, but at the expense of the integrated, living culture Yeats had hoped to achieve. He became increasingly depressed by the difference between the Ireland he had imagined and worked towards and the Ireland of "devout Catholicism and enthusiastic Gaeldom" he saw around him. He fought arduously and unsuccessfully against censorship, arguing that "no Government has the right, whether to flatter fanatics or in mere vagueness of mind to forge an instrument of tyranny and say that it will never be used." He worried that popular democracy meant "lawless vulgarity," materialism, and chaos. The materialism he had noticed long ago and continued to excoriate in speeches and articles. The vulgarity he feared was made vivid and poignant by the sale of Coole Park to the Forestry Department and by the subsequent decay and destruction of the old house itself. The anarchy was documented in 1927 by the assassination of Kevin O'Higgins, almost certainly in reprisal for the execution of seventy-seven Irregulars he had authorized as Minister of Justice. Yeats thought O'Higgins "the one strong intellect in Irish public life," and remembered his comment, "Nobody can expect to live who has done what I have," when he composed "Death," a poem meant to be an intransigent as Yeats thought O'Higgins was.

Practical politics — his serious, conscientious, regular work as a Senator—reinforced Yeats's belief in the need for authority. The conservative reflex solidified into a conservative bias. He becomes a public man, and not only a literary public man, in search of a new national philosophy, political ideology, and personal identity. He explores ideas of tradition, hierarchy, and power, trying to discover and articulate a different and renewed *polis*. Not always lonely and embattled, he attempts to be constructive and conciliatory, to help build a new nation as well as scolding the existing one. Back in 1914 he had asserted that "neither religion nor politics can of itself create minds with enough receptivity to become wise, or just and generous enough to make a nation." By 1925 he thought he had found just such a creative force. Drawing upon his experience as an official visitor to schools in the south of Ireland, he presented his program to the Irish Literary Society:

> There are two great classics of the eighteenth century which have deeply influenced modern thought, great Irish classics too difficult to be taught to children of any age, but some day those among us who think that all things should begin with the nation and with the genius of the nation, may press them upon the attention of the State. It is impossible to consider any modern philosophical or political question without being influenced knowingly or unknowingly by movements of thought that originated with Berkeley, who founded the Trinity College Philosophical Society, or with Burke, who founded the Historical. . . .
>
> In Gaelic literature we have something that the English-speaking countries have never possessed—a great folk literature. We have in Berkeley and in Burke a philosophy on which it is possible to base the whole life of a nation. . . .
>
> Feed the immature imagination upon that old folk life, and the mature intellect upon Berkeley and the great modern idealist philosophy created by his influence, upon Burke who restored to political thought its sense of history, and Ireland is reborn, potent, armed and wise. Berkeley proved that the world was a vision, and Burke that the State was a tree, no mechanism to be pulled in pieces and put up again, but an oak tree that had grown through the centuries.

Yeats does not repudiate Gaelic, but it is an unequal partnership. Gaelic is recommended for "the immature imagination" and Burke and

Berkeley for "the mature intellect." He felt that Irishism, Catholicism, and democracy had sufficiently numerous and voluble advocates, and came increasingly to speak for Protestant Anglo-Ireland and an aristocratic sense of values. Georgian Ireland, he claimed, "re-created conservative thought" and has "regained its importance...now that Ireland is substituting traditions of government for the rhetoric of agitation."

During these years Yeats was system-building as well as nation-building, and inevitably the two preoccupations came together. He was not satisfied with the first version of *A Vision* and kept revising until the second edition of 1937. He was reading a great deal, for confirmation and expansion: Kant, Husserl, Hegel, Bergson, Whitehead, Croce, Gentile, Spengler, Henry Adams, and Toynbee. He read or reread the eighteenth-century giants—Swift, Berkeley, and Burke. He must have reread or again thought about W. E. H. Lecky, the historian and Member of Parliament for the University of Dublin whose support he had tried to enlist for the Irish Literary Theater. He admired Lecky's immense learning and organic sense of history, conformable to his own developing theories. He was now ready to respond to some of the major notes in Lecky's writing: the guarded nationalism combined with a patrician anxiety that democratic politics and a Catholic majority meant mob rule; the celebration of the Anglo-Irish aristocracy and gentry, the "people" of Lecky as well as, now, of Yeats; the awareness that that class was disintegrating, which gives a melancholy bite to the writing of both men.

He was also trying to accommodate his system to his emotional life, to incorporate into both *A Vision* and his idea of the nation the switch from the mood of *The Tower* to the affirmations of *The Winding Stair.* He worked on an earlier idea, that the soul should strive towards a state of "Unity of Being," the full and harmonious development of the individual personality, where every thought and action expresses the whole man. But true Unity of Being, he realized, depends upon a unity of culture that is no longer possible. It had been possible in the Renaissance, but Ireland had had no Renaissance and no unity of culture until the Anglo-Irish community of the eighteenth century. In that one century, "a renaissance echo" he decided, Ireland's "mind became so clear that it changed the world," and he now urges himself and his countrymen to "study the great problems of the world, as they have been lived in our scenery, the re-birth of European spirituality in the mind of Berkeley, the restoration of European order in the mind of Burke."

In 1927 Yeats wrote to Sturge Moore about Thoor Ballylee: "I like to think of that building as a permanent symbol of my work plainly visible to the passerby. As you know, all my art theories depend upon just this—the rooting of mythology in the earth." The "all" is an overstatement, but the rooting of mythology is a central and vital impulse. It had driven him to the Irish peasantry and their stories. It now impelled him to the Crazy Jane series of *Words for Music Perhaps*—earthy, idiomatic, and highly charged; ballads, but rhythmically complex; simple in form and complicated in ideas; embodying a commitment to life, to rampant and randy sexuality after the pessimism, other-worldliness, and vacillation of *The Tower*. He could have added that his theories depended upon the rooting of mythology in his own and his friends' lives and loves, and in his nation's history and prospects. One of the impressive things about Yeats's mythmaking is its increasing comprehensiveness, vitality, and magnitude. If romantic Ireland was not quite dead and gone, it had paled since the turn of the century. So, during the twenties, Swift, Berkeley, and Burke replace Cuchulain, Cathleen and Bran Boru. As he attempts to bring the eighteenth century "back into the tapestry" of Irish life, it becomes, in Yeats's imagination and through his invocations, a new and different kind of heroic period.

The two most impressive public poems of the period, those that most fully embody the impulses and forces of national life and Yeats's response to them, are "Meditations in Time of Civil War," which confronts that event, and "The Tower," which faces death and loss and then lays claim to a historically formed identity for the poet-senator in a new State. In March 1922, planning his return from Oxford to Dublin and Galway, Yeats wrote to Mrs. Shakespear that "we shall have a pleasant energetic life, if the treaty is accepted at the general election, and turmoil if it is rejected." It was rejected, turmoil followed, and Yeats wrote seven poems, separately titled, different in tone, perspective, rhythm, and rhyme, which he published in January 1923 as "Meditations in Time of Civil War." Though written later, it was placed before "Nineteen Hundred and Nineteen" in *The Tower*, which emphasizes the formal, emotional, and political similarities, as well as the distinct ways in which the two long poems place the poet, the poetic imagination, and poetic vocation in the tissue of contemporary events. The varied sections are united by the occasion of their composition and by the drama of their speaker's response. The scene narrows from the wide perspective of "Ancestral Houses" to the particularized "My House" and "My Table," expands slightly with "The Road at My Door," more significantly with "The Stare's Nest by My Window," and explodes into the visionary conclusion, "I See Phantoms of Hatred and of The Heart's Fullness and of the Coming Emptiness." Time shifts from the past ("Ancestral Houses"), to present ("The Road at My Door"), to future ("My Descendants"), but the last poem is out of time. The sequence is further held together by the consciousness of the speaker as he defines relationships and meditates: what is one to do; how can he salvage the past and accommodate the present; how can ideas of grace and sweetness be set against adversity, violence, and emptiness? The major sets of images — figuring order and grace, sweetness and contemplation; violence and disorder; emptiness and vengeance — mirror that consciousness and its pained, complex search for a voice, a stance, and a realized self.

We begin in the past, in the middle of a dialogue, and amid qualification, the first word already a concession to a countering argument:

> Surely among a rich man's flowering lawns,
> Amid the rustle of his planted hills,
> Life overflows without ambitious pains;
> And rains down life until the basin spills,
> And mounts more dizzy high the more it rains
> As though to choose whatever shape it wills
> And never stoop to a mechanical
> Or servile shape, at others' beck and call.

It is a world of privileged enclosure, spatial and auditory, as the self-defining and sustaining fountain is encircled by "flowering lawns," themselves protected by "planted hills." The association with the great estates ("Lady Gregory is planting trees," "Gregory's wood") is inevitable, as is the Georgian ambiance, richness within richness, proud independence, Burke's "unbought grace of life." But that world is as precarious as it it privileged — "Mere dreams, mere dreams!" Nevertheless, as the second stanza piles counterassertion upon qualification, it is a dream fundamental and necessary to artistic creation, and the image, one of Yeats's most valued, briefly detaches itself from historical or class particularity:

> Mere dreams, mere dreams! Yet Homer had not sung
> Had he not found it certain beyond dreams
> That out of life's own self-delight had sprung
> The abounding glittering jet;

but history and social decline are inescapable, and the present moment returns with *its* symbol, double-edged, a seashell both marvelous and empty, aptly figuring a glory inherited but not quite earned or sustained.

> though now it seems
> As if some marvellous empty sea-shell flung
> Out of the obscure dark of the rich streams,
> And not a fountain, were the symbol which
> Shadows the inherited glory of the rich.

The next three stanzas explore and complicate an historical puzzle. It required violent, bitter, powerful men to create the sanctuaries of sweetness and gentleness with their gardens, lawns, walks, "escutcheoned doors," "great chambers and long galleries." The poet wonders "what if" the sanctuaries themselves, concrete objects and personified ideals like "slippered Contemplation," "But take our greatness with our violence" and "our bitterness?" The verb is troublesome. How can gardens and doors "take"? If it means "accept" or "receive," then nature and art are required to accept the human acts that create and shape them, no matter how violent. If it means "absorb" or "take on," then nature and art are conditioned by the human acts and human cost that mould and engender. Either way, or both, the speaker is angry and anxious. The "our" is a class assertion, a declaration of allegiance in the face of decline and decay, expressed with casual contempt:

> And maybe the great-grandson of that house,
> For all its bronze and marble's but a mouse.

The second section moves from the ancestral scene to a particular scene ("My House"), from past to present and opulence to austerity, and from privileged enclosure to rugged impenetrability:

> An ancient bridge, and a more ancient tower,
> A farmhouse that is sheltered by its wall,
> An acre of stony ground,
> Where the symbolic rose can break in flower,
> Old ragged elms, old thorns innumerable,
> The sound of the rain or sound
> Of every wind that blows;
> The stilted water-hen
> Crossing stream again
> Scared by the splashing of a dozen cows.

It is an almost off-hand collection of Yeats's favorite symbols and words ("break" again) suggesting life and time, wishing for connections with eternity, defining the uses of adversity, laying claim to a territory. The landscape is precisely located at Thoor Ballylee and caught in a particular moment of time, the bridge, as Yeats ruefully notes, having been blown up by the Republicans before the poems were finished: "They forbade us to leave the house, but were otherwise polite, even saying at last 'Good-night, thank you,' as though we had given them the bridge." The water-hen may recall the third stanza of "Easter, 1916" and so suggest natural energy and abundance; but it is "stilted" (both senses) and "scared," an ironic figure of the poet and citizen in bad times.

Palmer's illustration to Milton provides an heroic identity: the poet, alone in his tower, light glimmering, as the shepherds gaze uncomprehendingly and farmers pass by unnoticing, recreating the world in "daemonic rage." But in the engraving, and in this poem, like Coleridge in the first stanza of "Frost at Midnight," the poet is cut off. The travelers, "benighted," do not understand him; he cannot even see them. Yeats then reaches for an historical community, a romantic parallel between soldier and poet, both isolated in the warring West, both holding out from forces they cannot understand or master, both anxious to leave a legacy but unable to build ancestral houses.

The third poem, "My Table," moves inside to contemplate his writing "board" and the objects upon it, pen, paper, and an ancient ceremonial sword recently presented to Yeats. As the great houses led to thoughts about historical process and social decline, these objects occasion a brief meditation about art and the social and political conditions—traditional, hierarchical, coherent — that foster it. But the scene is too static, too self-consciously arranged. The sword is there "that it may moralize/ My days out of their aimlessness" and the poet knows that the scene is as stilted as the water-hen, an evasion of the grim realities that surround him. The slightly effete, ninetyish decor and the comfortably melancholy tone is blasted by "it seemed/ Juno's peacock screamed" which also announces "the loss of control...the last surrender, the irrational cry, revelation," the end of an epoch of civilisation.

The fourth poem ("My Descendants") considers the Yeats dynasty and brings together the poem's preoccupations with ancestry and progeny. After a qualified assertion ("it seems") that as power and bitterness are necessary for luxury, so waste and loss are necessary for art and life, he concentrates all the implications of social and generational decay:

> And what if my descendents lose the flower
> Through natural declension of the soul,

Through too much business with the passing hour,
Through too much play, or marriage with a fool?
May this laborious stair and this stark tower
Become a roofless ruin that the owl
May build in the cracked masonry and cry
Her desolation to the desolate sky.

After such a terrible injunction, the Tower becoming a curse rather than a
legacy, there is an instant of panoramic vision—"The Primum Mobile that
fashioned us/ Has made the very owls in circles move"—and a return to the
present and the remote self searching for family and community. It is the
chilly comfort of lessened expectations. He does not feel prosperous; love
and friendship are manifestly not enough to this "ambitious heart" which
likens itself to Homer, Milton, and (later) Wordsworth; the stones are
decaying not monumental; threat is everywhere, as the next poem makes
clear, with its shift to the most tangible, concrete present, "The Road at my
Door," visits of Republican and Free State soldiers:

An affable Irregular
A heavily-built Falstaffian man,
Comes cracking jokes of civil war
As though to die by gunshot were
The finest play under the sun.

A brown Lieutenant and his men,
Half dressed in national uniform,
Stand at my door, and I complain
Of the foul weather, hail and rain,
A pear-tree broken by the storm.

The tone is much the same as Yeats's letters of the period, wry, urbane, a
little detached and stiff upper-lipish. Soldier and poet are now separate
beings, one unselfconscious, the other humiliated. He turns first toward
the nervous little bird, then toward his lonely tower, two mocking self-
images, as there are no productive visions for this Platonist:

I count those feathered balls of soot
The moor-hen guides upon the stream,
To silence the envy in my thought;
And turn towards my chamber, caught
In the cold snows of a dream.

"Meditations in Time of Civil War" turns on the sixth section, "The Stare's Nest by My Window," one of Yeats's most deeply felt and moving poems:

> The bees build in the crevices
> Of loosening masonry, and there
> The mother birds bring grubs and flies.
> My wall is loosening; honey-bees,
> Come build in the empty house of the stare.

Sweetness is to be found not in the privileged enclosure of the Big House and its demesne, but in the "cracked masonry" the poem has earlier seen as a lament and a threat. The lines convey an extraordinary sense of longing, a yearning for the healing richness and amber viscosity of the honey coupled with the protective domesticity of the starlings. The following year, accepting the Nobel Prize, Yeats talked about life in the country: "alone with your own violence, your own ignorance and heaviness, and with the common tragedy of life," you feel most strongly the countering desire for "beautiful emotion"; he then recalled these lines and the "tumultuous" situation that occasioned them: "One felt an overmastering desire not to grow unhappy or embittered, not to lose all sense of the beauty of nature. A stare... had built in a hole beside my window and I made these verses out of the moment." In "Meditations in Time of Civil War," loneliness is existential as well as geographical:

> We are closed in, and the key is turned
> On our uncertainty; somewhere
> A man is killed, or a house burned,
> Yet no clear fact to be discerned:
> Come build in the empty house of the stare.

Private uncertainty reflects public murder:

> A barricade of stone or of wood;
> Some fourteen days of civil war;
> Last night they trundled down the road
> That dead young soldier in his blood:
> Come build in the empty house of the stare.

In the final stanza Yeats begins to moralize his own and his country's days out of their aimlessness:

> We had fed the heart on fantasies,
> The heart's grown brutal from the fare;
> More substance in our enmities
> Than in our love; O honey-bees,
> Come build in the empty house of the stare.

The pronouns are crucial. *I/My,* which heavily and anxiously punctuate the poems, becomes *We.* As in "Nineteen Hundred and Nineteen," but with feelings of shared responsibility and desired reconciliation rather than mocking, embittered complicity, the poet accepts his nationality and its burdens. The stanzas are parallel to a letter Yeats wrote to Herbert Grierson while composing them: "I think things are coming right slowly though very slowly; we have had years now of murder and arson in which both nations have shared impartially. In my own neighborhood the Black and Tans dragged two young men tied alive to a lorry by their heels, till their bodies were rent in pieces. 'There was nothing for the mother but the head' said a countryman and the head he spoke of was found on the road side. The one enlivening Truth that starts out of it all is that we may learn charity after mutual contempt. There is no longer a virtuous nation and the best of us live by candle light."

Charity depends upon the recognition of the humanity of others and upon shared responsibility and aspiration: "O honey-bees,/ Come build in the empty house of the stare." The candle light is what "we" share, not the exclusive property of the en-towered poet, perched lonely above his be-nighted countrymen. Yeats has at last made good his claim at the conclusion of *Samhain* for 1904: "In a country like Ireland, where personifications have taken the place of life, men have more hate than love, for the unhuman is nearly the same as the inhuman, but literature, which is a part of that charity that is the forgiveness of sins, will make us understand men no matter how little they conform to our expectations." It is fitting that these lines provide the epigraph to the most distinguished history of modern Ireland. At his best, Yeats participates in national, not merely class history.

In this poem, however, for this poet, as, alas, in Irish history, such achieved reconciliation cannot last, and the final section sees "Phantoms of Hatred and of the Heart's Fullness and of the Coming Emptiness":

> I climb to the tower-top and lean upon broken stone,
> A mist that is like blown snow is sweeping over all,
> Valley, river, and elms, under the light of a moon
> That seems unlike itself, that seems unchangeable,
> A glittering sword out of the east. A puff of wind
> And those white glimmering fragments of the mist sweep by.
> Frenzies bewilder, reveries perturb the mind;
> Monstrous familiar images swim to the mind's eye.

It is a nightmare landscape only surrealistically attached to Galway particularity. The tower is broken, the moon unreal, and the sword a threat rather than an emblem of permanence and art. Fatigue, defeat, and guilt lead to frenzy rather than reconciliation. The first "monstrous familiar image," Yeats says in a note, draws on eighteenth-century reports of the murder of a Masonic Grand Master and so "seems to me fit symbol for those who labour from hatred, and so for sterility in various kinds." It is also fit symbol for sectarian bloodthirstiness and mindless brutality, a poetic analogue to Picasso's great mural, *Guernica*.

> 'Vengeance upon the murderers,' the cry goes up,
> 'Vengeance for Jacques Molay.' In cloud-pale rags, or in lace,
> The rage-driven, rage-tormented, and rage-hungry troop,
> Trooper belabouring trooper, biting at arm or at face,
> Plunges towards nothing, arms and fingers spreading wide
> For the embrace of nothing; and I, my wits astray
> Because of all that senseless tumult, all but cried
> For vengeance on the murderers of Jacques Molay.

The poet is almost drawn into that perverse, destructive fury, but reels away to another, apparently antithetical vision:

> Their legs long, delicate and slender, aquamarine their eyes,
> Magical unicorns bear ladies on their backs.
> The ladies close their musing eyes. No prophecies,
> Remembered out of Babylonian almanacs,
> Have closed the ladies' eyes, their minds are but a pool
> Where even longing drowns under its own excess;
> Nothing but stillness can remain when hearts are full
> Of their own sweetness, bodies of their loveliness.

The scene is informed by Gustave Moreau's "Women and Unicorns," a reproduction of which Yeats owned. But sweetness, fullness, loveliness are even less sufficient than love, friendship, or daemonic isolation. Images of murderous brutality have given way to images of narcissism, which are one term in the problems faced by the poem, not a resolution of them, an "empty sea-shell" not an "abounding glittering jet." In the fourth stanza the nightmare builds as the troopers and ladies "Give place to an indifferent multitude, give place/ To brazen hawks," which Yeats's note associates with the machine, and the poem, like Picasso, with machines of destruction. Then a highly compressed summary of the section, perhaps of the whole sequence, as the mechanical hawks replace thought and feeling, and eclipse the moon, emblem here of both Eastern permanence and Western process:

> Nor self-delighting reverie,
> Nor hate of what's to come, nor pity for what's gone,
> Nothing but grip of claw, and the eye's complacency,
> The innumerable clanging wings that have put out the moon.

Once more the poet turns away from the realities—political, social, familial, historical, phantasmagorical—he has been forced to face, and gathers together his themes: action or contemplation, friendship and love, solitude and conscience, ambition and desire:

> I turn away and shut the door, and on the stair
> Wonder how many times I could have proved my worth
> In something that all others understand or share;
> But O! ambitious heart, had such a proof drawn forth
> A company of friends, a conscience set at ease,
> It had but made us pine the more.

None seem resolved or resolvable:

> The abstract joy,
> The half-read wisdom of daemonic images,
> Suffice the ageing man as once the growing boy.

Of course the lines parody Wordsworth. "Suffice" emphasizes limits, explicitly recognized by Yeats and implicitly by the "Intimations Ode." We are invited to remember the conclusion to *Anima Hominis:*

> A poet, when he is growing old, will ask himself if he cannot keep his mask and his vision without new bitterness, new disappointment.... Surely, he may think, now that I have found vision and mask I need not suffer any longer. He will buy perhaps some small old house, where, like Ariosto, he can dig his garden, and think that in the return of the birds and leaves, or moon and sun, and in the evening flight of the rooks he may discover rhythm and pattern like those in sleep and so never awake out of vision. Then he will remember Wordsworth withering into eighty years, honoured and empty-witted, and climb to some waste room and find, forgotten there by youth, some bitter crust.

Yet there is an authentic—because enormously hard-won—strength in that "suffice." "Meditations in Time of Civil War" recognizes and accepts the full complexity and pain of the poet-senator's situation. It achieves, briefly but deeply, a genuine moment of community. It hazards, amid great risks, a qualified assertion of poetic vocation. In rare moments literature can make us understand and forgive; its candlelight, if shared, can achieve charity after contempt; the daemonic images can illuminate rather than obscure our collective experience.

"The Tower," like "Meditations in Time of Civil War," is located upon those battlements, but its arrangement and argument, the issues it confronts, its tone and stance, are very different. It was written in 1925, with revisions continuing into '26, after the "Meditations," but placed before it in *The Tower,* as Yeats, rearranging chronology to emphasize themes, reverses the order of the first four poems: "Sailing to Byzantium" (written in 1927), "The Tower" (1925–26), "Meditations in Time of Civil War" (1922), and "Nineteen Hundred and Nineteen" (1919). The first section, like the first stanza of "Sailing to Byzantium" and hence of the volume, faces a condition even more galling than civil war, that "bodily decrepitude" that always (and prematurely) nagged at Yeats and now, in his sixties, enrages him. You can turn away from politics more easily than from the body. The difficult task of this poem will be to absorb age and decay into consciousness, as "Meditations" absorbs violence and bitterness:

> What shall I do with this absurdity—
> O heart, O troubled heart—this caricature,

Decrepit age that has been tied to me
As to a dog's tail?

The first, reflexive answer to that question is probably Yeats's recollection of what he once called "the most beautiful of all the letters" of Blake: "I have been very near the gates of death, and have returned very weak, and an old man feeble and tottering, but not in spirits and life, not in the real man, the imagination which liveth forever. In that I am stronger and stronger as this foolish body decays":

> Never had I more
> Excited, passionate, fantastical
> Imagination, nor an ear and eye
> That more expected the impossible.

Those are bold expectations. They are also, as "Meditation in Time of Civil War's" devastating commentary on fantasy reminds us, precarious. "Sailing to Byzantium" seems to create a more secure sanctuary than a tower or ancestral houses, a world "out of nature" in which to sing. "The Tower" radically questions that sanctuary. It recognizes, as Harris says, that "the choice is not between an art which accepts the body and an art which ignores it, but between an art which accepts the body and no art at all":

> It seems that I must bid the Muse go pack,
> Choose Plato and Plotinus for a friend
> Until imagination, ear and eye,
> Can be content with argument and deal
> In abstract things; or be derided by
> A sort of battered kettle at the heel.

The "or" is stark: Plato and his distrust of the imagination, or, as the price of continuing to court the muse and affirm the imagination, the battered kettle of the body. The second section of the poem, a long, wild, elliptical reverie in which Yeats returns to the *ottava rima* he had used in "Robert Gregory" and "A Prayer for My Daughter," does not appear to offer much help. It hardly seems to address, to say nothing of answer, the Draconian choice posited by the opening stanza. The poet paces upon his battlements, notes the uninviting landscape, "where/ Tree, like a sooty finger, starts from the earth," and sends "imagination forth" to call up "Images and memories/ ... For I would ask a question of them all." The question, or rather questions as there are two, is delayed by nine stanzas of extravagant evocation, personal and historical. He first recalls (in both senses) Mrs. French, a flamboyant figure out of Sir Jonah Barrington, chronicler of the "relics of Feudal arrogance" of the Ascendancy, whom Mrs. Yeats was reading aloud. At a dinner party the lady had imprudently remarked about an insolent neighbor, "I wish the fellow's ears were cut off! That might quiet him":

> Beyond that ridge lived Mrs. French, and once
> When every candlestick or sconce
> Lit up the dark mahogany and the wine,
> A serving-man, that could divine
> That most respected lady's every wish,
> Ran and with the garden shears
> Clipped an insolent farmer's ears
> And brought them in a little covered dish.

It is an extraordinary tone, from the off-rhyme of "once/sconce" to the "little covered dish," to the later, outrageous "Mrs. French,/ Gifted with so fine an ear," a celebration of flamboyance, energy, and assurance tinged with revulsion. Then comes Mary Hynes, the peasant beauty Yeats had heard of while collecting folklore in Galway, and memorialized in "Dust hath closed Helen's eyes" of *The Celtic Twilight,* and remembered again in "The Bounty of Sweden": "They say she was the handsomest girl in Ireland, her skin was like dribbled snow ... and she had blushes in her cheeks" sounds like a comfortable recollection, yet the peasant beauty turns out to be as destructive as the lady of the Big House. Whether from her beauty, the poem which commends it, or drink which toasts it, "certain men" went in search of the reality, but, no poets,

> ... they mistook the brightness of the moon
> For the prosaic light of day —
> Music had driven their wits astray —
> And one was drowned in the great bog of Cloone.

Mary leads to the other poet-admirer, Blind Raftery, the Gaelic poet Lady Gregory had translated for Yeats — "It is Mary Hynes, the calm and easy woman,/ Has beauty in her mind and in her face" — and thence to rapid generalization:

Strange, but the man who made the song was blind;
Yet, now I have considered it, I find
That nothing strange; the tragedy began
With Homer that was a blind man,
And Helen has all living hearts betrayed.

The inclusiveness—Raftery and Mary, Homer and Helen, blindness and desire, the earthly beauty and the muse—is also autobiographical, as it recalls Maud Gonne, his own living heart, and the fiction upon which he projected all that turmoil:

And I myself created Hanrahan
And drove him drunk or sober through the dawn

as Mary/ Raftery/ drink drove the farmers in "horrible splendor of desire." With studied casualness—"I thought it all out twenty years ago"—Yeats recapitulates the title story of *Stories of Red Hanrahan* where his hero, seduced from his human love, Mary Lavalle, into the quest for an ideal beauty, comes upon some gamblers and bewitches the cards onto a pack of hounds and a hare.

Hanrahan rose in frenzy there
And followed up those baying creatures towards—

O towards I have forgotten what—enough!

It is an odd gesture, like the "Lion and woman and the Lord knows what" of "The Circus Animals Desertion." Is it imperfect memory, impatience, repression, or all three? "The Tower," for the moment, does not account for the gesture but hurries on to its remaining memories, "An ancient bankrupt master of this house," nearly anonymous, who lived there a hundred years earlier, and the "Rough men-at-arms" before him, whose "images, in the Great Memory stored" still haunt the poet.

These fabulous figures have much in common. All are associated, Yeats's note says, "by legend, story and tradition with the neighborhood of Thoor Ballylee ... where the poem was written." They too are "Excited, passionate, fantastical." They present balanced emblems of Anglo-Ireland and Celtic Ireland: Mrs. French and Mary Hynes, Barrington and Raftery, the gentry in decline and the tribal warriors of an earlier age. Hanrahan neatly includes both worlds; he is the creation of and emblem for the poet who is about to declare again (in section III) his allegiance to Protestant, Augustan Ireland; he is also based on the Gaelic peasant poet Eoghan Ruadh O Suileabban. All are intimately known by Yeats, "to the bone," as he says in another poem. They have been taken into the imagination from his sources, and recreated. Yet all drive him into a frenzy, seem to possess him as he possesses them.

He can now ask his questions with their implied answers:

> Did all old men and women, rich and poor,
> Who trod upon these rocks or passed this door,
> Whether in public or in secret rage
> As I do now against old age?

The wild and "impatient" eyes give the answer and Yeats dismisses everyone but Hanrahan, "For I need all his mighty memories":

> Old lecher with a love on every wind,
> Bring up out of that deep considering mind
> All that you have discovered in the grave,
> For it is certain that you have
> Reckoned up every unforeknown, unseeing
> Plunge, lured by a softening eye,
> Or by a touch or a sigh,
> Into the labyrinth of another's being.

More striking and cagey rhymes, as "eye/sigh" mimes "thigh." The "old lecher" with his "broken knees for hire/ And horrible splendour of desire" is an apt respondent for a poet driven to questions about sex and the body, struggling desperately to accommodate "decrepit age" and to over-awe or seduce the muse rather than send her packing. *Now* he remembers Hanrahan's frenzied and frustrated quest:

> Does the imagination dwell the most
> Upon a woman won or a woman lost?
> If on the lost, admit you turned aside
> From a great labyrinth out of pride,
> Cowardice, some silly over-subtle thought
> Or anything called conscience once;
> And that if memory recur, the sun's
> Under eclipse and the day blotted out.

Memory calls up memory (lost youth, Maud Gonne, old defeats, surrenders and evasions) and the self-answering question taunts this figure from local legend who is also creation and double, not *hypocrite lecteur,* but *hypocrite personnage,* and no less than with Eliot and Baudelaire, *mon semblable — mon frère.* Interrogator-informant, speaker-audience, Hanrahan-Yeats—he (they? all?) have turned away from the labyrinth of experience, sexual and imaginative, out of pride, cowardice, thought, conscience; that is, out of Ego and Super-ego, what the opening section associates with Plato, argument, and "abstract things." He had earlier prayed (the lines seem almost a parody of "O honey-bees" in "Meditations in Time of Civil War" and "May she be granted..." in "A Prayer for My Daughter"),

> O may the moon and sunlight seem
> One inextricable beam,
> For if I triumph I must make men mad.

Now the madness comes home, "the sun's/ Under eclipse and the day blotted out." In a reversal of the Wordsworthian situation, the act of memory leads to imaginative loss, and there are no soothing, compensatory thoughts. This stark recognition does not bring acceptance. But it does, by a process of negation, affirm am embittered, determined commitment. There is no choice. The wild reverie of Section II has blown away the either/or of Section I. Eye and ear will never be content with argument ("For wisdom is a butterfly and not a gloomy bird of prey") and the body, with all its frustrated yearning, is unavoidable. However outrageous and destructive its operations, the imagination cannot be dismissed.

That decision elaborately and painfully reached, he turns, relaxed, to declaration: "It is time that I wrote my will." Section III is not a will, but a series of makings, testaments of allegiance, faith, and acceptance that refute the choice offered by the first section. He begins by choosing as heirs and audience "upstanding men" who skillfully fish the streams of his territory. "Upstanding" must be a Yeatsian coinage, a new word combining virility, virtue, and achievement. Given the resonance of subsequent allusions and the crisis of "The Tower's" situation, the fisherman may seem a little flat, or strained. But Yeats's intention is clear enough; as far back as "The Song of the Wandering Aengus" and "The Fisherman," the figure has stood for both an active self and an ideal audience. Such men "shall inherit my pride," pride no longer desperate or destructive, not associated with Ascendancy arrogance or country sexuality, but with the magnanimity of the great Georgian Irish and their public accomplishments:

> I declare
> They shall inherit my pride,
> The pride of people that were
> Bound neither to Cause nor to State,
> Neither to slaves that were spat on,
> Nor to the tyrants that spat,
> The people of Burke and of Grattan
> That gave, though free to refuse.

The past tense signals an internalized sense of civic virtue and pride, a Burkean move, history absorbed and made ethics. "History is necessity," Yeats soon wrote, "until it takes fire in someone's head and becomes freedom or virtue." Furthermore, that pride is instantly generalized, made less personal and removed from class consciousness, by its association with a cluster of natural symbols: the glorious dawn and summer shower, the "fabulous horn" of "A Prayer for My Daughter," and the swan singing in the face of certain destruction.

He then turns to an explicit and aggressive refutation of abstract thought:

> And I declare my faith:
> I mock Plotinus' thought
> And cry in Plato's teeth,
> Death and life were not
> Till man made up the whole,
> Made lock, stock and barrel
> Out of his bitter soul,
> Aye, sun and moon and star, all,
> And further add to that
> That, being dead, we rise,
> Dream and so create
> Translunar Paradise.

It is a bold assertion both philosophically and rhetorically (the punctuation and caesural pause of "lock, stock and barrel" rescues the cliché). One mentor of the "learned school" is surely Blake. In drafts of the poem — "That Eternal Man/ Rested the seventh day" — Yeats had been unguarded about the divine powers of the human mind. In the final version his language is less biblical and usurpatious. It also draws on Bishop Berkeley, another Irish predecessor, whom Yeats was currently confounding with Blake, and whose immaterialism he had revised into the subjective idealism of this passage. Locke joins Plato as the purveyor of abstractions. Berkeley joins Burke, in the century when Ireland's "mind became so clear it changed the world," countering forces who "found in England the opposite that stung their own thought into expression and made it lucid," leaving to the poet a new sense of political order and ultimate reality. It is a forced association and a willful epistemology. It is also exhilarating; it hovers on the edge of solipsism, but does not tumble because of the poem's engagement, its rich and varied historical sense, and because of the poet's passionate commitment to its imaginative possibilities.

Such assertions triumphantly made, he can claim that

> I have prepared my peace
> With learned Italian things
> And the proud stones of Greece,
> Poet's imaginings
> And memories of love,
> Memories of the words of women,
> All those things whereof
> Man makes a superhuman
> Mirror-resembling dream.

A collection of fragments shored aginst what are looking less and less like ruins, and a compressed definition of art in which realism succumbs to Yeats's own combination of romanticism and symbolism. He now comes closer to an orthodox will, the generosity of accepted age, what Erikson calls integrity, with a saving edge of sardonic self-portraiture, saving because Yeats is not a man who can give way smilingly, and should not pretend to:

> I leave both faith and pride
> To young upstanding men
> Climbing the mountain-side,
> That under bursting dawn
> They may drop a fly;
> Being of that metal made
> Till it was broken by
> This sedentary trade.

Now he is ready for the poem's final testament:

> Now I shall make my soul,
> Compelling it to study
> In a learned school
> Till the wreck of body,
> Slow decay of blood,
> Testy delirium
> Or dull decrepitude,
> Or what worse evil come—
> The death of friends, or death
> Of every brilliant eye
> That made a catch in the breath—
> Seem but the clouds of the sky
> When the horizon fades,
> Or a bird's sleepy cry
> Among the deepening shades.

"Make my soul" is not only colloquial Irish for "prepare for death," but a literal statement, the last of the poem's impressive makings. After this confrontation with history, the imagination, and his own condition; facing once again ("till" — "until" introduces an extraordinary subordinate clause) all the evils of age, he is able to create decrepitude, death, and loss, so that they seem no more substantial ("but") than the landscape ("the clouds of the sky/ When the horizon fades") or "a bird's sleepy cry/ Among the deepening shades." At the same time they are no less substantial, and birds and landscape give "The Tower" its fine, final, ambiguous resolution. The first bird appears at dusk

> When the swan must fix his eye
> Upon a fading gleam,
> Float out upon a long
> Last reach of glittering stream
> And there sing his last song.

It is one of Yeats's most heroic emblems of the soul in time facing eternity, like Cuchulain shouting "I come!" at the end of *At the Hawk's Well*. It recalls the marvelous definition of history in "Meditations in Time of Civil War," "the obscure dark of the rich streams," and the much more imperiled swan of "Nineteen Hundren and Nineteen" leaping "into a desolate heaven." It also anticipates that last letter to Elizabeth Pelham: "Man can embody truth but he cannot know it." Like Homer, Raftery, and the speaker in "A Dialogue of Self and Soul," it is committed, no matter how battered and blind, to song, singing into the void.

The second set of birds are more domestic and more ambiguous, the daws of the third to last stanza, set in oppostition to the "superhuman/ Mirror-resembling dream" created by the romantic imagination.

> As at that loophole there
> The daws chatter and scream.
> And drop twigs layer upon layer,
> When they have mounted up,
> The mother bird will rest
> On their hollow top,
> And so warm her wild nest.

From the widest possible reach in the first stanza, he returns "there" to the Tower. The revisions add the "As," which show Yeats insisting that the daws are a simile for the "dream," as the honey-bees have been an emblem of reconstruction and reconciliation. The late Curtis Bradford thought that the daws' nest, "a mere heap of trash which yet serves life's obscure purpose well enough," is an appropriate image "of the somewhat ramshakle nature of this 'faith' as compared with Judaism and Christianity." It is a tempting interpretation. But Yeats gave little to orthodox consistency and rarely worried about ramshakle ecclecticism as long as he could absorb and transform it. He wrote in *A Vision,* as if he had been thinking about such objections: "My imagination was for a time haunted by figures that, muttering 'The great systems', held out to me the sun-dried skeletons of birds, and it seemed to me that this image was meant to turn my thoughts to the living bird. That bird signifies truth when it eats, evacuates, builds its nest, engenders, feeds its young; do not all intelligible truths lie in its passage from egg to dust?" The living birds, who occupy the tower that he possesses, signify more truth than the abstract systems. Death comes, but life chatters on. The body decays but still makes superhuman dreams. "You can refute Hegel but not the Saint or the Song of Sixpence."

The landscape is half-lit throughout. The poet remembers "the brightness of the moon" and "the prosaic light of day". But the reverie begins "under the day's declining beam" and ends "among the deepening shades"; the swan sings while regarding the "fading gleam." The imagination, more particularly the imagination gathering allegiances, making declarations, and facing death, is as half-lit, as ambiguous, as the landscape. It is magnificent, creating everything. It is threatening, driving its possessors and claiming its victims. It is precarious, having a tenuous and anxious hold over its own possessions, just as memory has an inconclusive hold over the past, and society over its achievements. So the relaxation at the end of the poem, its combination of triumph and quiet acceptance, is honestly earned. The body decays, but work goes on. Eggs turn to dust, but the young daws chatter and scream. The imagination transfigures, but its limitations are recognized. History takes fire, the past comes alive, but the conflagration cannot last.

3

On March 9, 1932, Eamon deValera and his party came to power removing Cosgrove and the party which had signed and fought for the Treaty of 1922, attempted to direct an orderly state and achieve some reconciliation with England, created the Senate, and appointed Yeats a Senator. DeValera began to dismantle the treaty, formulate a new constitution, and establish a policy of neutrality. His government, naturally wanting to incorporate the Republican forces which had been losers in the Civil War, ended the Military Tribunal and allowed the order outlawing the I.R.A. to lapse. The I.R.A. soon began drilling, recruiting, and threatening its old enemies. At the same time, the forces most hostile to deValera and Republicanism, most friendly to England, most concerned with law and order, and most closely connected with property began to organize. Dr. T. F. O'Higgins, brother of the assassinated Minister of Justice, founded the Army Comrades Association, originally a kind of alumni organization for members of the Free State Army, which now opened its ranks and soon claimed a membership of 30,000 men. In 1933 General Eoin O'Duffy, recently dismissed as Commissioner of Police, became the nominal leader of a reorganized, disciplined, quasi-military group now called the United Ireland Party or, after its unofficial uniform, the Blueshirts. For a few months it seemed possible that O'Duffy, his advisers, and their followers might be able to impose on Ireland the Corporate State and totalitarian rule, on continental models, with the I.R.A. providing the "Communist menace."

   Yeats was intensely interested. He had been out of the Senate for four years and largely out of politics, praising "the happiness of finding idleness a duty. No more opinions, no more politics, no more practical tasks." Now an old friend, Captain Dermot MacManus, brought O'Duffy to see and learn from him. For about a year (February 1933–February 1934) he was actively engaged with the new movement. It appealed to his old conservative reflex, his recent conservative ideology, and his fears about democracy. With the help of Ezra Pound he had been, for at least ten years, curious and enthusiastic about the beginnings of Fascism in Italy and Germany. Lady Gregory's death in 1932 was a crisis which made him feel even more old and alone, and he reaches for new sources of energy and community, including theatrical politics. In some ways the Steinach operation for sexual rejuvenation he underwent in 1934 is the physiological equivalent of his excited, furtive fascination with Fascist politics. He creates and celebrates the unguarded sexuality of Crazy Jane at the same time that he imagines himself Gentile to O'Duffy's Mussolini. His fury about "decrepit age" had for some time been coupled with more abstract, though nightmarish, intuitions of power and destruction let loose in the world. For a brief, dismal moment he convinced himself that association with the Blueshirts might allow him to be an agent rather than victim of those forces. He often wrote to Olivia Shakespear about his adventures:

> If I were a young man I would welcome four years of conflict, for it creates unity among the educated classes, and force DeValera's Ministers, in all probability, to repudiate the ignorance that has in part put them into power.

> The great secret is out — a convention of blue-shirts — "National Guards" — have received their new leader with the Fascist salute and the new leader announces reform of Parliament as his business. ... Italy, Poland, Germany, then perhaps Ireland. Doubtless I shall hate it (though not so much as I hate Irish democracy) but it is September and we must not behave like the gay young sparks of May or June.

> The organization is for an independent Ireland within the commonwealth. Whether it succeeds or not in abolishing parliamentary government as we know it today, it will certainly bring into discussion all the things I care for.

He wrote three "Marching Songs" for the Blueshirts, and two commentaries upon them, which express more aggressively and less playfully the sentiments of the letters, with the additional assertion that he writes in the name of artistic integrity and for a national policy of "unity of culture.... If any Government or party undertake this work it will need force, marching men ... ; it will promise not this or that measure but a discipline, a way of life; that sacred drama must to all native eyes and ears become the greatest

of the parables. There is no such government or party today; should either appear I offer it these trivial songs and what remains to me of life."
The "songs" are trivial; they are also repulsive:

> The soldier takes pride in saluting his Captain,
> The devotee proffers a knee to his Lord,
> Some back a mare thrown from a thoroughbred,
> Troy backed its Helen; Troy died and adored;
> What's equality? — Muck in the yard:
> Great nations blossom above;
> A slave bows down to a slave.

Six months after writing the "Songs," Yeats added a note saying that he wrote them "because a friend belonging to a political party wherewith I had once some loose associations, told me that it had, or was about to have, or might be persuaded to have, some such aim as mine.... Finding that it neither would nor could, I increased their fantasy, their extravagance, their obscurity, that no party might sing them." Conor Cruise O'Brien, whose circumstantial and controversial essay has focused the issue and caused chagrin to apologists for Yeats's politics, argues that this and similar statements do not constitute a repudiation of Fascist ideology, but a shrewd recognition that O'Duffy was a clown and that Fascism stood no change of prevailing in Ireland. The recognitions were certainly shrewd and self-protective, and their expression was often arch; but they were also more genuine than O'Brien allows, in touch with personal need and at least aware of political morality. During the winter of 1933, well before O'Duffy's exposure and resignation, even while he was working on the "Songs," Yeats experiences reservations, some remorse, and begins to withdraw from the movement. He seems to have completed the "Songs" out of the momentum and expectations created by their inception, and immediately been embarassed by them. Their ranting is so self-parodic that they contain the seed of their own repudiation, which the too sly note makes explicit. The letters of 1934–35 cease talking about politics and become preoccupied by his health and excited about his work, particularly his idiosyncratic compilation of the *Oxford Book of Modern Verse,* his reworkings of *A Vision,* and his return to writing poetry, which he had been unable to do since Lady Gregory's death. "I long for conversation on something else but politics" (November 1933) becomes "Your life is too tranquil, mine too exciting" (January 1934), but excitement stems from plays and *A Vision* rather than politics. He repeats the old lament, "I long to escape from this practical life," but "this life" now means the Abbey and the Irish Academy, not the Blueshirts. By 1936 he is both longing for the lost quiet of Coole—"It was part of the genius of that house"—and happily reporting, "I am writing much and sleeping little ... writing better and more than I have done for years."

He was relieved that General O'Duffy had gone to Spain and worried that he might come back at the head of a "Christian Front" (O'Duffy's term) or "Catholic Front" (Yeats's), "gathering all the bigots together" to impose morality on Ireland. His concern for intellectual freedom and artistic integrity, accurately prompted by anxieties about censorship and State control of the Abbey, overcame any lingering appeal of a strong man leading a mass movement. Now his comments have none of the urbane, adventuresome tone he had adopted about the Blueshirts: "The political situation here is unexpected and threatening. ... I am convinced that if the Spanish war goes on, or if [it] ceases and O'Duffy's volunteers return heroes, my 'pagan' institutions, the Theatre, the Academy, will be fighting for their lives against combined Catholic and Gaelic bigotry. A friar or monk has already threatened us with mob violence."

The withdrawal from Fascism, cagey and timely though it may be, is also sincere. As he realizes that he cannot and will not be an agent of a new, imposed order, he cultivates an anarchy of will, a determination to be no victim despite all the murderous forces gathering around him. He fondly recalls Blake's "'And he his seventy disciples sent/ Against religion and government,'" and adds, to Ethel Mannin, "I hate more than you do, for my hatred can have no expression in action. I am a forerunner of that horde that will some day come down the mountains." He insists that programs and ideologies offer no salvation and turns instead to personal will, a new version of the "interior personality created out of the tradition of myself" he had cultivated in *Estrangement:*

> When there is despair, public or private, when settled order seems lost, people look for strength within or without. Auden, Spender, all that seem the new movement, *look* for strength in Marxian Socialism, or in Major Douglas; they want marching feet. The lasting expression of our time is not this obvious choice but in a sense of something steel-like and cold within the will, something passionate and cold.

At the same time he was reworking some bitter controversies. He read Harrison's *Parnell Vindicated,* which argued that Captain O'Shea had been bribed and Parnell betrayed by the Party and the clergy, and Maloney's *The Forged Casement Diaries,* which attacked as bogus the diaries circulated by the British in 1916 to justify the execution of Sir Roger Casement. Yeats must have remembered Lady Gregory's quiet, decisive remark, "I defy anyone to study Irish history without getting a dislike and distrust of England," and he published, during the winter of 1936–37, five furious, virulent, anti-English ballads about Casement, the O'Rahilly, killed in 1916, and Parnell. The ballads were political acts, as O'Brien says, as potentially explosive as *Cathleen ni Houlihan;* and they are far more serious than the "Marching Songs." The Casement ballads in particular would remind readers on both sides of the channel and in America that Sir Roger was executed for attempting to bring German support to Ireland's rebellion. The sea was no longer the old sea beacause "the nation from which Casement had tried to bring help now possessed a powerful air-force." The ballads gave Yeats a measure of public popularity he had not enjoyed for some time, and they risked the loss of friends in England. They offered eccentric by clear support to deValera and his policy of neutrality. The ballads may have contributed to what became, in a year or so, the IRA "policy" of random bombings in England and declared intention of replacing, by whatever means necessary, Ireland's elected leaders. There is no positive evidence that the Republican extremists read Yeats or any poetry; he certainly did not write with them in mind; but the mood of the poems, their combination of rage and threat, is not wholly removed from acts of violence.

He is also feeling, once again and more fiercely, that other rage— against age and loneliness. AE died in 1935, and Yeats "had to use all my powers of intrigue and self-assertion to prevent a fanatical woman from making it a political demonstration by draping the coffin with the tricolour." Olivia Shakespear went in 1938; "all other lovers being estranged or dead," she was the last contact with his youth. He had written her, in one of the letters marking his disengagement from the Blueshirts, that he was working on a play "that I might write lyrics out of dramatic experience, all my personal experience having in some strange way come to an end." For such a relentlessly autobiographical poet that is the recognition of a crisis. Institutions disappeared as friends died. The Irish Senate, where he had found a role, a platform, and some ideology, was abolished after a struggle in 1936, which must have seemed, like the destruction of Coole, the sacrifice of one more monument of the Old Order. The rage and lust he writes about to Dorothy Wellesley and Ethel Mannin constitute a half-apology for the Casement ballads; it is also part of a personal apocalypse, a sense of himself as "the first of the final destroying horde." In the context of the letter in which it appears "The Spur" is not a playful poem:

> You think it horrible that Lust and Rage
> Should dance attendance opon my old age;
> They were not such a plague when I was young;
> What else have I to spur me into song?

What has happened is a kind of internalization of fascism. It begins with the withdrawal, lasts for the rest of his life, and proceeds simultaneously with more healthy feelings and statements. A letter to Olivia Shakespear from the summer of 1934 illustrates the process:

> I had a Swedish compliment the other day, that has pleased me better than any I have ever had. Some Swede said to my wife "Our Royal Family liked your husband better than any other Nobel prize winner. They said he has the manners of a Courtier." I would like to think this true but I doubt — my kind of critical mind creates harshness and roughness. Which somehow reminds me, have you read *Hadrian the Seventh* by Lionel's friend or acquaintance "Baron Corvo"? — it is quite cheap and nearly a great book, my sort of book, the love of the ruling mind, the ruling race. An imaginary Pope is the theme, with enough evil to be a great man. I hate the pale victims of modern fiction—that suffer that they may have minds like photographic plates.

That sounds like an aristocratic pose descending through alienation into fascism, but it is attached to gossip and a book, not to a movement which Yeats has already judged and found insufficient. The Blueshirt song writer is becoming the "Wild Old Wicked Man." Yeats creates speakers who are directly autobiographical:

> I pray—for fashion's word is out
> And prayer comes round again—
> That I may seem, though I die old,
> A foolish, passionate man.

and others, like Ribh in "Supernatural Songs," who dramatize his own needs:

> Why should I seek for love or study it?
> It is of God and passes human wit.
> I study hatred with great diligence,

For that's a passion in my own control,
A sort of besom that can clear the soul
Of everything that is not mind or sense.

The internalization is distressing—frequently repulsive, often hysterical, sometimes self-parodic — but it represents a fictive identity not a
political program. The identity is problematical but so far removed from
ordinary politics that it is not a public danger. It can provide an acid
imaginative strength, as Yeats sees himself "ravening, raging, and uproot-
ing that he may come/ Into the desolation of reality" and cultivates "the
brutality, the ill-breeding, the barbarism of truth" which he claimed for
On The Boiler, his last prose work, "a *Fors Clavigera* of
sorts — my advice to the youthful mind on all manner of things, and
poems." Yeats worked hard on the series of five tracts and his letters,
written between the fall of 1937 and the following summer when he
expected publication (it came posthumously), show an odd combination
of motives and emotions. He hopes for commercial success to endow the
Cuala Press so it will not be a burden on his family. He writes with some
anxiety ("I wonder how many friends I will have left") but more gaiety
about the ruckus he antitipates ("The boiler is going to very hot"). He
delights in new sources of energy. The letters both tease and apologize, but
finally come down on seriousness of purpose: "For the first time in my life I
am saying what are my political beliefs." The results are depressing, except
for those who want a stick with which to beat the old poet and his
admirers, like Harold Bloom who advertises "that very late and grotesque
tract all good Yeatsians should re-read once a year." In fact, *On the Boiler*
justifies neither the enthusiasm of Yeats's letters nor the pouncing of his
detractors. It is a sad and silly document, repetitious, dull, an almost senile
rehearsal of various Yeats doctrines on art, education, politics, and science:

> A City Father of a defeated Spanish town said that he could not
> understand it because their commander was not less well born than his
> opponent.

> Eugenical and psychical research are the revolutionary movements
> with that element of novelty and sensation which sooner or later stir
> men to action.

> Desire some just war, that big house and hovel, college and public-
> house, civil servant — his Gaelic certificate in his pocket —
> and international bride-playing woman, may know that they belong
> to one nation.

That is not thought but a parody of thought, just as "Under Ben Bulben" ("Scorn the sort now growing up/... Base-born products of base beds") is a parody of late Yeats, not "an old man's eagle mind," but an old man's self-indulgent rant, WBY as Cecil B. DeMille.

4

Poems and tracts like those are not serious art, or thought, or politics. Their alienation and impotence are coy and stylized, pose not mask. Unlike *Cathleen Ni Houlihan* and perhaps the Casement ballads they have had — fortunately—no discernible impact on Irish life. Unlike "Easter, 1916" and "Meditations in Time of Civil War" they do not participate in history by representing national consciousness at a moment of crisis. But they have to be taken seriously as literary biography, as an episode in the history of Yeats's imagination. What resources do such attitudes provide and at what cost? How do certain poems and plays embody a political consciousness, a confrontation with and translation of the various forces of his time? We can begin to answer these questions and to face the problem of Yeats's politics by looking at two poems and a play written during the last twenty years of his life. They are public statements and they contain responses to public issues. Considering them from a political point of view ignores other impulses but does help to define Yeats's situation and response, and ours to his.

"On a Political Prisoner" is about Constance Markiewicz, confined in Halloway Gaol for her part in the Easter Uprising. "I am writing one on Con," Yeats told his wife in 1918, "to avoid writing one on Maud. All of them are in prison." The poem follows those about the Uprising in *Michael Robartes and the Dancer* and shares their worries about the price of revolutionary dedication and popular leadership; but its diction, phrasing, and mood are more akin to "In Memory of Major Robert Gregory"; and the last two stanzas are sympathetic and moving as gull and prisoner, past and present, coalesce:

> When long ago I saw her ride
> Under Ben Bulben to the meet,
> The beauty of her country-side
> With all youth's lonely wildness stirred,
> She seemed to have grown clean and sweet
> Like any rock-bred, sea-born bird:

Sea-bore, or balanced on the air
When first it sprang out of the nest
Upon some lofty rock to stare
Upon the cloudy canopy,
While under its storm-beaten breast
Cried out the hollows of the sea.

Nine years later both the Countess and her sister had died, the country had been through terror and civil war, and Senator Yeats had hardened reservations about the forces let loose by the Rebellion and its participants. "In Memory of Eva Gore-Booth and Con Markiewicz" expresses essentially the same argument as the first poem, that the sisters have bartered the unbought grace of their earlier lives for abstractions, programs, and mass popularity. But the reservations are a bit hysterical, and more than a bit nasty; a touching memory has dried into contempt:

The light of evening, Lissadell,
Great windows open to the south,
Two girls in silk kimonos, both
Beautiful, one a gazelle.
But a raving autumn shears
Blossom from the summer's wreath;
The older is condemned to death,
Pardoned, drags out lonely years
Conspiring among the ignorant.
I know not what the younger dreams—
Some vague Utopia—and she seems,
When withered old and skeleton gaunt,
An image of such politics.

The poem begins in nostalgia not sympathy, an attachment to the women's past not their situation or their very considerable accomplishments in politics and economics, administration and art. The attachment is also to his past; Lissadell was the first Big House to receive the young poet: "We were merchant people of the town. No matter how rich we grew, no matter how many thousands a year our mills or our ships brought in, we could never be 'country.'...the long-settled habit of Irish life set up a wall": Even the nostalgia is vitiated by bitterness and bullying. The conclusion begins in snobbery, moves through contemptuous dismissal of commitments (social welfare, revolutionary nationalism, woman's suffrage, trade unionism) which the two women sincerely and effectively maintained, and ends in a forced, theatrical cry for destruction:

Dear shadows, now you know it all,
All the folly of a fight
With a common wrong or right.
The innocent and the beautiful
Have no enemy but time;
Arise and bid me strike a match
And strike another till time catch;
Should the conflagration climb,
Run till all the sages know.
We the great gazebo built,
They convicted us of guilt;
Bid me strike a match and blow.

Friendship and the imagination's apprehension of public events are equally betrayed by reactionary pique.

Solitude and rage reach their climax in Yeats's penultimate play, *Purgatory*, written between March and August 1938, when it was performed at the Abbey and Yeats made his last public appearance at the theater. It was originally intended for publication in *On the Boiler*, where it belongs, as it shares most of the attitudes of that tract. It is, however, a completed work of art, one of Yeats's most successful plays in purely dramatic terms. It is tightly constructed who no extraneous exposition, powerfully realized images, and a dominating central character. The verse, after so many years of experiment, achieves the lucidity and immediacy necessary for poetic drama. "I have put nothing into the play because it seemed picturesque," Yeats told his opening night audience, "I have put there my own conviction about this world and the next." Unlike *On the Boiler*, *Purgatory* justifies Yeats's claims for seriousness of purpose and skill of execution. It was written very rapidly for Yeats, which does not mean that he has finally gained facility; rather, like Dr. Johnson composing *Rasselas* in the evenings of one week, he was dramatizing some of his central preoccupations, asserting intensely held convictions, and drawing upon vitally significant experiences and images; it also means, as Curtis Bradford first said, that *Purgatory* allows violent and usually contained feelings to explode. If the play is a triumph for Yeats, it is a problem for his readers: how can anything so good he so deeply repellent?

The plot is simple and probably derives from a ghost story Yeats long ago heard and retold. An old man and his son approach "a ruined house and a bare tree in the background." The boy complains and the father issues instructions: "Study that house.... Study that tree." House and tree tell a story. Sixty-three years ago the old man's mother, the "rich inheritor" of this house, formed a *mesalliance* (Yeats's term) with a local groom and betrayed her class and outraged her family by marrying him. She dies giving birth to the child who would become the Old Man. Her husband let the house go and sold off land to meet debts and buy drink. When the Old Man was sixteen his father "burned down the house when drunk" and his son murdered him. The Old Man has returned with his own son, now just short of sixteen, driven by obsessions of sexual guilt and class decay, and by a belief that some act of his may release the spirit of his mother from continual reliving of her transgression. The window lights up once more for "desecration and the lover's night" and the Old Man, in spite of his outburst—"Do not let him touch you!"—is unable to prevent the reenactment of his conception by a drunken father and mother morally debilitated by desire. The Boy cannot see the scene, thinks his father cracked, and starts to make off with the money. He does see the window when it next lights up with an image of his grandfather, "like some tired beast," finding whiskey after sex. The horrified boy covers his eyes, and his father then murders him with the same knife he used to kill his father. The Old Man momentarily believes he has released the soul of his mother from its bondage and plans to clean his knife and escape. But the hoof beats of his father's horse, as he rides home in anticipatory lust years ago, return and the play ends with his despairing, confused prayer, as bleak as Job's and Swift's "Perish the day on which I was born":

> Her mind cannot hold up that dream.
> Twice a murderer and all for nothing,
> And she must animate that dead night
> Not once but many times!
> O God!
> Release my mother's soul from its dream!
> Mankind can do no more. Appease
> The misery of the living and the remorse of the dead.

Purgatory "occurs" in a few minutes but covers all of the Old Man's life: his conception and birth; his mother's degradation and death; his murder of father and son. It also implies much modern history and dramatizes the existence of souls in Purgatory. It is one of Yeats's signal accomplishments in combining an intensely realized present and a simultaneity of many past moments, all powerfully *there* as the crazed Old Man and his doomed, uncomprehending son gaze at the window.

Purgatory is at least five different things, all important to Yeats. It is a reworking of Irish folklore with the personal experience decidedly overcoming the traditional. It is a study of spirits in Purgatory informed by

"The Soul in Judgement" of *A Vision* and dramatized in *The Dreaming of the Bones* and *The Words upon the Window-pane;* but *Purgatory* can dispense with the lengthy prose exposition of the Swift play, and with the familiar legend of the other; it provides the necessary doctrine in a dozen crisp lines:

> The souls in Purgatory that come back
> To habitations and familiar spots.... Re-live
> Their transgressions, and that not once
> But many times; they know at last
> The consequence of those transgressions
> Whether upon others or upon themselves;
> Upon others, others may bring help,
> For when the consequence is at an end
> The dream must end; if upon themselves,
> There is no help but in themselves
> And in the mercy of God.

It is also an appalling, surrealist meditation upon Oedipal conflict by a man whose children had recently reached maturity (Anne, who did the sets, was twenty, Michael eighteen) and who had been increasingly preoccupied by ideas of generational decay. The Old Man hates his father, hates him many years after killing him, for his vulgarity, selfishness, and opportunism; but mostly hates him for his virility, for the desire he excited in his wife: "She is mad about him," the Old Man cries in revulsion as he watches the spirits begin to "renew the sexual act." He loves and loathes his mother for her sexuality and her pliability. He hates his son for being the consequence of his own and his parents' sexuality, for his recent virility, and for his recognition that "now I am young and you are old." Father and son always speak at cross purposes; the Old Man never addresses his son as anything other than "you" and the son only says "father" once, and then it sounds wrong. The Old Man's contempt is complete:

> I gave the education that befits
> A bastard that a pedlar got
> Upon a tinker's daughter in a ditch.

The death of the boy, grim enough in the scenario, is revised into sickening horror, Oedipal lust reenacted as murder, and collapsing into gibberish:

> My father and my son on the same jack-knife?
> That finishes—there—there—there—
> > *He stabs the boy again and again. The window grows dark.*
> 'Hush-a-bye baby, thy father's a knight,
> Thy mother's a lady, lovely and bright.'
> No, that is something that I read in a book,
> And if I sing it must be to my mother,
> And I lack rhyme.

Purgatory is also a parable about the decline of the Anglo-Irish gentry, a view of the play Yeats stressed when interviewed about it. The Old Man, deprived of an education by his father, found it where he could:

> A gamekeeper's wife taught me to read,
> A Catholic curate taught me Latin.
> There were old books and books made fine
> By eighteenth-century French binding, books
> Modern and ancient, books by the ton.

It is the old alliance of peasant, priest, and noble, here in its final decay. The boy is thieving, stupid, and blind. He cannot see the glorious past of his grandmother or hear the destructive hoof-beats of the *mesalliance*. He can only apprehend the drunken bestiality of his grandfather, of which he is the inevitable consequence. The implied dates of the play, surely self-conscious, punctuate recent Anglo-Irish history. "Fifty years ago" when the Old Man last saw the house and tree would be just before the Parnell split of 1891. The son would have been born in 1922 during the summer when the Treaty was signed and the Free State began. He, too, is "an image of such politics." The Old Man recreates the ruined house with intense feeling and wide resonance. Yeats may be recalling the ruined Castle Dargan of his youth and *Reveries*, but the primary reference is more recent, "In my play," he said after the first performance, "a spirit suffers because of its share, when alive, in the destruction of an honoured house; that destruction is taking place all over Ireland today. Sometimes it is the result of poverty, but more often because a new individualistic generation has lost interest in the ancient sanctities." He was thinking of all the Big Houses lost since 1916 or now vulnerable, especially Coole and his and Lady Gregory's recollections and celebrations of it. As Yeats grows older and Ireland changes, it is the loss rather than the aristocratic strength and sanctity he most feels, as in this play, or *The King of the Great Clock Tower*, or the defeated last stanza of "The Curse of Cromwell."

At the end of his essay on Swift Yeats had found another significance for "the ruined castle lit up." It was, he argued along with Plotinus, proof of the "'limitlessness of the individual'. ... If we accept this idea many strange or beautiful things become credible. ... All about us there seems to start up a precise inexplicable teeming life, and the earth becomes once more, not in rhetorical metaphor, but in reality, sacred," an assertion dramatized in "Crazy Jane on God":

> Before their eyes a house
> That from childhood stood
> Uninhabited, ruinious,
> Suddenly lit up
> From door to top:
> All things remain in God.

The lit-up house becomes an emblem for the active imagination just as the purgatorial state in *A Vision* is "a symbol of the imagination at work." But this *Purgatory* is a symbol of the imagination under duress and recoiling. The old man is crazed in very late-Yeatsian ways. He is driven into fury by his own despair, by the intractability of his circumstances, and by horror at what grows around him. His son is the new Ireland and the Old Man, like his creator, is interested in "certain problems of eugenics":

> I killed that lad because had he grown up
> He would have struck a woman's fancy,
> Begot, and passed pollution on.

He wants to annihilate history and so perpetuates it. Obsessed by the thought that his long dead mother *enjoys* the ghostly repetition of sex, he cannot forgive her. He cannot cast out remorse, purge hatred by murder, and his loathing is as much a product of the *mesalliance* as his son, and not eradicable. The young soldier in *The Dreaming of the Bones* cannot forgive either, but he is not so entangled in the story of Diarmuid and Dervorgilla. The Old Man has wholly internalized the history of decay and betrayal. He is not really a dramatic creation like Therisites or the Swift of *The Words upon the Window-pane*. He is hardly even a "speaker" or *persona*. As Bradford's study of the manuscripts shows, Yeats began by speaking of the Old Man in the third person and soon moved into direct discourse, becoming his distraught protagonist. As the Old Man cannot forgive his mother, accept his son, or save himself, Yeats cannot accept his country, resolve the Oedipal drama, or acknowledge his decaying body. The conflagration wished for at the climax of "In Memory of Eva Gore-Booth and Con Markiewicz" receives its powerful, profoundly pessimistic realization here, in this house and this play.

5

Given poems and plays as impressive and troublesome as these and others like them, it is not surprising that "the problem of Yeats's politics" — the nature of those politics and their relationship to his imaginative life and literary achievement—has been addressed frequently, variously, and for the most part inadequately. Neither is it surprising that a reader's response is likely to depend upon his own assumptions and upon the contexts he brings to bear upon his understanding of Yeats. There is the relatively simple approval of shared politics. In 1933 the Blueshirts, presumably, admired Yeats *for* his politics. Neo-conservatives ever since have been given to unguarded celebration of what they consider Yeats's eternal verities like his "passionate attachment to tradition and continuity." There is the more complicated approval of true belief. Kathleen Raine accepts and endorses Yeats's "System" as a coherent escatalogy, "a source of... strength and... lucidity in the New Age we are entering," and argues that "when he wrote 'In Memory of Eva Gore-Booth and Con Markiewicz,' he was passing upon the politics of time the judgment of the politics of eternity as he had come to understand it. The judgment is one those who make a religion of politics at all times resent, but is nonetheless the teaching of every religon which holds the soul to be immortal." We need to understand the implications of that belief, of commitment to a system which holds itself superior to and liberated from "the politics of time." It seems unlikely that Yeats ever wholly shared that belief. Given the argument, tone, and feeling of "In Memory," one does not have to make a religion of politics (or literary criticism, or biographical scholarship) to be worried if this is the Yeats we are to cherish in the new age adawning.

There is also a touching and naive notion, occasionally felt by almost everyone, that poets we admire, even love, must be nice people. This leads to the not very persuasive excuses offered in behalf of Yeats that he was "only playing" at politics, that anyone who prayed to "seem, though I die old,/ A foolish, passionate man" would find his occasion in sex or politics or both. This is surely an injustice to Yeats, a failure to take him seriously enough. It also fails to consider what it might mean to "play" with sinister ideas and prescriptions. Equally naive, though arrogant rather than touching, is the view that we should reject all of Yeats because of his politics: "Don't read that fascist!" John Harrison has made a much more ambitious and open-minded attempt to consider and judge the "reactionary" writers of modern British literature. Unfortunately he misrepresents Yeats, quotes badly out of context, and cannot make good his claim to demonstrate a relationship between poetic style and authoritarian politics.

More complex judgments attempt to begin with understanding and often conclude with acceptance, frequently reluctant, of a great poet flawed by bad politics, or tolerance of that flaw, or chagrin at those politics. They usually posit a distinction — sometimes sharp, sometimes fuzzy — between the apprehending imagination and achieved language of the poet, and the ideas and reflexes of the political being. Auden's "In Memory of W. B. Yeats," along with the argumentative "Defense" of the poet written at the same time, is also an elegy to the 'Thirties, a public withdrawal from the idea of poetry as a mode of action. History cares little about a poet's politics, good or bad, but "Worships language and Forgives/ Everyone by whom it Lives":

> You were silly like us; your gift survived it all;
> The parish of rich women, physical decay,
> Yourself; mad Ireland hurt you into poetry.
> Now Ireland has her madness and her weather still,
> For poetry makes nothing happen; it survives
> In the valley of its saying where executives
> Would never want to tamper; it flows south
> From ranches of isolation and the busy griefs,
> Raw towns that we believe and die in; it survives,
> A way of happening, a mouth.

George Orwell might have been answering Auden (one more time and on another issue) in 1943 when he argued that a poet's politics do matter, that they "leave their mark on the smallest detail of his work," and that Yeats's are unacceptable: "Throughout most of his life, and long before Fascism was ever heard of, he had had the outlook of those who reach Fascism by the aristocratic route. He is a great hater of democracy, of the modern world, science, machinery, the concept of progress—above all, of the idea of human equality." Yeats is "too big a man to share the illusions of Liberalism," knows that Fascism means injustice and inequality "and acclaims it for that very reason. But at the same time he fails to see that the new authoritarian civilization, if it arrives, will not be aristocratic, or what he means by aristocratic. It will not be ruled by noblemen with Van Dyck faces, but by anonymous millionaires, shiny-bottomed bureaucrats and murdering gangsters." Characteristically generous as well as blunt, Orwell notes Yeats's death in 1939 and thinks that he might well have changed his views if he had lived to see the full implications of fascism. Orwell also acknowledges the difficulty of tracing the connection between political "tendency" and literary style, begs the question in his one essay about Yeats, and concludes that the problem "remains to be worked out."

Conor Cruise O'Brien works it out by positing a "diplomatic" relationship between the political manager, with his cunning, cautious, skeptical engagements and disengagements, understandings and misunderstandings, and the poet with his passionate, intuitive apprehensions and expressions. Manager and poet are united by history, by the violence, cruelty, and chaos of the twentieth century in Ireland and Europe.

But this is too dualistic, envisioning too complete a split between the "pure" poet and "impure" politician. It makes manageable the hard questions about politics and style by seeing them both as expressions of something else. So severe on the Senator, O'Brien may be a little too forgiving of the apprehending imagination. Yeats's politics get expressed tonally and stylistically; often the politics are *in* his style, not behind it. It is not a question of particular programs (Yeats once called practical politics "the dirty piece of orange peel in the corner of the stairs as one climbs to some newspaper office"), but of political feelings, the absorption of public issues into consciousness, and the transformation of them to an expression that is political and personal at the same time. The rhetoric of "Easter, 1916" mimes the difficult, admirable ambivalence of its speaker. The images of "The Stare's Nest at my Window" convey that deep desire not to hate. "The Second Coming" carries accents of bourgeois hysteria as well as prophetic intuition. The violent aggression of the "Marching Songs" (the rhythms imitate boots striking pavement), the shrill snobbery of "A Bronze Head," the nihilism of *Purgatory,* the apocalyptic rage of other late poems are willed not accidental, and have political causes and political implications. Failures and accomplishments in political thought and expression, for a poet, are also failures and accomplishments of the imagination.

The two contexts of understanding most usefully brought to bear on the problem are the two traditions that most influenced Yeats — the modernist in literature and aesthetic theory and the Anglo-Irish in culture and politics. Astute readers—Frank Kermode, Thomas Whitaker, Dennis

Donoghue—have noted some of the ways in which authoritarianism is the underside of the modernist movement and in which Yeats "had both a healthy sense of an ideal unity and a dangerous need to replace it with its totalitarian shadow." It is dangerous, they remind us, to see politics from the point of view of art, to claim, as Yeats often does, that the primary function of politics is to foster conditions of artistic achievement and appreciation. It is even more dangerous to impose aesthetics on politics, and some of the central assumptions of modernism, when translated into political terms, do have an authoritarian thrust: the superiority of art and the artist to ordinary life; the autonomy of art and the overriding power of individual vision; the primacy and imperialism of the imagination; the idealization of a mythic past; the driving thirst for commitment in the absence of fully realized belief. It is not an accident that Yeats reread Nietzsche in the mid-thirties and he becomes, as Kermode says, "our first example of that correlation between early modernist literature and authoritarian politics which is more often noticed than explained: totalitarian theories of form matched or reflected by totalitarian politics." Kermode's conclusion is stark: when the sense of crisis and need for order is treated as a paradigm rather than a fiction, "its ideological expression is Fascism; its practical consequence is the Final Solution." To these gloomy and accurate observations we need to add two more. First, whatever Yeats's intent, totalitarianism denies and is denied by some of the same modernist assumptions and impulses. Second, Kermode and critics who have learned from him, for good reasons admiring Yeats as they do, resort to the same explanation by division as does O'Brien. The good poet "was proof against enchantment by the dream," the political thinker "was not. ... In speaking of the great men of early modernism we have to make very subtle distinctions between the work itself, in which the fictions are properly employed, and *obiter dicta* in which they are not, being either myths or dangerous pragmatic assertions." But when the myths and assertions get made in "the work itself," the distinctions are not easy, and the problem, however subtle our response, will not go away.

Enough has already been said about the Anglo-Irish tradition and Yeats's sense and use of it, except, perhaps, to emphasize that his invocations are political acts, and that they are inevitable, or at least deeply consistent. Except for his father, whose nationalism was gentle and whimsical, the family with which he grew up—Pollexfens and Middletons—were Unionists. His friends were Anglo-Irish Protestants as were the great majority of his political exemplars and allies, "radical" in relation to England and English dominion, but conservative in relation to the social order of Ireland. Studying at "the school of John O'Leary," pursuing

Maud Gonne and so attending to her politics, were departures and crises, not inevitable stages of development. The return to Anglo-Ireland represented by "September, 1913" liberated political feelings, reclaimed a tradition, and indicated the direction he was to take for the rest of his life. "The old Ascendancy feeling" never really vanished, but sublimation metamorphosed into other strategies of emotion and expression: tactical repression ("baptism of the gutter") during the Celtic Twilight; vociferous anger in *Responsibilities;* aggression in the Divorce Speech; determined and exhilarating commitment in "The Tower"; old-fasioned snobbery in "A Bronze Head" and "Under Ben Bulben"; destructive rage in "The Curse of Cromwell" and *Purgatory;* embattled, lonely heroism in "The Black Tower."

Yeats maintained that the most resounding political figure of that tradition was Edmund Burke, in one way an awkward choice as Burke spent most of his life excoriating the "Job Ascendancy," that "Junto of robbers," which Yeats sublimated. The choice of Burke in spite of the discrepency reveals a good deal about Yeats's situation and needs in the twenties and thirties and about the waywardness and resourcefulness of his appropriations. The figure of Burke can tell us something about the nature of Yeats's politics. Both men, to vary Arnold's famous phrase about the earlier, saturate politics with imagination, and both illustrate the complexities, achievements, and costs of the imagination's apprehension of political myths and realities. One career illuminates the other and an awareness of Burke (and of Yeats's idea and use of him) helps us to think about Yeats's politics and his poetry without straining to separate them from one another.

Yeats began reading Burke in the early 1920s, purchased the Bohn's Standard Library edition, probably with some of his Nobel Prize money, read widely and marked many passages, particularly in *An Appeal From the New to the Old Whigs* which was, according to Mrs. Yeats, his political bible. He also read and marked *Thoughts on the Cause of Present Discontents;* some of the speeches about Hastings and India; *Reflections on the Revolution in France; Thoughts on French Affairs;* and *A Letter to a Noble Lord.* He was probably familiar with the *Speech on Conciliation with the Colonies,* the *Letter to the Sheriffs of Bristol,* and the *Letters on a Regicide Peace.* He knew many of the Burke anecdotes and said, in a Senate Speech of 1924, that Burke's hurling a scalping knife onto the floor of Parliament was "a fact which has been burning in my imagination." Burke is explicitly invoked in Yeats's three Georgian poems—"The Tower," "Blood and the Moon," and "The Seven Sages"; he was included in an early draft of "The Second Coming"; and he is implied or echoed in several other poems. Yeats mentions him in *Autobiographies* and some letters, is preoccupied by him in the 1930 *Diary*, discusses him in the essays on Swift and Berkeley, and raises his example in three Senate speeches, a lecture, and *On the Boiler*.

Yeats is wrong about Burke in some important and instructive ways. He does not see that Burke's priorities—affection for Ireland, especially her Catholics; greater loyalty to England; overriding commitment to the Empire—are almost the reverse of his own. He mostly ignores those abiding practical commitments which shape Burke's public life, and therefore he does not grasp the depth and scope of Burke's political philosophy. He is particularly insufficient about those features of Burke's thought associated with America, India, and Ireland, and which teach utility, equity, expediency, and decency in political affairs. Yeats makes much of Burke's hatred of abstraction, but does not see beyond that to what Lord Morley called his "conscious and noble utilitarianism," his great lesson that the well-being of actual individuals is the final test of government. "Haughtier-headed Burke" does not convey, nor does Yeats recognize, the cautiousness of his thought, the continual qualifications, and the acute sense of circumstance. When one of the "Seven Sages" proclaims that "whether they knew it or not," Burke and his Anglo-Irish peers "hated Whiggery," he betrays both Yeats's discomfort with the good party man and his failure to perceive the ethical and moral basis of Burke's political thought. A fuller understanding might not have modified Yeats's later politics, but, like the continued presence of Lady Gregory, it would have chastened them. Instead, under the pressure of his own circumstances, he read "the eighteenth century" as "his eighteenth century." He ignores or too blandly explains away Ascendancy selfishness and corruption, the "singular condition" of Burke's Ireland, and his generous and passionate efforts to improve it.

In spite of these misunderstandings and limitations Yeats is right about Burke — responsive, acute, inventive — in a number of remarkable ways. From his point of view, Burke had all the appropriate phobias. He hated Jacobinism, feared democracy, and condemned theorizing and abstraction. Yeats is especially attentive to the ideas of Burke which run counter to characteristic ideas of the Enlightenment, which modify or contradict them and offer new perspectives in their place. Yeats is much more astute about Burke in the context of Europe (of the history of ideas and of large social, political and religious movements) than in the context of Ireland. Burke's "Irishness" becomes a metaphor for his *otherness*, his antagonism to "English" materialism and empiricism, to Locke, Newton, Descartes and the *philosophes* of France. In Burke Yeats found the most authoritative and exciting analogue to his own reactions against powerful forces of the twentieth century. As Berkeley refuted the materialists and effected "the rebirth of European spirituality," so Burke indicted the revolutionaries and "restored to political thought its sense of history" and to Europe its sense of order. They stand together in Yeats's imagination as the discovery and articulation of something which England has never possessed: "a philosophy on which it is possible to base the whole life of a nation."

Burke also had the right answers and became England's and Ireland's greatest spokesman for the leadership of an aristocracy, for the lessons of history and the wisdom of tradition, for "the riches of convention," and for an idea of the national community embracing all the generations and virtues. In "The Child and the State" and "Blood and the Moon" (except for "haughtier-headed") the lesson of Burke — sharply recognized yet elaborated so inventively that it becomes Yeats's own — is all there: the insistence that everything begins with the nation; the belief that "the whole life of a nation" incorporates its history and is expressed by its genius; the quest for unity that brings together past and present, state and art, thought and action, imagination and intellect—that merges the child and the citizen with his surroundings and his horizons. The defining emblem—the great tree—is justly Burke's. It reminds us of his prior assertion that only historic communities, not absolute states or separate individuals, can be potent, armed and wise; it reminds us, too, that Burke is present in Yeats's imagination even when he is not named, as he must surely be present in "Among School Children," with its own harmonies and synthesis, educational setting, and great tree.

Yeats and Burke, to alter Thoreau's metaphor, often march to the tune of the same drummer. Yeats maintained that Burke "recreated conservative thought," and it is certainly true that he defines the conservative imagination of Great Britain and America, defines it in its moments of excess as well as in its moments of insight and harmony. Yeats follows him and the curve of one political imagination illumines the other. Both meditate upon the past and seek to recover and shelter it. Both place their faith in intuitions about history, in received tradition and felt experience, rather than in theory and abstraction. Both celebrate the national community, men in civil society. Both believe in the leadership of an aristocracy (though Yeats is understandably more nervous about its power) and in the virtue of hierarchy. Both have an abiding sense of the mysteries of individual and corporate life.

It is a position of great strength and attractiveness. It contains a sense of harmony and permanence, of deeper communal life and loftier human possibilities, than Lockean or consensus politics can understand. But it is also given to cant, to hysteria, narrowness and obsessiveness, to loss of control and sometimes blood-thirstiness. Yeats understood about the will doing the work of the imagination. As Burke reacted to the French Revolution and all that, he felt, it had let loose, something tragic happened to him. In the French writings he is nowhere as happy, valiant and assured, as in touch with corporate and communal reality and possibility, as he is in the great speeches on America. In later writings, like the *Letters on a Regicide Peace,* he calls for total war — a "long war" — and urges the adoption of Jacobin means, and the emulation of Jacobin energy, to combat the Jacobin threat. In *A Letter to William Elliot,* driven to the contemplation of unconstitutional and extra-parliamentary responses to Republicanism, he almost calls for a citizens' movement to place in power a few strong men, or "a single man," capable of meeting the crisis. It is a sad and frightening flirtation with the idea of an English Directory or a British Bonaparte. At the end of *his* life, and his tether, Yeats mocks the lassissitude of Parliamentary democracy, admires the vigor of National Socialism, and calls for the rule of "a few able men." He becomes interested in power as power and calls for war — "Love war because of its horror, that belief may be changed, civilisation renewed." He lusts after energy and spills into hysteria and self-parody, just as Burke's measured prose turns barbarous.

So Burke defines the conservative imagination when it is threatened and out of joint. He is our model of the pathology of that imagination as well as its strength. His reactions in the nineties, like his accomplishments in the seventies, are representative. In complex ways they are also seminal and archetypal. When Yeats writes the "Marching Songs" Burke's tree, with its Berkeleyan foliage, has rotted away. In "A Prayer for My Daughter" the poet-father articulates and acts out a way of life that will maintain the rich horn and spreading laurel and so protect the innocent and self-delighting soul from the murderous winds of anarchy and disintegration. But in the "Songs" the destruction is willed not apprehended; it is a marching not a levelling wind, a wind of the ego not the imagination, or nature, or history, a call to arms rather than a defense. The poems request and rhythmically act out violence and aggression, not protection. All temperaments react when threatened; all imaginations, or most, at one time or another go out of joint and succumb to extravagant despair, or grotesque irony, or weary resignation. Some are simply struck dumb. The shared reaction of Burke and Yeats is general, almost mythic: a compulsive and emotional attachment to the past and the established; a corresponding distrust of theory and innovation; a feeling of personal isolation; an intelligence in uncertain relationship to reality; a tone obsessive, paranoic, or hysterical; a vision usually gloomy and often apocalyptic. This is what happens to the conservative imagination under threat and recoiling, and it happens to twentieth-century poets as well as to eighteenth-century politicians.

6

The Occult and *A Vision*

In 1884 Yeats met AE and received his first introduction to spiritualism and the occult. He was soon deeply involved in interests and activities which brought together Celticism, neo-Platonism, Indian philosophy and magic, and which were then experiencing a rejuvenation in Europe and Great Britain. He became a founding member of the Dublin Hermetic Society and one of his first published writings is an article on esoteric Buddhism in *The Dublin University Review*. He experimented with psychical research, attended séances, and in 1887 met Madame Blavatsky, joined the London Lodge of Theosophists, became a leading member of its esoteric section, but was soon asked to resign because of his heterodox interest in magic and magical evocation. In 1890 he met MacGregor Mathers and joined the hermetic Order of the Golden Dawn. The Order was more appealing than the Lodge because it emphasized magic and ritual, initiation and secrecy, and Yeats remained a member for thirty years. By 1892 he could write to O'Leary that his "magical pursuits" were "the centre of all that I do and all that I think and all that I write," and he was soon practicing the evocation of spirits with Mathers in Paris, and astrological prediction with George Pollexfen in Sligo. He inducted Maud Gonne into the intricacies of the occult, as she took the lead in nationalist politics; together they experienced astral communication and the spiritual marriage; and Yeats conceived and cherished a plan for a select initiate to study the Celtic Mysteries at a kind of occult monastery, the Isle of Heroes, to be established in the Western counties. The Blake edition of 1893 was influenced by these activities, as were the stories published in 1897 as *The Secret Rose*.

In 1893 Yeats had become a member of the Inner Order of the Golden Dawn; by 1900, with the code name DEDI ("Demon Est Deus Inversus") he was an "Instructor in Mystical Philosophy" and (without irony) a "Statesman of the Second Order," achieving the degree of 5–6, then 6–5, in the Golden Dawn. He was also centrally involved in the fierce infighting within the Order in 1900 which led to the expulsion of Mathers, the attempts of various schismaticsists to start new branches and initiate new rituals, and the strenuous arguments for tradition, discipline, and continuity for which he was the principal spokesman. Those battles resolved, he continued his commitment to the occult, and to spiritualism and psychical research, writing articles, attending séances, investigating miracles, and thinking about magic. In 1914 he published "Swedenborg, Mediums, and the Desolate Places," a long and lovely reverie which connects his reading (Swedenborg, Blake, neo-Platonists) with the occult, especially spiritism, Irish folklore and the Noh plays to which Ezra Pound had recently introduced him. *Per Amica Silentia Lunae* followed in 1917. It is his most successful doctrinal text, an enactment of his interests as they are filtered through his occult speculations, in a prose of enchanting beauty. In the same year he married Georgie Hyde-Lees who shared his interests and who soon attempted automatic writing. The results, fragmentary at first, developed into fifty manuscript books, provided his chief preoccupations for the next seven years, and were organized into *A Vision* in 1925 and, after substantial revision, again in 1937. Several plays and numerous poems grow out of or are commentaries upon the same concerns.

A slight but still arresting Yeats anecdote is that when the Nobel laureate was appointed to the Senate of his newly formed state, his first act was to cast his horoscope. What can be made—what has been made—of the prolonged and passionate commitment of this extraordinary intelligence to "magical pursuits"? There is a good deal of embarrassment and hostility: his father, Pound ("very, very, very bughouse"), Orwell ("hocus-pocus"), Auden ("Southern Californian"), Bloomsbury (delicious, malicious anecdotes which, unlike Auden, do not admit the snobbery), Edmund Wilson who works hard to find a saving skepticism. There is honest, neutral scholarship which acknowledges and documents the commitment without judgment or interpretation. Some practical criticism sees *A Vision* as an intermediate stage between the raw data of experience and the finished poems and plays, and reads the texts in light of the beliefs; this works well for texts associated quite directly with Yeats's system and less well for other texts.

It is possible, and often fruitful, to read the occult or visionary works as an analogue to the creative process, an exploration of the nature and value of symbolism, and a form of imaginative or literary history. Literary interpretation takes most seriously the "metaphors for poetry" Yeats's in-

structors said they had been sent to deliver, and sees *A Vision* and the associated poems and plays as a representative Romantic achievement—the
vision of history, the self in history, and eshcatology as art. One of the
first distinguished commentaries on the problem occupies several posi-
tions at once. Northrop Frye suggests that *A Vision* "is to the student of
Yeats what *De Doctrina Christiana* is to the student of Milton: an
infernal nuisance that he can't pretend doesn't exist" and proceeds to use it
as the key (though a "fragmentary and often misleading" key) to the
structure of Yeats's symbolic language and guide to his imaginative
achievement. In this way the occult works can be seen as a model of Yeats's
mind and sensibility and as a symbolic structure which both underlies and
corresponds to the *Collected Poems* and *Plays*. There is also the tactic of
substitution. Harold Bloom discovers in Yeats his own version of Gnosti-
cism, as well as his own history of Romanticism, and castigates Yeats for
promulgating the first and failing to achieve the second. F. A. C. Wilson
reads the entire canon as if Yeats were a more fully learned and thoroughly
committed neo-Platonist than it is possible to imagine him being. There is
finally the true belief of readers like Kathleen Raine which, as we have
seen, raises a good many more difficulties than it solves. A survey of the
major doctrinal texts culminating in *A Vision* and the related poems and
plays—what can aptly be considered Yeats's occult canon—will define the
issues, his commitments and achievement, and the range of sensible response.

2

In 1897 Yeats published three stories, dedicated to AE, which provide a
terminus ad quem for that canon: "Rosa Alchemica," "The Tables of the
Law," and "The Adoration of the Magi." The tales seem very dated,
especially given what was about to happen to the short story in Ireland. It is
not easy to take the suave style, the nineties tone and the decor of *The
Savoy,* where parts of them were published. The ironies are a little too pat.
The narrator is too timid and aesthetical to be Yeats, even the Yeats of
1897. He may represent that part of Yeats which fears commitment, or the
modern imagination resisting the old mysteries, or an exaggeration of the
"London" half of Yeats which his other fiction was setting against the
"Dublin" half. Yeats's loyalties are not to characters, but to texts: the
sacred books of the Order of the Alchemical Rose and of Joachim of Flora,

the words spoken through the voice of a possessed old man. They include much that Yeats believes some of the time, and several things he believes almost all of the time and is to develop over the next thirty years. These mannered stories are interesting and important because they define ideas and attitudes held long before the ghostly instructors spoke through Mrs. Yeats. He caresses words that are to return in both *A Vision* and the Byzantium poems and he discovers the situation of "Leda and the Swan." He is already convinced that thoughts have an independent reality and that identity is to be achieved through a pursuit of one's opposite, the wearing of a mask, whether Robartes' or the mask of a realized self seen in a dance of initiation. Robartes can plunge into the abyss to discover that self; Aherne can too, but only for a moment; the narrator cannot and vacillates between aesthetical detachment and conventional piety. Yeats is working on ideas of psychological types, the subjective and objective, which will develop into the *Antithetical* and *Primary* as well as on alternating historical cycles, the Pagan and the Christian. He is attracted to ritual and secrecy and the sense of an elect or élite set against the multitude. He is fascinated by ideas and images of annunciation, sudden and unanticipated revelation, alchemical transmutation of dross into gold, matter into essence, life into art. He is already convinced that the natural and supernatural worlds interpenetrate and that the imagination can apprehend the process and experience the ecstasy. They are controlling ideas and compelling intuitions, to be elaborated in *Per Amica Silentia Lunae* and codified into the system of *A Vision*.

First, however, there were the bitter battles over the membership, organization, discipline, and ideology of the London chapter of the Order of the Golden Dawn. In 1901, as the crisis ended, Yeats wrote two polemical essays. The first, "Is the Order of R. R. & A. C. (Rosae Rubeae et Aureae Crucis) to remain a Magical Order?," was privately printed, distributed "to the Adepti of the Order," and never published by Yeats. The second, "Magic," is a public statement of convictions which appeared in *The Monthly Review* and was included in *Ideas of Good and Evil* in 1903 and *Essays and Introductions* in 1961. The two essays, read together, are instructive about his public and private expressions of occult belief.

The "R. R. & A. C." tract is revealing but not interesting. With its intense, argumentative concern for what now seem trivial issues, it sounds like nothing so much as academic politics, with all the limitations of that dreary genre. Yeats is especially stern about the need for obedience and strict observation of the hermetic orders and honors. He writes with contempt for his opponents' insistence on choice: "I have preferred to talk of greater things than freedom. In our day every idler, every trifler, every bungler, cries out for his freedom; but the busy, and weighty minded, and skilful handed, meditate more upon the bonds that they gladly accept, than upon the freedom that has never meant more in their eyes than right to choose the bonds that have made them faithful servants of the law."

The prose is bureaucratic and the argument is not very persuasive. But "R.R. & A.C." does reveal his concern with some fundamental points of doctrine. A Magical Order is "an Actual Being, an organic life holding within itself the highest life of its members now and in past times," and Adeptship is a spiritual discipline which will link initiates to "that Supreme life" which is always in conflict with ordinary, incarnate life. Its enemies are real, probably evil beings who would create "centres of death to this greater life; astral diseases sapping up, as it were, its vital fluids." Yeats is fierce about the dangers of meditation as a way of joining two souls into one "communion of mood," which suggests some second thoughts about the spiritual marriage to Maud Gonne as well as objections to the Golden Dawn schismaticists. He is also messianic about the potentially boundless power of the Order, if the ancient rules are obeyed and unity preserved, to expand and to prosper and to "be of incalculable importance in the change of thought that is coming upon the world."

There are a few moments when the poet almost overcomes the embattled Adept. "The central principle," he writes at the close of one attack, "is that everything we formulate in the imagination, if we formulate it strongly enough, realizes itself in the circumstances of life, acting either through our own souls, or through the spirits of nature." In "Magic" he makes the same assertion, without the petulance, and in a more pliant and persuasive prose:

> I cannot now think symbols less than the greatest of all powers whether they are used consciously by the masters of magic, or half unconsciously by their successors, the poet, the musician and the artist.... Surely, at whatever risk, we must cry out that imagination is always seeking to remake the world according to the impulses and the patterns in that Great Mind, and that Great Memory? Can there be anything so important as to cry out that what we call romance, poetry, intellectual beauty, is the only signal that the supreme Enchanter, or some one in His councils, is speaking of what has been, and shall be again, in the consummation of time?

The essay begins with the "three doctrines" Yeats claims are "the foundation of nearly all magical practices" and which are central to his idea of the poetic imagination:

(1) That the borders of our mind are ever shifting, and that many minds can flow into one another, as it were, and create or reveal a single mind, a single energy.
(2) That the borders of our memories are as shifting, and that our memories are part of one great memory, the memory of Nature herself.
(3) That this great mind and great memory can be evoked by symbols.

He then recounts some experiments in symbolic evocation, examples of thought transference, Glanvil's story of the Scholar Gypsy made famous (and respectable) by Arnold's poem, folk beliefs in the Western Counties, and other mysteries and revelations ignored by conventional historians — not, he says, "to prove my arguments, but to illustrate them." The arguments conform to the doctrine of the private essay, but the emphasis and tone have changed. The language is evocative rather than aggressive, the stance exploratory (even slippery) rather than dogmatic. The impulse to set rules and impose orders has become the openness of an inquiring mind: "I have come to believe so many strange things because of experience, that I see little reason to doubt the truth of many things that are beyond my experience." Blake rather than "Frater S.R.M.D." is the authority, the Romantic imagination instead of "degrees and seniority." As folklore, the collective unconscious, and a poet's belief in symbols replace the endless gradations of hermetic authority, the artist overcomes the adept.

In the first essay Yeats is constrained by a felt need to obey the Golden Dawn rules of secrecy and by some anxiety about the consequences of violating those rules; in the second he is aware of a wider audience and of more supple tactics of persuasion. But there is more to the difference than that, and it concerns the way in which truth can be located, for Yeats about the imagination and the spiritual life, and for us about Yeats. He never published "R.R. & A.C.," kept track of the few copies, and was unhappy when Quinn purchased Florence Farr's. He did not publish most of his occult or esoteric manuscripts. To decline to publish is not necessarily a repudiation, but it is a decision, and it does say something about Yeats's attitude toward particular works. Readers — especially scholarly readers—often assume that the unpublished material they have worked so hard to discover, acquire (and in Yeats's case, transcribe) gives them some special access, the drop on the poet, an insight into hidden thought or feeling. In most cases the reverse is true, the most *done* and public writing the most revealing, as Yeats knew when he wrote Sean O'Faolain that "the origins of a poet are not in that which he has cast off because it is not himself, but in his own mind and in the past of literature." When he said that doing revisions meant remaking a self, he was being entirely serious;

and rejection or suppression or neglect is a form of revision. However committed to the battles of the Golden Dawn, he knew that he was a writer, not a mage; he knew that writing provides its own discipline and that he was approaching or approximating his most important self when he was writing well; he knew that the real sources of his power came from the imperatives of his imagination and from the literary and national traditions that inform it.

"Swedenborg, Mediums, and the Desolate Places" illustrates that knowledge. This remarkable and beautiful essay was written in 1914 and first appeared in Lady Gregory's *Visions and Beliefs in the West of Ireland*. It is a serene and confident reverie which brings together many private thoughts and desires at the same time that Yeats is embattled on all those public issues angrily addressed in *Responsibilities* and the *Autobiographies*. Worthy of comparison to Browne and Pater, it is written in a supple and evocative prose without the mannered quality of *Rosa Alchemica* or the stiffness of the occult papers. It is also cagey, punctuated by the saving skeptical phrase (the "gravity and simplicity" of séances "depend on all, or all but all, believing that their dead are near"), the vague formulation ("one remembers," "one does not doubt"), and the rhetorical question. There is the peculiar Yeatsian irony—playful, outlandish, self-protective — that often characterizes his talk of the mysterious. So Swedenborg's "cold abstract style" is "the result, it may be, of preoccupation with stones and metals, for he had been assessor of mines to the Swedish Government. ... He considered heaven and hell and God, the angels, the whole destiny of man, as if he were sitting before a large table in a Government office putting little pieces of mineral ore into small square boxes for an assistant to pack away in drawers." Irony can become faintly grotesque comedy: whole bodies never appear at séances, only pieces, "for the dead are economical." The essay explores, without dogmatism, ideas which were a little obscured in *Rosa Alchemica* and which are to become the formulas of *A Vision*. Spirits truly exist and affect for good or evil this life, which is one of many incarnations. Spirits are often the opposites, or daimons, of a particular incarnate being: "we are each in the midst of a group of associated spirits who sleep when we sleep and become the *dramatis personae* of our dreams, and are always the other will that wrestles with our thought, shaping it to our despite." After death the soul lives through a series of purgatorial states which are analogous to acts of imagination.

The next important essay was originally called "An Alphabet" and renamed *Per Amica Silentia Lunae*, from Book II of *The Aeneid* where Virgil sees the moon "as the symbol of cyclical human life." It is Yeats's most successful doctrinal text, along with parts of the *Autobiographies* his major achievement in prose. It is another example of that Yeatsian combination of persuasion, evocation, and equivocation as he exercises his privilege to call habitual thoughts "convictions." Yeats is too skeptical, or too aware of skeptical readers, to claim that he has discovered irrefutable truths; like the wan narrator of *Rosa Alchemica,* he writes a "little book" for idle moments; but the propositions that follow have his emotional and imaginative assent, and he skillfully goes about enchanting ours.

The first section is "Ego Dominus Tuus," a poem written in 1915, which anticipates the second section, "Anima Hominis," completed in 1917; they were published along with the third section, "Anima Mundi," in 1918 and together reflect the crucial discoveries of these exciting and consolidating years. It is one of a very few poems which really does depend on the doctrinal prose and which dramatizes and illuminates the doctrine. The title comes from the *Vita Nuova* where Love, the "Lord of Terrible Aspect," suddenly appears to Dante and says "I am thy Lord." The first speaker, *Hic,* taunts the second, *Ille* (Pound liked to call it a dialogue between Hic and Willie) for his occult researches and for the unproductive middle age mocked in *Responsibilities* and lamented in *Autobiographies.* In response *Ille* posits the existence of a second self or mask which is neither projection nor compensation; it has a separate, external, objective existence. When thinking psychologically Yeats calls it the anti-self; metaphysically it resembles the Daimon, or spirit from the other world that mirrors and completes particular beings in this world. In either case it is actual and palpable. "That which comes as complete," the ideal forms beyond the trembling of the veil "must come from above me and beyond me."

Hic—who is later called the *Soul* as opposed to the *Self,* or *Primary* as opposed to *Antithetical,* and who embodies nineteenth-century ideas of art and identity which Yeats resisted and is in the process of revising— replies "And I would find myself and not an image." *Hic* offers the conventional wisdom of "sincerity and self-realisation" which drove Yeats, with help from Oscar Wilde, to his countering ideas of mask and anti-self. When *Hic* mocks that "unconquerable delusion" he is probably recalling "the unconquerable hope" and "inviolable shade" pursued by Arnold's "Scholar Gypsy," a poem Yeats used in both "Magic" and "Swedenborg." Arnold, admiring the Gypsy's hope, vigor and natural piety but despairing of its possession, wrote one of the great Victorian poems of Romantic protest against "the sick fatigue, the languid doubt" of his times—"Its heads o'ertaxed, its palsied hearts"—and its intellectuals, "Light half-believers of our casual creeds,/ Who never deeply felt, nor clearly willed." *Ille* appropriates that argument, though he searches for stronger models than the reclusive gypsy. Yeats's "we" is less felt than Arnold's; he uses the argument without accepting the Victorian identity, though his resistance is not yet made manifest:

> We are but critics, or but half create,
> Timid, entangled, empty and abashed,
> Lacking the countenance of our friends.

Hic now plays his trump, claiming that "The chief imagination of Christendom,/ Dante Alighieri" shared his views and "so utterly found himself" that he achieved fame and sanctity second only to Christ's. *Ille* and Yeats reply that Dante neither found nor sought a "sincere" self but "fashioned from his opposite" an image that shaped his hunger for earthly and heavenly beauty and drove him to the hardest of all possible tasks. The supreme example of tragic art, "he fought a double war," struggling with his visionary desires as well as with impossible love and political exile, "his unjust anger and his lust." "Anima Hominis" presents a series of such antithetical definitions of imaginative activity, beginning with Yeats argumentative in company and dreaming and composing when alone with his "Marmorean Muse"; Lady Gregory, whose "only fault is a habit of harsh judgment" writes comedies that are "a high celebration of indulgence." Synge—silent, gentle, scrupulous, debilitated by long ill health — writes voluable, physical, death-defying plays. William Morris, "a happy, busy, most irascible man" followed "an indolent muse," while Landor wrote with "calm nobility" but lived in violent passion. Keats, in the most notorious formulation of both poem and prose

> sank into his grave
> His senses and his heart unsatisfied,
> And made—being poor, ailing and ignorant,
> Shut out from all the luxury of the world,
> The coarse-bred son of a livery-stable keeper—
> Luxuriant song.

It is, as everyone has said, too far off about Keats to be interesting, even as creative distortion, but the comparison between Keats and Dante reveals a good deal about Yeats in 1915. *Ille*'s Keats is rather like the poet Yeats worries he has been, his Dante the mask-wearing quester he was trying to become. Twelve years later, restudying Blake's Dante designs, he found "my own mood between spiritual excitement, and the sexual torture and the knowledge that they are somehow inseparable!" *Ille* puts it this way:

> Being mocked by Guido for his lecherous life,
> Derided and deriding, driven out
> To climb that stair and eat that bitter bread,
> He found the unpersuadable justice, he found
> The most exalted lady loved by a man.

"Bitter bread" may come from Rossetti's paraphrase of Dante, but Yeats here associates it with a greater poet, one he also needs to judge and revise. "Anima Hominis" concludes with the brief, self-consciously false hope that a poet, "growing old," may "keep his mask and his vision without new bitterness, new disappointment," that he "need not suffer any longer" and "may discover rhythm and pattern like those in sleep and so never awake out of vision. Then," in the passage already noted in connection with "Meditations in Time of Civil War," "he will remember Wordsworth withering into eighty years, honoured and empty-witted, and climb to some waste room and find, forgotten there by youth, some bitter crust." In an earlier section Yeats prepared for this harshness by asserting that "Wordsworth, great poet though he be, is so often flat and heavy partly because his moral sense, being a discipline he had not created, a mere obedience, has no theatrical element." At the same time, he wrote to his father, who had liked to tease Dowden by disparaging Wordsworth, that he was reading "The Excursion" and "The Prelude." Like many readers, he wanted "to get through all the heavy part that I may properly understand the famous things."

Yeats will accept the Wordsworthian sublime no more readily than its sequel, the Arnoldian depressed. What Wordsworth does not understand, Dante achieves, and Yeats seeks is the knowledge that both art and identity depend upon the discovery of an anti-self, that such a being has a separate existence, and that the quest involves continual conflict and continual loss. *Hic* taunts *Ille* for his dependence on Michael Robartes's occult research, as Robartes taunts the narrator of "Rosa Alchemica," and as Yeats and Hanrahan taunt each other in "The Tower." The Daimon, he writes in "Anima Hominis," "comes not as like to like but seeking its own opposite, for man and Daimon feed the hunger in one another's hearts:

> The Daimon is our destiny. When I think of life as a struggle with the
> Daimon who would ever set us to the hardest work among those not

impossible, I understand why there is a deep enmity between a man and his destiny, and why a man loves nothing but his destiny.... We meet always in the deep of the mind, whatever our work, wherever our reverie carries us, that other Will.

Ille next responds to *Hic*'s pious hopes for happy poets, "lovers of life,/ Impulsive men that look for happiness/ And sing when they have found it," with the strongest assertion of the poem:

> No, not sing,
> For those that love the world serve it in action,
> Grow rich, popular and full of influence,
> And should they paint or write, still it is action:
> The struggle of the fly in marmalade.
> The rhetorician would deceive his neighbours,
> The sentimentalist himself; while art
> Is but a vision of reality.
> What portion in the world can the artist have
> Who has awakened from the common dream
> But dissipation and despair?

That is a conflation of his father's aphorisims, his experience with the Tragic Generation, and his current insights. In "Anima Hominis," as we have seen, Yeats builds on letters back and forth from New York to formulate a distinction between the "practical men," who are the true sentimentalists, and the poets who "sing amid our uncertainty" and who, in their quest for the antithetical self, discover that their "passion is reality" and their intermittent reward ecstasy. JBY's experience with the sick mother and dying child becomes the occasion for that moving and seductive meditation on the dependence of beauty on pain, vision on dread: "I shall find the dark grow luminous, the void fruitful when I understand that I have nothing, that the ringers in the tower have appointed for the hymen of the soul a passing bell." It is a central and permanent insight which appears again in his last poem, "The Black Tower," and in a letter of 1929 to Sturge Moore occasioned by rereading some old favorites: "I am reading William Morris with great delight, and what a protection to my delight it is to know that in spite of all his loose writing I need not be jealous for him. He is the end, as Chaucer was the end in his day, Dante in his, incoherent Blake in his. There is no improvement: only a series of sudden fires, each though fainter as necessary as the one before it. We free ourselves from obsession that we may be nothing. The last kiss is given to the void."

Yeats insistently repeats the need for and the inevitability of "new bitterness, new disappointment": "the poet finds and makes his mask in disappointment, the hero in defeat. ... for a hero loves the world till it breaks him, and the poet till it has broken faith," which it surely will. Artists must seek passion, not originality; every fire is necessary, and they are bound to be new "because no disaster is like another." Passions become vision "when we know that they cannot find fulfilment." He believes with Blake (and Wordsworth may be the text for both) that "we perceive in the pulsation of the artery, and after slowly decline." Poetic inspiration is sudden, evanescent, debilitating and humbling: "I think that we who are poets and artists, not being permitted to shoot beyond the tangible, must go from desire to weariness and so to desire again, and live but for the moment when vision comes to our weariness like terrible lightning, in the humility of the brutes." *Ille* makes the same case as he concludes the dialogue, responding to *Hic*'s prescription of "sedentary toil" and "imitation of great masters":

> Because I seek an image, not a book.
> Those men that in their writings are most wise
> Own nothing but their blind, stupefied hearts.
> I call to the mysterious one who yet
> Shall walk the wet sands by the edge of the stream
> And look most like me, being indeed my double,
> And prove of all imaginable things
> The most unlike, being my anti-self,
> And, standing by those characters, disclose
> All that I seek; and whisper it as though
> He were afraid the birds, who cry aloud
> Their momentary cries before it is dawn,
> Would carry it away to blasphemous men.

It completes the thought of this poem and the first three lines anticipate some of the "famous things" in late Yeats: "A Dialogue of Self and Soul," "The Circus Animals' Desertion," "The Man and the Echo." We arrive at a reconstituted self through pursuit of and conflict with an image which is psychologically the anti-self and metaphysically the Daimon. Both exist "above me and beyond me" and the quest presupposes loss. For Wordsworth memory and imagination, or perception and creation, coalesce to recapture an earlier self and so to compensate for loss. For Yeats the imaginative act is also, and at the same time, seeking and conflict and defeat. Discovering an anti-self, making a self, and creating art are dialectical, but so intermeshed as to be nearly synonymous. Yeats separates the acts for understanding, then elides them again for persuasion and evocation.

"Anima Mundi," completed a little more than two months after "Anima Hominis," develops its implications, is the metaphysics to the first book's epistemology. Yeats effects an amalgamation of the "general mind," or the "subconscious," to the "Great Memory" or "Anima Mundi" and so comes to the realization he later describes in *The Trembling of the Veil:* "I know now that revelation is from the self, but from that age-long memoried self, that shapes the elaborate shell of the mollusc and the child in the womb, that teaches the birds to make their nests; and that genius is a crisis that joins that buried self for certain moments to our trivial daily mind." He insists upon the independent existence of Daimons, of souls, ghosts, spirits, shape-changers and apparitions. Their lives after death or beyond time affect the various incarnate beings who are their chosen vehicles, though "Anima Mundi" leaves the elaboration of particular purgatorial stages to Book III of *A Vision,* as "Anima Hominis" leaves "those heaving circles, those winding arcs" of history to Book V. "All souls have a vehicle or body," and, as Blake said, " 'God only acts or is in existing beings or men.' " Yeats can be playfully suggestive — "it is the dream martens that, all unknowing, are master-masons to the living martens building about church windows their elaborate nests" — or pictorial: "all our mental images ... are forms existing in the general vehicle of *Anima Mundi,* and mirrored in our particular vehicle.... I think of *Anima Mundi* as a great pool or garden where it moves through its alloted growth like a great water-plant of fragrantly branches in the air."

The realization of contact with the "vast luminous sea" is the epiphany, which derives from the ultimate epiphany "when all sequence comes to an end, time comes to an end, and the soul puts on the rhythmic or spiritual body or luminous body and contemplates all the events of its memory and every possible impulse in an eternal possession of itself in one single moment."

At the conclusion of "Anima Mundi," which he later turns into section IV of "Vacillation," the sense of radiant connection with the General Mind—the mind of all humanity—is so intense that hatred, "the common condition of our life," disappears. "I am in the place where the Daimon is, but I do not think he is with me until I begin to make a new personality, selecting among those images ... and yet ... I am full of uncertainty, not knowing when I am the finger, when the clay:

At certain moments, always unforeseen, I become happy, most commonly when at hazard I have opened some book of verse. Sometimes it is my own verse when, instead of discovering new technical flaws, I read with all the excitement of the first writing. Perhaps I am sitting in some crowded restaurant, the open book beside me, or closed, my excitement having overbrimmed the page. I look on the strangers near as if I had known them all my life, and it seems strange that I cannot speak to them: everything fills me with affection, I have no longer any fears or any needs; I do not even remember that this happy mood must come to an end. It seems as if the vehicle had suddenly grown pure and far extended and so luminous that the images from *Anima Mundi*, embodied there and drunk with the sweetness, would, like a country drunkard who has thrown a wisp into his own thatch, burn up time.

3

There is more introductory matter for *A Vision* than for *A Tale of a Tub*, and Yeats's rather anxious citation of Swift ("this way of publishing introductions to books, that are God knows when to come out") does not provide a saving irony. The three sections of "A Packet for Ezra Pound" give an account of "the incredible experience" of his wife's automatic writing, his excited response, and a few explanations and justifications that are more usefully considered after reading the whole book. The "Stories of Michael Robartes and his Friends: an Extract from a Record Made by His Pupils" have an aptly circular structure; a student of Robartes, Yeats's creation forty years past, writes to Yeats about the old tales; but social comedy is not Yeats's strength and the stories are too arch and prolix. The portrait of Giraldus Cambrensis, sage and author of yet another sacred text, looking very much like W. B. Yeats almost winking, is the only funny moment, happy evidence of the "impish humor" which, AE maintained, partly animates this strange book. "The Phases of the Moon," *A Vision*'s introductory poem, is just what Yeats called it — "a text for exposition"; unlike "Ego Dominus Tuus," it does not transcend the limitations of the genre and is, like the stories, rather too coy. It is most interesting as a poem of rooting, like "The Tower" or "A Prayer for my Daughter," but far less successful. So an open-minded reader is best advised to begin at page sixty-seven and the first of the five significant books. Book I: "The Great Wheel" owes most to "Anima Hominis" and is Yeatsian psychology or character definition. Book II: "The Completed Symbol" is about religion and proceeds from "Anima Mundi." Book III:

"The Soul in Judgment" is eschatology and defines the stages of Purgatory mentioned in "Anima Mundi." Book IV: "The Great Year of the Ancients" is about learning and literature, Yeats's search for authorities, the discovery of large historical patterns. Book V: "Dove or Swan" is about the multiple patterns in history and explores those arcs and circles not developed in *Per Amica Silentia Lunae.*

Yeats's "Great Wheel," which he liked to think "a form of science for the study of human nature" combines astrology, an eclectic psychology that began with JBY's more casual classifications, and a highly personal and flexible geometry. The basic unit is the gyre or cone; or rather a double cone, the apex of one located at the furthest expansion of the other; they whirl in opposite directions, "dying each other's life, living each other's death" in the often repeated thought of Heraclitus. Yeats turns the cones on their side in order to present two superimposed planes where they intersect. That is the Great Wheel of the twenty-eight phases of the moon which determines character, personality and destiny. He associates the line with time and subjectivity, the plane with space and objectivity, the spiral (later the sphere) with fully comprehended reality. At a particular moment every being has four dominant qualities, which Yeats calls *The Faculties,* two whirling right to left, and two left to right. Like other psychological classifications they are not so much personality traits as they are ways of organizing observation. They are:

1) *Will* — or *Is* or energy, analogous to Ego.
2) *Mask* — or *Ought,* Other, Anti-self.
3) *Creative Mind* — Thought, Knower, under certain conditions the Imagination.
4) *Body of Fate* — Object, Known, chance and circumstance; the environment.

Location on the wheel is determined by *Will;* but in a complex dialectic *Will* draws on *Mask* which is opposite to it, and on *Creative Mind* and *Body of Fate* which are placed on a line which intersects the *Will-Mask* line. Hence if *Will* is at Phase Twelve, *Mask* is opposite at Phase Twenty-six, *Creative Mind* to the right at Phase Eighteen, and *Body of Fate* to the left at Phase Four. The lines converge at the four cardinal points of the wheel (One, Eight, Fifteen, Twenty-two) or the "four phases of crisis." Phases One and Fifteen, however, are abstractions, definitions of complete objectivity and complete subjectivity, where human life is impossible. The clearest analogy for all of this (one of *A Vision*'s few clear analogies) comes from the *"Commedia dell' Arte* or improvised drama of

Italy. The stagemanager, or *Daimon,* offers his actor an inherited scenario, the *Body of Fate,* and a *Mask* or role as unlike as possible to his natural ego or *Will,* and leaves him to improvise through his *Creative Mind* the dialogue and details of the plot."

It is very flexible and it has a very inclusive sense of time: "This wheel is every completed movement of thought or life, twenty-eight incarnations, a single judgment or act of thought." There are wheels within wheels as each group of three phases can comprise its own circular unit; a being goes through several rounds of the Great Wheel; opposed phases weave and unweave each other; and there are *True* or *False Masks* and *Creative Minds* depending on whether a being is in or out of phase. The Great Wheel divides itself into two fundamentally opposed categories as Yeats develops the antinomies explored in *Per Amica.* Phases Eight through Twenty-two belongs to *Antithetical* or subjective man; phases Twenty-two through Twenty-eight and One through Seven to *Primary* or subjective man. The system permits an almost endless listing of oppositions:

Antithetical	*Primary*
Moon	Sun
Vision	Reality
Unity	Plurality
Personality	Character
Freedom	Necessity
Emotion	Reason
Aristocracy	Democracy
Aesthetics	Morals
Self-realization	Service
Self-dramatization	Sincerity
Ecstasy	Wisdom

It may all seem too easily schematic, the dialectical chart conquering reality, but Yeats's involvement with the distinctions is intense and personal. "I think that two conceptions," he wrote in his diary while revising *A Vision,* "that of reality as a congeries of beings, that of reality as a single being, alternate in our emotion and in history, and must always remain something that human reason, because subject always to one or the other, cannot reconcile. I am always, in all I do, driven to a moment which is the realisation of myself as unique and free, or to a moment which is the surrender to God of all that I am."

The categories are shifting rather than static and they do not represent facile organization but struggle. In Yeats's system as in his experience, "human life is impossible without strife" and the ghostly instructors "identify consciousness with conflict, not with knowledge, substitute for subject and object and their attendant logic a struggle towards harmony, towards Unity of Being. Logical and emotional conflict alike lead towards a reality which is concrete, sensuous, bodily." That reality is the *summum bonum* of *A Vision* and its apprehension is the goal of much of Yeats's mature thought. The diary entry moves from the "two conceptions" of reality to a sense of "the ultimate reality" which "must be all movement, all thought, all perception extinguished, two freedoms unthinkably, unimaginably absorbed in one another." Unity of Being is the condition sought for in certain privileged historical epochs, like Byzantium under the rule of Justinian, and in equally privileged personal experience, like that recorded at the end of *Per Amica* or in "Vacillation." Dante compared it "to a perfectly proportioned human body" and JBY to the moment when "all the nature murmurs in response if but a single note be touched." *A Vision*'s categories, apparently rigid and abstract, exist in the service of that concrete, sensuous reality. Its cones and planes form a singularly ingenious set of symbols for a poet whose sense of character and history is both organic and dialectical, and who has rejected the myths of historical progress and personal sincerity. They allow Yeats free play for the exfoliation of antitheses, at the same time setting it in a pattern of development rather than the static tables of so much psychology and sociology, which are thin and unconvincing precisely because they leave little room for history and no room for mystery. The wheels also allow and support "an early conviction of mine, that the creative power of the lyric poet depends upon his accepting some one of a few traditional attitudes, lover, sage, hero, scorner of life." The *1930 Diary*, following the encounter with Swift, adds "some image of despair" and claims that "a good poet must ... be the last of a dynasty." Book I of *A Vision* is an elaboration, perhaps an overelaboration, of these insights; but it is the elaboration not the insight that obscures. The desire is clear enough: to order and so control experience; to develop the implications of masks and antitheses; to articulate a sense of the possibility of fullness, harmony and ecstasy; to achieve for the lyric something of the scope of the epic without succumbing to naturalism and positivism.

"The Great Wheel" is more or less temporal and secular. "Book II: the Completed Symbol" attempts to fit the gyres of character and destiny into a more transcendental scheme: "I may found an Irish heresy." Yeats wrote happily to Olivia Shakespear. The central figure is the *Daimon*, the "stage manager" of the analogy, whom Yeats's instructors called the "Ghostly Self," and who can also be seen as the soul in eternity or in the "period between lives," which includes "all the events of our life"; or as the ideal of the soul of man in one of its incarnations; or even as the archetype of "nations, cultures, schools of thought." Inherent in the *Daimon*'s eternal nature, apparently as its memories, are the four *Principles,* timeless counterparts of the four *Faculties.* They spin in a gyre of twelve revolutions (roughly corresponding to months but also defined by the seasons) which contains the gyre of the *Faculties* with its twenty-eight phases. This makes the geometry a little obscure, even for *A Vision:* "the *Principles* are the *Faculties* transferred, as it were, from a concave to a convex mirror, or vice versa." When Yeats says that he "can see" his whirling and counter-whirling, superimposed symbols "like jelly fish in clear water," the uninitiated reader is likely to find the image odd and the waters muddy. Elsewhere he is so Platonically inclusive that all prior distinctions seem to collapse: "for all things are a single form which has divided and multiplied in time and space." At any rate, as the "innate ground" of the *Faculties,* the *Principles* are:

1. *Husk* (corresponding to *Will*): sense, the human body, the past; the *Daimon*'s power of concentrating itself in an embodied, temporal life.
2. *Passionate Body (Mask):* object of sense; the sense world; the present.
3. *Spirit (Creative Mind):* Divine Mind, the future.
4. *Celestial Body (Body of Fate):* the object of the Divine Mind, and out of time.

The *Principles* may, at chosen moments, exist in timeless unity and perfection, like the Fifteenth Phase of The Great Wheel; but, consistent with the rest of the system and with Yeats's experience, they act on man— through the *Daimon*—as conflict: "the whole system is founded upon the belief that the ultimate reality, symbolised as the Sphere, falls in human consciousness ... into a series of antinomies." That sphere, or cycle, or *Thirteenth Cone* is the other major element of "The Completed Symbol." It represents the deliverance into unity from the whole cycle of birth and death, time and space, hence from all the apparatus of *A Vision,* "for always at the critical moment the *Thirteenth Cone,* the sphere, the unique intervenes." It is the freedom to the apparent determinism of *A Vision.* At times Yeats seems simply willful and rather too casual: "I substitute for God the Thirteenth Cone, the Thirteenth Cone therefore creates our perceptions—all the visible world—as held in common by our wheels." He has, however, some powerfully resonant precedents, including the perfect circle of Renaissance iconography and the symbolism of the *Paradisio,* and some intense personal experience, like that recorded in *Per Amica* or in a subsequent letter to Olivia Shakespear:

The night before...I went for a walk after dark and there among some great trees became absorbed in the most lofty philosophical conception I have found while writing *A Vision.* I suddenly seemed to understand at last and then I smelt roses. I now realized the nature of the timeless spirit. Then I began to walk and with my excitement came—how shall I say?—that old glow so beautiful with its autumnal tint. The longing to touch it was almost unendurable. The next night I was walking in the same path and now the two excitements came together. The autumnal image, remote, incredibly spiritual, erect, delicate featured, and mixed with it the violent physical image, the black mass of Eden.

He has, too, the precedent of Blake, and, though the language of *A Vision* often obscures it, the *Thirteenth Sphere* is also the realm of the imagination, the state of being where one discovers that "Man made up the whole,/ Made lock, stock and barrel/ Out of his bitter soul." Whether as God, or imagination, or "phaseless sphere," the *Thirteenth Cone* is eliptically defined by Ribh's fourth song, aptly called "There":

> There all the barrel-hoops are knit,
> There all the serpent-tails are bit,
> There all the gyres converge in one,
> There all the planets drop in the Sun.

While the relationships among the parts are constantly shifting and the symbolic correspondences are flexible to the point of confusion, there is an order to the elements of Book II, a hierarchy of spiritual magnitude or "eternality." The *Thirteenth Cone* is the ultimate, all-inclusive reality. The *Daimon* is the ultimate self, the eternal being or soul. The four *Principles* of the *Daimon* whirl in a gyre of twelve revolutions and determine the four *Faculties* of the individual soul or being, locked in time on its wheel of twenty-eight phases. That being at any particular moment is placed on the wheel by the position of its *Will.*

The first four sections of "Book III: The Soul in Judgement," like *Per Amica* and in a similarly allusive and evocative prose, seek to persuade us of the reality of lives after death and of the need for belief in personal immortality. The remaining seven sections describe the six stages between death and rebirth. The soul in Purgatory, influenced by the circular movement of the *Principles,* works over and absorbs the knowledge which the *Faculties* accumulated during life. This may take little or much time; the norm is three generations (death to birth) and it takes about two thousand years for a full cycle of lives.

The first stage is *The Vision of the Blood Kindred* when all the images and impulses of the life just completed are simultaneously present, like the dream or illumination said to occur just before death. Then comes the *Meditation* as the spirit goes over the whole of life's experiences in three sub-stages: in the *Dreaming Back* life is relived in order of intensity; in the *Return* in chronological order; in the *Phantasmagoria,* the life past is completed, its implications fulfilled. The third stage is *The Shiftings.* The emotion of bodily life now over, the soul begins to understand its good and evil and relives life's moments in a new form, the tyrant becoming victim and the victim, tyrant. In the *Marriage* or *Beatitude* good and evil vanish (the stage is similar to Keats's Negative Capability); all is understood and perfect equilibrium is achieved. The *Purification* is the first movement towards rebirth as the spirit finds its next particular aim and begins to shape its next incarnation. The final stage is *Foreknowledge,* an anticipatory vision and acceptance of the next incarnation. The object of this complex phasal judgment is not happiness or virtue, but freedom from the circle of current experience, as the system again emphasizes stress and conflict.

The terms of this Purgatory, and its lines of demarcation, may be a little arbitrary, but its substance is neither fantastical nor foolish. For his firm belief in lives after death Yeats is drawing upon a neo-Platonic tradition that included Plotinus, Henry More, Swedenborg, and Blake, and a literary tradition that began, for him, with Irish folklore and most recently expressed itself in the Noh plays. "The Soul in Judgement" is psychologically acute about the stages of growth and about identity formation. The spirits keep reliving ordinary life, and Yeats is not so much making the quotidian into the eternal as he is making the eternal into the phenomenal. For all the elaboration, he keeps coming back to the idea that experience is all we have. "I think I have done one good deed," he wrote in 1931, "in clearing out of the state from death to birth all the infinities and eternities, and picturing a state as 'phenomenal' as that from birth to death. I have constructed a myth, but then one can believe in a myth—one only assents to philosophy." Yeats's Purgatory is also an image of and analogue to the creative process. As the imagination combs over life, facing the conflict and experiencing the loss, trivia can become ecstasy and the poet can be reborn, for the moment at least intended, whole, radiant. Furthermore, the notions in Book III lead to some of the pathos of *The Words upon the Windowpane* and the power of *Purgatory.* Yeats said that "The Soul in Judgment" was the "most unfinished" section of *A Vision.* It is completed in those plays and there demonstrates its value for him.

"The Great Year of the Ancients," Yeats's search for authorities, is the least coherent and interesting book of *A Vision.* It seems to wander about two ideas that are important to him, but which he cannot quite pin down here. The first is the idea of the Great or Platonic year with its associated, antithetical ideas of eternal recurrence and perfect harmony or stability. He offers an uncharacteristically homely example: "It is though innumerable dials, some that recorded minutes alone, some seconds alone, some hours alone, some months alone, some years alone, were all to complete their circles when Big Ben struck twelve upon the last night of the century." But he immediately adds, "my instructors offer for a symbol the lesser unities that combine into a work of art and leave no remainder" and that lesser unity, at least graspable, is what moves him, and us, most. Amid the patterns of endless recurrence there may be an imaginable moment of perfect order, but history usually reveals itself as conflict: *Antithetical* and *Primary;* Caesar (or Eros) and Christ; East and West: "At the birth of Christ religious life becomes *primary,* secular life antithetical—man gives to Caesar the things that are Caesar's. A primary dispensation looking beyond itself towards a transcendent power is dogmatic, levelling, unifying, feminine, humane, peace its means and end; and antithetical dispensation obeys imminent power, is expressive, hierarchical, multiple, masculine, harsh, surgical." That unpleasant formulation reminds us that *A Vision* is also a political book. It should further remind us that Yeats did not choose his values according to what he thought the new dispensation would be. Rather, like most prophets, he projects the antithesis of what he dislikes about present civilisation onto his sense of the coming order.

"Book V: Dove or Swan" remained unchanged from the 1925 edition. It is by far the most satisfying section of *A Vision*. Yeats organizes and meditates upon his vast and unsystematic reading and thinking about the idea and uses of history. He draws upon Heraclitus, Plotinus, Swedenborg; Swift and Berkeley; Blake, Coleridge and Pater; Balzac and Goethe; Vico, Nietzsche, Gentile and Whitehead. He was pleased and excited to find confirmation in Spengler and Henry Adams. It is prophetic, speculative and ironic in a prose that is not quite as seductive as *Per Amica's*, but less rigid and more inviting than the rest of *A Vision,* and enormously confident. It begins in Yeats's conviction that "all knowledge is biography" and that history is drama and takes its strength from its central insight, also dramatized in poems like "The Tower" and recorded in the 1930 Diary: "History is Necessity until it takes fire in someone's head and becomes Freedom or Virtue." It is, as Thomas Whitaker has demonstrated, not a coherent philosophy of history but a vision of history as art, an acceptance of history without loss of freedom or creativity, a projection of the necessarily limited human condition upon the panorama of recorded events, from the swan who impregnated Leda and so inaugurated the classical age, to the Dove of the Christian annunciation, to the present disintegration.

The most inclusive temporal unit is the Great Year of Book IV, here seen as twelve revolutions of the Wheel of twenty-eight incarnations, the completion of the heavenly circuit when the Zodiac falls into place, about 26,000 years, though the math is variable. That is unmanageable, even for Yeats: "An historical symbolism which covers too great a period of time for imagination to grasp or experience to explain may seem too theoretical, too arbitrary, to serve any practical purpose." So there are smaller units, wheels within wheels: 4000 years, or the entire epoch with which *A Vision* is concerned; 2000 years for a full sweep of the wheel of the *Principles;* 1000 years, the basic unit of analysis, for the sweep of a double gyre through its *primary* and *antithetical* phases, or rise and fall of *A Vision*'s three major eras. The first phase is from about 2000 B.C. until the birth of Christ. Early, legendary Greece (initiated by Zeus and Leda) leads to the age of Homer, the pre-Socratic philosophers and Phidias, and reaches its height in Periclean Athens, the full moon on the wheel, as close to the ideal Phase Fifteen as a civilization can attain. Then comes a decline through Aristotle and abstract thought ("to die into the truth is still to die") into the most completely primary expression of this phase, the Roman Empire and its rigid order. The annunciation to Mary and the birth of Christ beginning a new, primary dispensation which continues to about Phase Eight, becomes antithetical, reaches its peak with the visionary art of Byzantium near the year 1000, and degenerates into the Middle Ages. Our own epoch began with Romance Literature and Romanesque, then Gothic architecture, achieved a stage close to perfection with the Italian Renaissance, then declined through the spiritual chaos and strife of the seventeenth century, eighteenth-century rationalism, nineteenth-century materialism, into the disintegration — or *Hodos Cameliontos* — of the present, a grimly primary age anxiously awaiting an antithetical annunciation. The dates are approximate and the eras overlap as each phase is also a different phase of another cycle, which allows for variation and conflict. Phase Fifteen on one circuit is Phase Eight or Twenty-two on another; the perfection embodied in Byzantium occurs at the same time as the fall of Rome. There are numerous gaps as Yeats is primarily interested in the cardinal points of the wheels, moments of particular intensity or revelation, fulfillment or disintegration. Of course it is an eclectic, quirky and willful scheme. It is also extraordinarily flexible, capacious and—for Yeats —liberating. It is resourceful and satisfying on its own terms, as a meditation upon history, and it organizes the thought of some rich and complex poems. It meets Yeats's desire "for a system of thought that would leave my imagination free to create as it chose and yet make all that it created, or could create, part of one history, and that the soul's."

"The End of the Cycle," *A Vision*'s prose epilogue, is far shorter and more interesting than all the introductory matter. (It is also more compelling than "All Souls' Night," the concluding poem, another "text for exposition" which never quite gets around to saying its "marvellous thing" or revealing its "mummy truths.") Yeats is alone, turning over in his mind not a system but a symbol, "attempting to substitute particulars for an abstraction like that of algebra" or of one of the currently available ideologies: "Then I draw myself up into the symbol and it seems as if I should know all if I could but banish such memories and find everything in the symbol. But nothing comes—though this moment was to reward me for all my toil. Perhaps I am too old." "But nothing comes." It is like the feeling at the close of *Reveries over Childhood and Youth* when "all life weighed in the scale of my own life seems to me a preparation for something that never happens." At the end of this book there should be triumph, but there is instead an overriding sense of loss, a negative, very Yeatsian epiphany. Then a moment of recovery: "Then I understand. I have already said all that can be said. The particulars are the work of the *thirteenth sphere* ... but it has kept the secret." It is not a convincing recovery at the end of a book which has been trying to tear out and codify the secrets. Conviction does not come from the system but from an image which returns Yeats to "Swedenborg," which has closed with the same thought, and to his affectionate reading of William Morris. It is posed as a question—"Shall we follow the image of Heracles that walks through the darkness bow in hand, or mount to that other Heracles, man not image, he that has for his bride Hebe, 'The daughter of Zeus, the mighty, and Hera, shod with gold'?"— but it follows and claims "that other Heracles," or reconstituted being, something intended, complete, a vision of art as transformed history and achieved identity.

In the "Introduction" Yeats worried that "some, perhaps all, of those readers I most value, those who have read me many years, will be repelled by" that "arbitrary, harsh, difficult symbolism." Contemporary letters call *A Vision* "the skeleton in my cupboard," wonder if people will think him a "crazed fanatic," and worry again about "the disgust and bewilderment of my friends." In truth, *A Vision* is not an inviting book. It is more difficult than it needs to be, and we are justified in being put off by such "rules" as this: "*When the will is in antithetical phases the True Creative Mind is derived from the Creative Mind phase, modified by the Creative Mind of that phase; while the False Creative Mind is derived from the Creative Mind phase, modified by the Body of Fate of that phase.*" Whatever it does for Yeats it does not cohere in our minds. We read it, lose it, have to go back again, and the difficulty does not seem to be as rewarding or rewarded as it is with the more complex poems and plays.

There is a genuine problem about its determinism. There is some release, some carefully plotted moments of escape, choice as well as chance. *Will* at times seems to select its *Mask, Creative Mind* its *Body of*

Fate, the *Daimon* its incarnations. The *Thirteenth Cone* affords ultimate release from almost everything, though its imposition is arbitrary and its operations obscure or secretive. While Yeats was revising *A Vision,* Kevin O'Higgins was assassinated, and he wrote to Mrs. Shakespear about some premonitions: "Had we seen more he might have been saved, for recent evidence seems to show that those things are fate unless foreseen by clairvoyance and so brought within the range of free-will." Yeats's grief, anger and helpless guilt were surely sincere; but the "clairvoyance" that brings free will was uniquely his and no help to O'Higgins; so with *A Vision* where the power to see and be free seems so privately, eccentrically the poet's that we are not invited or allowed to share it. The liberty Swift served, Yeats thought, "was that of intellect, not liberty for the masses but for those who could make it visible." True enough perhaps, but *A Vision* too often darkens rather than illuminates. Whatever Yeats's intention, it feels deterministic, and it too often recalls "R.R. & A.G.'s" contempt for the freedom of lesser hermeticists, and *On the Boiler* or "Under Ben Bulben's" for lesser beings, "base born products of base beds." Orwell was not being fanciful or simply ideological when he noted the conjunction between occultism and authoritarianism. Yeats was not pointing to mere coincidence when he wrote that he was ready to talk with "the Fascist organiser of the blue shirts ... for I had just re-written for the seventh time the part of *A Vision* that deals with the future."

The book is full of valuable insights (such as the fine, thrown-away phrase about "Jane Austen's privileged and perilous research") and even possesses some comic moments (like the curious man of Phase Eighteen, probably Arthur Symons, who says, "I was never in love with a serpent-charmer before"), but too many judgments are willfull and wayward, Yeats the prisoner of his own system. Lady Gregory and Synge deserve better as friends and allies, Keats and Shelley as predecessors. It is not free from penny-astrology prescriptions—"He should seek to liberate the *Mask* by the help of the *Creative Mind* from the *Body of Fate*—that is to say, to carve out and wear the now free *Mask* and so to protect and to deliver the Image"—or rules of the game—"it is stated that the individual may have to return to this phase more than once, though not more than four times, before it is passed"—which sound suspiciously like cosmic *Monopoly.* The ghostly wisdom can be rationalization of a rather perverse kind: "we get happiness, my instructors say, from those we have served, ecstasy from those we have wronged." Late in his life Yeats said that a good deal of his "private philosophy" had not gotten into *A Vision.* Perhaps we may be pardoned if we remember Dr. Johnson on *Paradise Lost* and do not wish it longer.

What is objectionable about *A Vision,* then, is its over-determination and elaboration, its willful obscurity, and its arch tone. It is not really a problem of belief or doctrine, which are neither so outré nor fanciful as they at first seem. With only slight oversimplification it is possible to list Yeats's Articles of Belief, the creed to which *A Vision* subscribes, under four headings:

1. Immortality, reincarnation, and purgatory. There is a "Communion of the Living and the Dead" and both history and psychology are supernaturally conditioned. The mode of the communion is characteristically an annunciation or a revelation.

2. Mind is the animating principle of the universe. There is an ancestral or general memory (or collective unconscious) which can be evoked by symbol and by meditation. Our thoughts have a reality independent of our quotidian beings. The imagination can transform the trivial into the ecstatic and permanent.

3. There is form and pattern (for Yeats cycles and antitheses) to the record of human experience.

4. True identity can be achieved by pursuing the opposite or other, by wearing a mask.

There is a substantial tradition, or several traditions — religious, philosophical, literary — behind these beliefs, which, as Denis Donoghue points out, are not necessarily "more fanciful than a philosopher's belief in innate ideas, a geneticist's belief in heredity, or a linguist's belief in a child's possession of generative grammar." Yeats held most of them all his life; the majority appear before 1900, and all of them by 1917, before his marriage and Mrs. Yeats's automatic writing. The terms belong to Yeats, not his instructors. The freshest material in *A Vision* is in "Dove or Swan"; that is informed by reading not ghosts; and it is the least eccentric and most fruitful of the five books.

Yeats worried about incredulity and mockery as well as disgust and bewilderment: "Some will ask whether I believe in the actual existence of my circuits of sun and moon." He responds, at first, with the same kind of justification he had made in "Magic," a plea for openmindedness in the face of experience, and then with a concession to rationalism: "I can but answer that if sometimes, overwhelmed by miracle as all men must be when in the midst of it, I have taken such periods literally, my reason has soon recovered." He concludes his "Introduction" with a new definition of the matter of *A Vision* and with a more conventional, though still personal, justification:

> Now that the system stands out clearly in my imagination I regard
> them as stylistic arrangements of experience comparable to the cubes

in the drawing of Wyndham Lewis and to the ovoids in the sculpture
of Brancusi. They have helped me to hold in a single thought reality
and justice.

That is not safety in derision but in the subjective viability of an
intellectual and imaginative construct. Frank Kermode has rightly
suggested that the last phrase is most clearly understood as "reality and
order." Yeats's half-parodic version is "an unexplained rule of thumb that
somehow explained the world." It is a familiar idea in modern literature—
Conrad's codes, Stevens's fictions, Lawrence's myths — most succinctly
caught by Eliot's famous explanation of the Homeric parallels in *Ulysses.*

Placing people in schemes of psychology and events in patterns of
history requires really looking at both. For all their oddity, the ghostly
messages and exotic diagrams become a vehicle for what his father so
wished, a "poetry in closest and most intimate union with the positive
realities and complexities of life." Like form in the poems, like all of Yeats's
realized encounters, *A Vision* provides a way of confronting experience
and mastering it, achieving freedom out of necessity, rather than capitulat-
ing to naturalism or quietism or annihilation. For Yeats unlike Eliot it is an
exploitation of religious belief without religious faith and its consequent
demands on volition and behavior: "one can believe in a myth—one only
assents to philosophy"; "you can refute Hegel but not the Saint or the Song
of Sixpence."

When Yeats offered "to spend what remained of life explaining and
piecing together those scattered sentences" of automatic writing, his instructors replied: "'No ... we have come to give you metaphors for
poetry.'" Metaphors are not decorative figures but those rich and elaborate *makings,* a way to understand the significance of experience, a form of
truth. The "dry astrological bones" of *A Vision* do become "breathing
life" in poems and plays, just as the bird "signifies truth" rather than "the
great systems." As "a system of thought that would leave the imagination
free," a geometry that is "more than mathematical," *A Vision* is also an
analogy to the creative process and a renewal of it. It is a source of energy
for the poet, and for all that is unlikeable about it, it is a kind of moral
achievement. The "Muses resemble women," Yeats said "who creep out at
night and give themselves to unknown sailors and return to talk of Chinese
porcelain ... except that the Muses sometimes form in those low haunts
their most lasting attachments."

4

Yeats also said that he "put *The Tower* and *The Winding Stair* into evidence to show that my poetry has gained in self-possession and power" and that he owed the change to the "incredible experience" which culminates in *A Vision*. The strength of his poetry after 1917 is manifest, and we should be wary about disputing his evidence. Like "one has had a vision, one wants to have another, that is all," it is a hard claim to reject unless we are prepared to deny the possibility of vision, or the achievement of those two impressive volumes. We should instead look at some of the poems associated with the system and try to understand the nature and sources of their power. We can begin with texts that depend upon *A Vision* and then consider those which grow out of the same matrix but which do not really need the system to be understood. Five important poems punctuate *A Vision*'s idea of history. "Leda and the Swan" dramatizes the annunciation which begins the first or classical era; "Two Songs from a Play" focus on the annunciation to Mary which inaugurates the second, Christian era; "The Second Coming" contains the disintegration of this age and envisions the birth of the next dispensation. The two Byzantium poems are Yeats's most concentrated exploration of the relationships between this world and the Otherworld. Together they illustrate the various ways in which the poems—particular acts of imagination—expand, complete, and occasionally subvert the argument of *A Vision* and the uses of the occult.

"Leda and the Swan," which was written in September 1923, before the first edition but well into Yeats's organization, has connections with its view of history and became the introduction to "Dove or Swan," "the annunciation that founded Greece," the initiating event of the first great cycle. Zeus takes the form of a swan to rape the mortal Leda, eternity engendering upon time, and so produces Castor and Pollux, Clytemnestra and Helen, Love and War, the fall of Troy and the shaping of Greek civilization. Yeats apparently began it by joining some of his speculations about historical causation to his growing sense of contemporary decline, "but as I wrote, bird and lady took such possession of the scene that all politics went out of it." The possession is multiple—Zeus of Leda, Leda of the scene, both of Yeats's imagination (he owned a copy of Michelangelo's famous painting which he had also seen in Venice), and "Leda and the Swan" is a signal example of Yeats's transforming powers, breathing life into his instructors' designs. Its power derives from its attention to the intensely realized moment of violence and terror—Blake's "Pulsation of the Artery" which contains "all the Great Events of Time" — and to the genuine, altogether current question with which it ends.

The sonnet form achieves for "Leda" what the Great Wheel wants to achieve for *A Vision*: violence and historical sweep held in one of the most tightly controlled of poetic forms. The form exactly mirrors the drama. The octave carries the assault and the subduing; at the turn from octave to sestet the whole poem hangs suspended upon the moment of engendering, and the following three lines brilliantly figure the rape and prefigure its consequent history, sexual violence becoming "those heaving circles, those winding arcs":

> A shudder in the loins engenders there
> The broken wall, the burning roof and tower
> And Agamemnon dead.

The poem turns again in the middle of the sestet. As Zeus goes from violence to post-coital indifference, Leda moves from vague yet intense terror to a vague yet real sense of power, from victim to agent of divinity and historical force:

> Being so caught up,
> So mastered by the brute blood of the air,
> Did she put on his knowledge with his power
> Before the indifferent beak could let her drop?

The revisions show Yeats diminishing the role of Zeus and developing Leda's participation. "Helpless thighs" become "loosening thighs," suggesting at least some volition. The body feels the divine heart, and the mind begins to apprehend if not understand. In the first stanza Leda is merely "caught"; in the last she is "so caught up"; an early draft had "Being mounted so" and the revision changes Leda from stricken and debased animal to participating intelligence. An earlier twelfth line—"Did nothing pass before her in the air?"—explicitly raises the possibility of an answering and compensatory vision. The completed poem — rightly — is more agnostic: does Leda know? Is the power that she now carries accompanied by knowledge? Can we ever begin to understand the mysteries of divine intervention or the nature and implications of our pain and our terror? It is a real, open question and the poem does not posit a clear answer; but Yeats's sympathies and intuitions can be felt. When

Wordsworth wishes for knowledge purchased without loss of power, the grave of the Boy of Winander, over which he stands, provides a mute and poignant refutation. Only on rare occasions is Yeats flatly confident that it is possible to see beyond the veil into the temple, to both master and know experience; but he seldom disallows the possibility. If he wills the rough beast of "The Second Coming," he also wills the possibility that Leda knows.

The next annunciation poem in the scheme of *A Vision* is "Two Songs from a Play" which introduce and conclude *The Resurrection,* the powerful and unorthodox drama about Christ's first appearance after the crucifixion, the reactions to that event of a rationalist, a humanist, and a believer in inexplicable mysteries, and—more generally—about "the terror of the supernatural" experienced by the witness who feels the heartbeat of the risen man/God. The poems have an even wider sweep than "Leda," asserting parallels both uncanny and archetypal between the rebirth of Dionysus, Virgil's prophecy of the Golden Age, and the birth and death of Christ. The second song begins with a vision of Christ and His conse-quences which is dramatically the view of the old—Greek and Roman—order and conceptually the view of "Dove or Swan," Christ as the initiator of a Primary epoch:

> In pity for man's darkening thought
> He walked that room and issued thence
> In Galilean turbulence;
> The Babylonian starlight brought
> A fabulous, formless darkness in;
> Odour of blood when Christ was slain
> Made all Platonic tolerance vain
> And vain all Doric discipline.

The last stanza, added in 1931, four years after the first version of the play, returns all significant experience to the human heart and so accepts transience. Most of the stanza recalls the *Autobiographies'* account of the "Tragic Generation" and sounds too ninetyish for its context:

> Everything that man esteems
> Endures a moment or a day:
> Love's pleasure drives his love away,
> The painter's brush consumes his dreams;
> The herald's cry, the soldier's tread
> Exhaust his glory and his might:

But the concluding couplet could only have been written by the mature Yeats and encapsulates the most compelling theme of his later work:

> Whatever flames upon the night
> Man's own resinous heart has fed.

The lines rescue the poem from both the determinism of endless cycles and the shrugging decadence of the Rhymers. It is remarkable and instructive that only after working through *A Vision* is Yeats able to achieve this scope and this exhilaration, to assert again and again the subjective and the human in the face of the cycles of history and the mysteries of religion. It does not exactly subvert *A Vision*, but it does redeem it. If all those wheels sometimes seem the will doing the work of the imagination, here the imagination does its own.

Yeats's two most studied poems (studied in both senses) are probably "Sailing to Byzantium" and "Byzantium." They are certainly the two that most emphatically pose the antithesis between time and eternity, flux and permanence, the issue of much of *A Vision* and central to Books III and V. Byzantium was the capital of Eastern Christendom, the Eastern Roman Empire that rose politically and artistically in the fifth and sixth centuries after the fall of the Western Empire. Until the end of the nineteenth century British historians — most notably Gibbon with his Augustan ironies — regarded it as the epitome of decadence, artificiality and self-indulgence. Late in the century there was a rediscovery and reinterpretation of its history and especially its art, which appealed to the nineties because of its gorgeousness, elaborateness, consciousness of form and color, and its artifice—its insistence on being art rather than nature or an imitation of nature. Wilde codified the new attitude in *The Decay of Lying* which he read to Yeats over Christmas dinner and which worked its way, many metamorphoses later, into "Dove or Swan":

> I think that in early Byzantium, maybe never before or since in recorded history, religious, aesthetic and practical life were one, that architect and artificers...spoke to the multitude and the few alike. The painter, the mosaic worker, the worker in gold and silver, the illuminator of sacred books, were almost impersonal, almost perhaps without the consciousness of individual design. ... They could copy out of old Gospel books those pictures that seemed as sacred as the text, and yet weave all into a vast design, the work of many that seemed the work of one, that made building, picture, pattern, metalwork of rail and lamp, seem but a single image.

Romantic enthusiasm counters Gibbon's reductive irony, and a celebration of the aesthetic and the synthesizing is set against the Victorian predilection for the analytical, utilitarian, and naturalistic. For Yeats Byzantium defines both art and Unity of Being (though he has to juggle his dates a bit to make it correspond to Phase Fifteen) because it is *sui generis,* self-justifying, and synthetic: it joins East and West, public and private, observer and object, the matter of art and the vision of a whole people, the single image and the vast design, the complexity of time and the unity of creation. It is both his Grecian Urn and his perfected Ireland, an ideal he had held passionately and gave up bitterly; a mythical city based on an idea of history (he had seen the mosaics at Ravenna, Palermo and Cefala and concluded the first edition of "Dove or Swan" "finished at Syracuse in 1925," and the second, "written at Capri, February 1925"); a location for art so ideal it seems an art work itself; an expression of religious feelings without the need for submission to religious dogma; an embodiment of personal well-being. Yet, as Helen Vendler has said, there is a "curiously tentative and wistful tone" about the description, as if some part of Yeats knew how wholly remote such an ideal synthesis must be. The tone is more self-assured, the act of appropriation more complete, in the two notable poems that gather together these associations, impulses and desires.

The movement of "Sailing to Byzantium" is quite clear, and so are its essential terms. The poem begins with the familiar lament for lost bodily vigor and sexuality, a regret not overcome by the compensating sense of increased wisdom, a Yeatsian obsession which, in the earliest fragment, is exceedingly blunt:

> For many loves have I taken off my clothes
> for some I threw them off in haste, for some slowly & indifferently
> & laid on my bed that I might (— — — —) be
> (— — — —) they longed to see
> (— — — —) naked, but now I will take off my body
> That they might be enfolded in that for which they
> had longed
> (   ) I live on love (   ).

The remorse is professional as well as amatory, the old poet complaining that "all that men know, or think they know, being young/ Cry that my tale is told my story sung." It is exciting, as well as chastening, to watch what Yeats achieves in his endless, diligent, and intelligent revisions. What seems mere though understandable crankiness becomes his most eloquent, wholly objectified statement of a recurrent human feeling:

That is no country for old men. The young
In one another's arms, birds in the trees
—Those dying generations—at their song,
The salmon-falls, the mackerel-crowded seas,
Fish, flesh, or foul, commend all summer long
Whatever is begotten, born, and dies.
Caught in that sensual music all neglect
Monuments of unageing intellect.

In the early versions there was a defined *personna,* "a poet of the Middle Ages," who disappears as the drafts go through their permutations, so that the "I have sailed" of stanza II marks both the entry of the poet into the poem and the Keatsean shift in location from "that ... country" to the "holy city." There he prays to sages who are deliberately presented as both holy men and achieved figures of art, and realizes the idea dimly buried in the fragment. Now that the poet has achieved his location and articulated his prayer ("made his soul" as both "The Tower" and Irish idiom call the preparation for death), he can declare his own escatalogy:

Once out of nature I shall never take
My bodily form from any natural thing,
But such a form as Grecian goldsmiths make
Of hammered gold and gold enamelling
To keep a drowsy Emperor awake;
Or set upon a golden bough to sing
To lords and ladies of Byzantium
Of what is past, or passing, or to come.

Yeats's note says simply, and teasingly, "I have read somewhere that in the Emperor's palace at Byzantium was a tree made of gold and silver, and artificial birds that sang." Critics have not been so reticent and there is a large body of speculation and association. Perhaps it is enough to say that there are three kinds of significance appropriate to the birds of this poem, all of them appearing elsewhere in Yeats. They are natural birds in stanza I figuring life and the senses, what he called "the instinctive joy of human life," like the linnets in "A Prayer for my Daughter," moor-hens in "Easter, 1916," starlings in "Meditations in Time of Civil War," or that "living bird" of *A Vision* that "signifies truth." The bird of the last stanza, which Yeats called "a symbol of the intellectual joy of eternity," is related to the purified soul in medieval and occult lore and Eastern religion, and to several of Yeats's swans. It is also a created object, a work of art glimmering, gorgeous, incorruptible. It sits on a golden tree which perfects all natural trees; it reconstitutes the tattered scarecrow of the second stanza; it is related to the tree of unity in "Among School Children" and "A Prayer for my Daughter"; and it draws upon the tree of life in Celtic, Hebrew, and occult mythology, and the golden bough of comparative religion. Yeats, too, read his Frazer.

As in the Nightingale Ode, the geographical movement of the poem is complemented by the musical. The "sensual music" of stanza I, which catches the young as Zeus caught Leda, becomes the "singing school" that affords the only solace for the aged man of stanza II; in stanza III he finds his proper "singing masters" who will release his soul from bodily decrepitude and gather him (in a phrase remembered from "The Tables of the Law) "Into the artifice of eternity."

So where — and how — is this visionary voyager at the end of the poem? The ironies matter. There is surely an edge to "monuments" in the first two stanzas. A monument is just that—fixed, inert—especially in the context of that enormously attractive flux, and Yeats had had too much fun in his Senate speech on Divorce and in its companion poem "The three Monuments" (written the year before "Sailing to Byzantium") not to know it:

> They hold their public meetings where
> Our most renownéd patriots stand,
> One among the birds of the air,
> A stumpier on either hand.

"Monuments of its own magnificence" may seem direct, even boastful, as Yeats later associated Aristotle's definition of "magnificence" with Byzantium and with this poem. But the edge from the first stanza carries over; the old scarecrow is desperate; the only singing school *for him* in "that country" is solipsistic self-regard. In the scheme of "Dove or Swan" Byzantium replaces the disliked "formal Roman magnificence, with its glorification of physical power"; in an early draft either the sages or the aged man are "Rigid, abstracted, and fanatical," also qualities of Roman art, Roman power, and "Roman decay." The poet's task is to escape the monuments, not celebrate or emulate them.

There is a slighter edge, but edge nevertheless, in "artifice of eternity"; like the Urn, and for the same reasons, it is a "cold pastoral," remote, inhuman, static. Similarly, the drowsy Emperor and his lords and

ladies seem a poor audience, few enough but hardly fit for a poet who spent
so much of his time propagandizing and evangelizing and who dreamed of
a "subject matter" which would be "the vision of a whole people." The
poet sings to them not of frozen artifices or release from time, but "Of what
the Bard!/ Who present, past and future sees." The opening stanza of
"Sailing to Byzantium" calls it "Whatever is begotten, born, and dies."
Both poets know that "Eternity is in love with the productions of Time,"
and both, no matter how lofty and detached the perspectives they achieve,
commend the dying generations more than the monuments, or even the
mosaics.

   "Byzantium" apparently began in 1930 when Sturge Moore objected
that the last stanza of "Sailing to Byzantium" was a disappointment, "as
such a goldsmith's bird is as much nature as a man's body, especially if it
only sings like Homer and Shakespeare of what is past or passing or to
come to Lords and Ladies." Within two weeks Yeats entered in his diary a
"Subject for a poem. April 30th," which places this city about 450 years
later than Justinian's Byzantium of the first poem, hence further into the
antithetical phase:

> Describe Byzantium as it is in the system towards the end of the first
> Christian millennium. A walking mummy. Flames at the street corners
> where the soul is purified, birds of hammered gold singing in the
> golden trees, in the harbour, [dolphins] offering their backs to the
> wailing dead that they may carry them to Paradise.

By mid-June he had the first full version, completed the revisions in
September, and in October wrote to Moore that the poem originated in his
criticism, which had "showed me that the idea needed exposition." The
drafts show more rapid and confident progress than the long tinkering
with "Sailing." The ideas had been in his head "for some time," and several
images—especially the Great Dome of St. Sophia and the dolphins carrying
souls from one world to the next—had been reluctantly dropped from the
earlier poem. He chose a stanza form that he had already mastered in "In
Memory of Major Robert Gregory," section II of "The Tower," and "A
Prayer for my Daughter," and proceeded with speed and assurance.

   There has been a prolonged debate about whether "Byzantium" is a
description of Purgatory (or what it feels like to believe in Purgatory)
growing from Book III of *A Vision,* or an image of art and analogue to the
process of creation, refining the dross of experience and violence of nature
into the perfected work. It is neither necessary nor desirable to choose since
Yeats would allow for both interpretations: the perfection of art adum-

brates eternity; eternity expresses itself through art. One of his central impulses attempts to link his speculations about eternity with his rare moments of epiphany, and analogues with the Romantics—Blake, Shelley, Coleridge, Keats—inform both poems. In notes for *A Vision* he said that we attain Unity of Being ("the point in the Zodiac where the whirl becomes a sphere") "always in the creation or enjoyment of a work of art, but that moment though eternal in the Daimon passes from us because it is not an attainment of our whole being." "Byzantium" enacts such a passing attainment. It is aesthetics and escatalogy, and history and psychology as well. Reversing the perspective of "Sailing to Byzantium," the speaker has journeyed to and now stands in Byzantium, the ideal city, which is also a poem, and eternity, and his own mind.

The unpurged images of ordinary experience—Plato's appearances combined with Blake's London—recede from consciousness at the sound of the gong of St. Sophia whose great dome is an emblem of art and transcendence. It is either starlit or moonlit so it can be associated with Phase One or Phase Fifteen, the full embodiment of *Primary* or *Antithetical* being, saint or artist, absorption into the universal or realization of the Self. It disdains ordinary life and nature because of its achieved perfection of form and its release from the cycles of time. In the second stanza the speaker summons his guide, Virgil to his Dante, a spirit or mosaic figure, man/image/shade, "breathless" because out of time as the speaker is breathless with ecstasy and anticipation. The shade, like the Daimon, winds up experience in life and unwinds it in the stages between death and life. "I call it death-in-life and life-in-death" invokes both Phase One and Phase Fifteen and the Heraclitian formula reiterated so often in *A Vision* and again at the end of *The Resurrection*. In the third stanza he contemplates the bird he had imagined in "Sailing to Byzantium," only this "Miracle, bird or golden handiwork" is more fully perfected and released, with none of the ambiguity and poignance of its predecessor, so etherally and formally distanced that it need only "scorn aloud" the "mere complexities" of human "mire and blood." The next stanza enters the refining fire of Purgatory and the imagination:

> At midnight on the Emperor's pavement flit
> Flames that no faggot feeds, nor steel has lit,
> Nor storm disturbs, flames begotten of flame,
> Where blood-begotten spirits come
> And all complexities of fury leave,
> Dying into a dance,
> An agony of trance,
> An agony of flame that cannot singe a sleeve.

It is the rather terrifying "antique dance" of "Rosa Alchemica" or of the Noh play mentioned in *Per Amica* and again in *A Vision*, the "girl in a Japanese play whose ghost tells a priest of a slight sin, if indeed it was sin, which seems great because of her exaggerated conscience. She is surrounded by flames, and though the priest explains that if she but ceased to believe in those flames they would cease to exist, believe she must, and the play ends in an elaborate dance, the dance of her agony." "'We have no power,'" one of the spirits in the *Purification* told Yeats, "'except to purify our intention,' and when I asked of what, replied, 'Of complexity.'" The fires of Purgatory and of aesthetic transformation are not material, but they cause both agony and simplification through intensity.

The perspective of the last stanza dramatically changes as Yeats pictures, he said in a lecture, "the ghosts swimming, mounted upon dolphins, through the sensual seas, that they may dance upon its pavements":

> Astraddle on the dolphin's mire and blood,
> Spirit after spirit! The smithies break the flood,
> The golden smithies of the Emperor!
> Marbles of the dancing floor
> Break bitter furies of complexity,
> Those images that yet
> Fresh images beget,
> That dolphin-torn, that gong tormented sea.

The stanza is built around that Yeatsian word "break," and the syntax is tricky. The most persuasive reading is that the marbles created by the Emperor's golden smithies break or purify the bitter furies, and their images, and the new images created by them, the sea of mire and blood through which the souls pass and which the poet regards with new energy and awe. "Suddenly," Helen Vendler has said, "in a dazzling syntactical victory, the resolution, so unforeseeable, is accomplished: the two kinds of images, purged and unpurged, are not hostile but symbiotic." The poem ends not with a rejection of the "real" messy world for an impossibly—or intolerably—pure state, but a moment of poise between two whirling gyres and two states of consciousness, when "whirl becomes sphere." It returns the perspective to the close of "Sailing to Byzantium" and rescues the poem from something close to both incomprehensibility and inhumanity. Until this startling and marvelous moment, "Byzantium," for all its scenic and oratorical power, has been static, the geometry of *A Vision* rather than the drama of Yeats's reckless, passionate encounter with experience. The desire to elucidate the idea for Sturge Moore almost drove him into a radical separation of nature and art. But other impulses were at work as well. In a note for *Words for Music, Perhaps,* in which the poem first appeared, Yeats said that after an attack of Malta fever, "I warmed myself back into life with 'Byzantium.'" Here, at this moment, staring at those surging dolphins and raging seas, images of enormous evocative power on their own and which also recapitulate "Those dying generations—at their song,/ The salmon-falls, the mackerel-crowded seas," poem and poet live.

7

The Antinomies

Since "The Whole System" of *A Vision* "is founded upon the belief that the ultimate reality ... falls in human consciousness ... into a series of antinomies," and since he had long arranged his thought and disciplined his imagination by ideas of antithesis, it is not surprising that Yeats's later work plays out an extended series of oppositions: body and soul; self and other; East and West; life and death; time and eternity; day and night; personality and character; hero and saint; art and nature. Marriage was certainly a turning point in his life and *A Vision* a mode of intellectual and psychic organization. He went over all his poetry for the definitive edition of 1922, and in the same year completed *The Trembling of the Veil*, the central and most difficult section of *Autobiographies*. He had hammered his thoughts into unity and was ready for that most astonishing thing, a second career. He later paid "Gratitude to the Unknown Instructors" for the opportunity, and for the resources to meet it:

> What they undertook to do
> They brought to pass;
> All things hang like a drop of dew
> Upon a blade of grass.

We do not have to thank the ghostly teachers, and while reading *A Vision* often do not want to, but we should attend to the poet—in *The Tower, The Winding Stair* and *Last Poems* —creating the drop of dew. Formulations and insights that seem obscurantist or dogmatic in the prose receive in those volumes their richest, most fully embodied expression. The major poems after 1922 contain the imaginative rather than the strained synthesis and represent the true freedom from the determinism of *A Vision*, its achieved *Thirteenth Sphere*. They are what Yeats told his father he most sought, "not abstract truth, but a kind of vision of reality which satisfies the whole being."

"A Dialogue of Self and Soul" illustrates the difference. It is clearly informed by the System as *My Soul* is a voice of the *Primary* (Phase Twenty-Seven, the Saint, or Phase One, "complete plasticity") and *My Self* of the *Antithetical* (Phase Seventeen, the "Daimonic Man" whose "True Mask" is "simplification through intensity"). *Soul* commands a moral and spiritual self-analysis that has its roots in the stages of *The Soul in Judgment*, especially the *Dreaming Back*. It offers the same escape "from the crime of death and birth" as that represented by "Byzantium," a purgatorial stasis where

> intellect no longer knows
> *Is* from the *Ought*, or *Knower* from the *Known*.

The terms (and the italics) are the same as "The Great Wheel's" description of the relationship among the *Faculties;* but *My Soul* would dissolve the antinomies, collapse the dialectic, and so end conflict; that would also, of course, end consciousness. He demands that "imagination scorn the earth/ And intellect its wandering." His unity destroys the mind and the senses; his fullness strikes man "deaf and dumb and blind," turns the tongue into a stone.

Against this artifice of eternity *My Self* posits an ancient sword and a piece of a dress, "Emblematical of love and war." The Masculine sword— "consecrated...razor-keen...unspotted" is "bound and wound" by "That flowering, silken, old embroidery, torn/ From some court-lady's dress," conflict become art that "Can, tattered, still protect, faded adorn" just as the "broken, crumbling" tower is bound and wound by the stair. With these as his emblems *Self* can "claim as by a soldier's right/ A charter to commit the crime once more" and face the toil, ignominy, distress, pain, malice and decrepitude of life:

> I am content to live it all again
> And yet again, if it be life to pitch
> Into the frog-spawn of a blind man's ditch,
> A blind man battering blind men;
> Or into that most fecund ditch of all,
> The folly that man does
> Or must suffer, if he woos
> A proud woman not kindred of his soul.

I am content to follow to its source
Every event in action or in thought;
Measure the lot; forgive myself the lot!
When such as I cast out remorse
So great a sweetness flows into the breast
We must laugh and we must sing,
We are blest by everything,
Everything we look upon is blest.

In this psychic and rhetorical triumph the fiction of a dialogue and a speaker evaporates under intense autobiographical pressure. Yeats rejects *Soul*'s terms as well as his lust for transcendence in the name of nature and experience which he then redeems and reconstitutes. He had been seriously ill for some months when he composed the poem in 1927 and wrote to Mrs. Shakespear that it was "a choice of rebirth rather than deliverance from birth," an act of will against sickness and the possibility of death. This secular beatitude, the experience of sweetness and blessedness, is something that did happen, though rarely, to Yeats. One moment is recorded at the end of *Per Amica Silentia Lunae,* another in the letter realizing "the nature of the timeless spirit ... that old glow so beautiful with its autumnal tint." Such experience, the psychological experience of the poet and the literary experience he creates from it, is responsible for some of the major moments in Romantic literature: Keats joining the Nightingale, Wordsworth hearing the children, Blake's letters, Stephen Dedalus and the girl on the beach. The blessing—casting out remorse, despair, and repression—appeals to Blake and to Shelley, and to the moment that Coleridge and his readers desire for him but can only find mediated through others. The moments have in common an intensity of sense impression and association (the Daimonic Man of Phase Seventeen "assumes... an intensity which is never dramatic but always lyrical and personal"); a feeling of simultaneity or the stopping of time; an exultation of imaginative power; a sense of personal well-being as "all disagreeables evaporate, from their being in close relationship with Beauty and Truth"; and a voice unusually excited or exalted — an approximation of the sublime. The ecstasy is earned. In this poem it comes not from "the steep ascent,/ ... Upon the breathless starlit air" towards the dark of Soul's nirvana, but from the direct confrontation of "the frog-spawn of a blind man's ditch."

For all its persuasive power, however, "Self and Soul" is a triumph of rhetoric and feeling, not a fully enacted drama. *Self* and *Soul* do not really talk to one another. *My Soul* begins "I summon..." and *My Self* replies, "The consecrated blade upon my knees. ... " *My Soul* then asks "Why should the imagination?" and *My Self* counters with another anecdote about the sword. *My Soul* has no body, which is fair enough, but it has no presence either. There is not the sense of otherness that drama requires. The poem claims that experience can be transformed and redeemed but does not say how. Its conclusion is very appealing, but it does not account for the power and the privilege of being blessed and able to bless. For that we have to go to the poetry where the sense of otherness is more fully embodied and where Yeats develops his idea of the imagination's power and defines some of the insights and resolutions it affords.

The most impressive struggle to achieve that vision, to face and resolve the antinomies, is "Vacillation," the poem Yeats wrote between November 1931 and March 1932 in an effort to exorcise "that slut, Crazy Jane" whose language had become "unendurable." It was first called "Wisdom" and the title probably presented itself when he wrote to Mrs. Shakespear that he had "vacillated all day" over whether to begin a crucial line "And" or "What." The series of eight short poems reveals that for Yeats wisdom and vacillation are inseparable. The first five chronicle "All those antinomies": day and night; death of the body and remorse of conscience that had preoccupied him in *The Tower;* transfiguring joy and vitality that became *A Winding Stair*'s response; the aesthetic and the sensual life; conventional wisdom and its playful antithesis. The first poem sets the issues and concludes with an urgent question: since all experience, imaginative as well as practical, leads to remorse and death, and since the soul suffers even between lives, "What is joy?" It is the question that "Self and Soul" does not quite meet; it is close to the question of "Dejection: an Ode," and though Yeats's response and tone are different, Coleridge helps to shape "Vacillation" and to define its Romantic humanism.

The second poem finds an image and one elliptical answer:

> A tree there is that from its topmost bough
> Is half all glittering flame and half all green
> Abounding foliage moistened with the dew;
> And half is half and yet is all the scene;
> And half and half consume what they renew,
> And he that Attis' image hangs between
> That staring fury and the blind lush leaf
> May know not what he knows, but knows not grief.

This tree of life is from the *Mabinogian,* which Yeats had studied in Lady Charlotte Guest's translation, found again in Arnold's essay, and quoted in "The Celtic Element in Literature": "'They saw a tall tree by the side of the river, one half of which was in flames from the root to the top, and the other half was green and in full leaf.'" It is also Frazer's tree in *Adonis, Attis, Osiris,* where the disciples of the vegetation god castrate themselves in the annual fertility rites. It is related to the "Tree, of many, one" of the Intimations Ode, as this poem too confronts the problem of imaginative and perceptual loss. To ordinary consciousness half-life is the self-destructive sum of experience. The fury of the disciple or the vacillating consciousness of the poet can image a resolution of contraries; one achieves a self-immolating transcendence, the other an ecstasy of momentary comprehension. The poet can see the children on the shore, embody truth but not know it; the absence of grief is epiphany not rationalism or compensation, an approximation—but an intense one—of joy.

The third poem sets the subversive knowledge of the free individual ("All women dote upon an idle man") against the wisdom of the world ("Get all the gold and silver that you can") without being too serious about either. Seriousness is reserved for an injunction to the poet past his prime, "No longer ... caught" in the "Lethean foliage" of the sensuous life, preparing for death:

> Test every work of intellect or faith,
> And everything that your own hands have wrought,
> And call those works extravagance of breath
> That are not suited for such men as come
> Proud, open-eyed and laughing to the tomb.

It recalls the death of Mabel Beardsley, the heroism the poet half admired and half created, as well as his understanding that "strength of personality" gives a writer "precisely that symbol he may require for the expression of himself." Stoicism and strength are not joy either, but for the aging poet they are a precondition.

To this point the poem has been personal in reference but detached and dramatic in tone: "Man runs his course"; "A tree there is"; "your death"; "that thought." Yeats enters "Vacillation" with the fourth section, a rendering of the same experience recorded at the end of "Anima Mundi" and "A Dialogue of Self and Soul":

> My fiftieth year had come and gone,
> I sat, a solitary man,
> In a crowded London shop,
> An open book and empty cup
> On the marble table-top.

While on the shop and street I gazed
My body of a sudden blazed;
And twenty minutes more or less
It seemed, so great my happiness,
That I was blessèd and could bless.

These radiant lines were originally called "Joy" or "Happiness" and they dramatize his conviction that "the artist's joy ... is of one substance with that of sanctity," and just as rarely and briefly achieved (in an ironic but no less assertive formulation, art is "sanctity's scapegrace brother.") It is the epiphany that allows him to escape from hatred and to feel kinship with the rest of humanity, and Yeats aptly associated it with Coleridge's short poem — "She, she herself and only she,/ Shone through her body visibly" — and with the joy realized when men and women enter "upon the eternal possession of themselves in one single moment." A fleeting ecstasy for both poets, and the next section turns to the countering experience, experience most powerfully recorded in "Dejection: an Ode." Like Coleridge, Yeats cannot see the romantic landscape he so wonderfully describes:

Although the summer sunlight gild
Cloudy leafage of the sky,
Or wintry moonlight sink the field
In storm-scattered intricacy,
I cannot look thereon,
Responsibility so weighs me down.

The responsibility is creative as well as public and personal, the oppressive sense that all making, no matter how momentarily glorious, leads to further loss, Coleridge's:

grief without a pang, void, dark, and drear,
A stifled, drowsy, unimpassioned grief,
Which finds no natural outlet, no relief,
In word, or sigh, or tear —

Yeats puts it in terms that recall "Meditations in Time of Civil War" and anticipate "The Man and the Echo" — that is in terms central to his moral experience:

Things said or done long years ago,
Or things I did not do or say
But thought that I might say or do,
Weigh me down, and not a day
But something is recalled,
My conscience or my vanity appalled.

The next landscape is quintessentially Yeatsean, including the smell
of new-mown hay that goes back to "The Wanderings of Oisin" and his
recent decision to bring together East and West:

A rivery field spread out below,
An odour of new-mown hay
In his nostrils, the great lord of Chou
Cried, casting off the mountain snow
'Let all things pass away.'

This sixth poem faces the antinomies with the bold and precarious
humanism, at the edge of solipsism, that had characterized section III of
"The Tower," the ego's declarations into the teeth of personal decrepitude
and social disintegration. But again the ego is muted and solipsism avoided
by a plunge into history. The great lord of Chou, the Babylonian conqueror
of the second stanza, and the Western but highly assimilative poet of the
third pause to study the wreckage of time and declare "'Let all things pass
away.'" The equanimity of lord, soldier and poet depends upon the assertion that all the antinomies — the tree of life that contains them, human
history which records their transience, and song which investigates and
celebrates — all "From man's blood-sodden heart are sprung." It is the
Yeatsean truth that Swift could not endure ("Blood and the Moon"), that
made the assassination of O'Higgins bearable ("Death"), that redeems
fin-de-siècle defeatism ("Two Songs from a Play"), and which finally
explains the sources of his power ("The Circus Animals' Desertion").

Section VII introduces a debate between *The Soul* and *The Heart* — or
Self — the dialogue recapitulates "Self and Soul" but the sixth poem made
Heart the necessary term. In the letter to Mrs. Shakespear which an-
nounced the poem, Yeats said "I begin to think I shall take to religion
unless you save me from it." She apparently replied, knowing him well,
that he would be "too great a bore" if he got religion. Delighted, Yeats
contrasted "the choice of the saint...and the heroic choice," comedy and
tragedy, claimed to accept all the miracles, and concluded "I shall be a

sinful man to the end, and think upon my death-bed of all the nights I wasted in my youth." He included a draft of the poem in which, when completed, *Heart* wins a close but real victory:

> *The Soul.* Seek out reality, leave things that seem.
> *The Heart.* What, be a singer born and lack a theme?
> *The Soul.* Isaiah's coal, what more can man desire?
> *The Heart.* Struck dumb in the simplicity of fire!
> *The Soul.* Look on that fire, salvation walks within.
> *The Heart.* What theme had Homer but original sin?

That coal, like the Heaven of "Self and Soul," is frightening as well as purifying. In the Old Testament passage the seraph flies to Isaiah, places a live coal against his mouth and says, "Lo, this hath touched thy lips, and thy iniquity is taken away and thy sin purged." The verses that follow are less familiar and less comforting. Yeats, acutely self-conscious about the relationships between poetry, prophecy, and community must have remembered them too:

> Also I heard the voice of the Lord, saying, Whom shall I send, and who will go for us? Then said I, Here am I; send me. And he said, Go, and tell this people, Hear ye indeed, but understand not; and see ye indeed, but perceive not. . . . Then said I, Lord, how long? And he answered, Until the cities be wasted without inhabitant, and the houses without man, and the land be utterly desolate, and the Lord have removed men far away, and there be a great forsaking in the midst of the land.

That is the "reality"—whether articulated by Solomon or Isaiah, the Lord or *The Soul* —that the poet of "Vacillation" has to confront. He appeals to Homer as a stay against it and as a way of transfiguring it. Isaiah's coal is a powerful, admonitory image in another way. In his diary Yeats wrote that "I do not ask myself whether what I find in Elizabethan English, or in that of the early eighteenth century, is better or worse than what I find in some other clime and time. I can only approach that more distant excellence through what I inherit, lest I find it and be stricken dumb." Literature as well as the Lord can intimidate the modern poet, inescapably and anxiously self-conscious about the accomplishments of his titanic predecessors. Yeats insists upon his Anglo-Irish heritage, his eclectic synthesizing, his unconventional beliefs, and his reckless humanism precisely because they are his, and so mitigate the burden of that distant excellence of the past.

The last stanza, in which Yeats returns to the long rhymed couplets he had used in "The Wanderings of Oisin," addresses the Catholic scholar and mystic, Baron Friedrich Von Hügel, who had argued that the Christian vision was the artist's. Yeats acknowledges the appeal of Christian doctrine, honors sanctity, and affirms his belief in miracles. Still, he plays a "predestined part" and must choose the mixed fortunes of life before the tomb:

> Homer is my example and his unchristened heart.
> The lion and the honeycomb, what has Scripture said?
> So get you gone, Von Hügel, though with blessings on your head.

In an early draft the unchristened heart was Yeats's, and it was also "fierce"; the revision saves the phrase, underscores the drama (Homer against Von Hügel), and adds poetic and religious tact. The Bible is made to serve Yeats rather than the orthodox. Sweetness and light come from terror and destruction. Yeats must also have had Samson's riddle in mind when he composed "Meditations in Time of Civil War" and, in a different key, when he animated those flamboyant characters from Barrington in "The Tower." He had certainly remembered it in the early 'twenties, when he recalled the Irish Literary Society and his attempts to infuse his country with the heroic personality this poem seeks:

> If we were, as I had dreaded, declamatory, loose, and bragging, we were but the better fitted — that declared and measured — to create unyielding personality, manner at once cold and passionate, daring long-premeditated act; and if bitter beyond all the people of the world, we might yet lie — that too declared and measured — nearest the honeyed comb.

"The swordsman throughout repudiates the saint," Yeats wrote as he revised his poetry in 1932, "but not without vacillation. Is that perhaps the sole theme—Usheen and Patrick—'so get you gone Von Hügel, though with blessings on your head'?" The honeyed comb, Homer's theme and way, this life and original sin is the poet's choice; just as it was "the crime of death and birth" demanded in "Self and Soul," the "crime of being born" ironically dismissed in "Consolation," the bad language of Crazy Jane, and the "dolphin-torn" and "gong-tormented sea" regarded in "Byzantium," written two years earlier but carefully placed just before "Vacillation" in *Collected Poems*. The mysticism of a saint, like the bodilessness of a sage, is a rejection of the world. Yeats's myth, he said, was rooted in the earth. Self can only bless and be blessed by pitching into "the frog-spawn of a blind man's ditch." Jane must be rent to become whole, and the soul which creates light by the lovers' union must have a body which is naked and a beast. What Yeats wants—and here struggles impressively to attain— is that joy which is the same as sanctity, a secular beatitude which invokes those major Romantic moments, and which absorbs and transforms the otherworldliness of Von Hügel as well as the drowsy Emperor's hammered gold.

2

In 1926 Yeats wrote to Olivia Shakespear that "my moods fill me with surprise and some alarm. The other day I found at Coole a reproduction of a drawing of two charming young persons in the full stream of their Saphoistic enthusiasm, and it got into my dreams at night and made a great racket there, and yet I feel that spiritual things are very near me." The conjunction of body and soul, insistence that they are inseparable, and the playfully confessional tone which carries urgent feelings, characterizes a recurrent and poetically fruitful mood until the end of his life. Sometimes the playfulness dominates and he enjoys being Uncle William, wearing the mask of Michael Robartes, to Iseult Gonne, seen as the dancer; or, in *propria persona,* he makes the same grand appeal to irrefutable but unspecified authority "For Anne Gregory." But avuncular advice is a limited genre and Yeats did not often so indulge himself and charm his audience. He did, however, write two volumes of erotic poetry, *Words for Music Perhaps* and *A Woman Young and Old.* They are most notable for the creation of Crazy Jane and for a unique combination of qualities. They celebrate sex as the completion of life and as a resolution of the antinomies, not forgetting the usefulness of arcane authorities.

Many of these short poems contain an extraordinary compression of Yeats's ideas; "thoughts so long habitual" become ballads. They bear the same relationship to his philosophical poetry as JBY's sketches do to his portraits: not notes or practice, but instantly, gaily rendered miniatures. "His Bargain," for example, is both a parody of and an answer to *The Republic,* and "Lullaby" turns his reading in comparative mythology into a lovely, traditional lyric. Crazy Jane, "founded upon an old woman who lives in a little cottage near Gort," goes back to his folk-lore collecting years ago, but the intensity comes from more recent experience: "sexual abstinence fed their fire—I was ill and yet full of desire. They sometimes came out of the greatest mental excitement I am capable of":

> 'Love is all
> Unsatisfied
> That cannot take the whole
> Body and soul';
> *And that is what Jane said.*
>
> 'Take the sour
> If you take me,
> I can scoff and lour
> And scold for an hour.'
> *'That's certainly the case,' said he.*
>
> 'Naked I lay,
> The grass my bed;
> Naked and hidden away,
> That black day'
> *And that is what Jane said.*
>
> 'What can be shown?
> What true love be?
> All could be known or shown
> If Time were but gone.'
> *'That's certainly the case,' said he.*

The excitement is certainly sexual; it is also impressively inclusive and characteristically dialectical. Yeats wrote the Crazy Jane and Tom the Lunatic series between the spring of 1929 and late 1931, toward the end of his encounter with Swift and Georgian Ireland. He began while recovering from his first illness, when "life returned to me as an impression of the energy and daring of the great creators," and their composition was interrupted by the writing of *The Words upon the Window-pane*, its "Introduction," and "Swift's Epitaph." He completed the series after his second collapse. Yeats frequently wrote to Mrs. Shakespear about Crazy Jane, which suggests that he was recalling as well as advocating passion, thinking of "Diana Vernon" and perhaps of Vanessa, too. He informed them with the same quality and intensity of affirmation that characterizes "Self and Soul," the same dialogue between body and spirit, the same choice of the impure ditches, the same insistence that an integrated personality can make them pure. Both Jane, whose body is "like a road that men pass over" and Tom, "a ranting roaring journeyman," reflect a deliberate earthiness that reinforces the commitment to life.

Perhpas Yeats reduces Jane to a bundle of rags and her idea of love to sexual intercourse for the same reasons that Swift supposedly reduced Vanessa—to make her see that unaccommodated man or woman must be stripped in just this way before wisdom can replace illusion. At any rate, the series is full of glances at Swift. When Crazy Jane talks to the Bishop her concluding stanza begins with a particularly Swiftian quatrain:

> A woman can be proud and stiff
> When on love intent;
> But love has pitched his mansion in
> The place of excrement;

and ends (except for the pun which Swift would have appreciated) with a particularly Yeatsian couplet:

> For nothing can be sole or whole
> That has not been rent.

The "place" where love has pitched his mansion is defined in *Gulliver's Travels* or in "Cassinus and Peter" or "Celia." It is also defined in Yeats's diary when he writes that "Descartes, Locke, and Newton took away the world and gave us its excrement instead. Berkeley restored the world." The materialists destroy; unaccommodated Jane and Anglo-Irish Berkeley restore. While they are indeed strange bedfellows (the metaphor would please Jane but probably not the Bishop of Cloyne), they do agree about the sanctity of the self and its perceptions; and they recognize the conflict of opposites that underlies love and the necessity of destruction in order to achieve—"sole or whole"—unity of being. Yeats seems to be saying that he will grant Gulliver's view of the world, embrace it even, but that he will transform it by adding his own doctrines and perceptions and affirmations. He wrote to Mario Rossi that "Swift's absorption in the useful (the contemporary decline of common sense), all that made him write *The Tale of a Tub,* compelled his nature to become coarse. The man who ignores the poetry of sex, let us say, finds the bare facts written up on the walls of a privy, or himself is compelled to write them there." Throughout *Words for Music Perhaps* Yeats is confronting and revising Swift's hatred and passion, putting the poetry back into sex without ignoring the privy walls. In "Consolation" (a poem made "not so innocent" by its last two lines), the first stanza repeats Crazy Jane's interest in anatomy; the quatrain of the second stanza recalls Swift, and the couplet could only be Yeats:

> O But there is wisdom
> In what the sages said;
> But stretch that body for a while
> And lay down that head
> Till I have told that sages
> Where man is comforted.
>
> How could passion run so deep
> Had I never thought
> That the crime of being born
> Blackens all our lot?
> But where the crime's committed
> The crime can be forgot.

Swift, the emperor of Byzantium, and the speaker of "A Man Young and Old" have this in common: they urge a rejection (or a scorn and horror intense enough to amount to rejection) of the complexities, depravity, and corruption of this life "fastened to a dying animal." So Yeats embraces "bodily lowliness" as well as "the heart's pride," the inside as well as the outside, the Swiftian reality as well as the appearance, rather than retreating from it or letting it drive him into blind frenzy.

There are any number of strategies Yeats adopts for thus having it both ways. One is the bold assertion of Crazy Jane or "Self and Soul," replacing the obsession with affirmation: the "profane perfection of mankind" that "Under Ben Bulben" discovers in the Sistine Chapel. There is the friendly irony of forgetting the crime of birth in the joy of "Consolation," a topic about which Swift's irony is never comfortable. There is the transforming ecstasy of fully realized romantic love. The woman of "A Last Confession" has had many lovers with whom she has like Jane with Jack the Journeyman, "lived like beast and beast":

> I gave what other women gave
> That stepped out of their clothes
> But when this soul, its body off,
> Naked to naked goes,
> He it has found shall find therein
> What none other knows,

And give his own and take his own
And rule in his own right;
And though it loved in misery
Close and cling so tight,
There's not a bird of day that dare
Extinguish that delight.

These poems link sex, death, and the dance and have an abiding and (odd as the word sounds) chastening sense of the transience and mystery of sexual fulfillment. Jane understands that "The more I leave the door unlatched/ The sooner love is gone" and the singer of "Her Triumph" concludes her account of realized love:

And now we stare astonished at the sea,
And a miraculous strange bird shrieks at us.

Transience can be accepted, even transfigured, by imaginative energy and by tenderness of feeling, as in this lovely, late gift to Olivia Shakespear:

Speech after long silence; it is right,
All other lovers being estranged or dead,
Unfriendly lamplight hid under its shade,
The curtains drawn upon unfriendly night,
That we descant and yet again descant
Upon the supreme theme of Art and Song:
Bodily decrepitude is wisdom; young
We loved each other and were ignorant.

Yeats's very considerable achievement as a love poet is marked by qualities not often brought together, at least not since the seventeenth century. He is entirely serious, even earnest and urgent, but also extravagant. He has a perfect mastery of form, phrasing, and rhythm—speech at once intimate, complex, and lyrical. His wit and good spirits, his allusiveness, his combination of gravity and mockery, complicates and distances emotion and so saves Yeats, as Ellmann noted, "from the too clamant sexuality of D. H. Lawrence," to say nothing of all the little Lawrences that followed. It is not easy to be unequivocally erotic without being prurient or strident, silly or clinical.

Yeats's greatest poem about body and soul has less to do with sex, and everything to do with love. "Among School Children" goes back to the problem first faced in "Adam's Curse," but locates itself in the schoolroom rather than the drawing room. It originates in Yeats's senatorial visits to Irish schools, an Arnoldian role he enjoyed but which could lead to dark thoughts, as in the diary entry for March 1926, a month after one such official visit: "Topic for poem—School children and the thought that life will waste them perhaps that no possible life can fulfill our dreams or even their teacher's hope. Bring in the old thought that life prepares for what never happens." The "old thought" occurs at the end of *Reveries* and again in *At the Hawk's Well*. The poem, completed in June, moves from a fairly simple situation to its complex, problematical, and triumphant ending. It begins with Senator Yeats, "a sixty-year-old smiling public man," feeling a little out of it, awkwardly aware of the radical disjunction between his appearance to the children and his wandering thoughts and vague regret. The children, especially their eyes, make him "dream" of a long past moment of kinship with Maud Gonne, the spiritual marriage recollected with longing rather than the anxiety it then entailed, the poem's first image of ideal unity:

> it seemed that our two natures blent
> Into a sphere from youthful sympathy,
> Or else, to alter Plato's parable,
> Into the yolk and white of the one shell.

But that unity is lost, perhaps illusory, and he is brought back to the schoolroom for a coalescence of the present and the recollected, actual, and ideal, children and Maud. He is conscious of time and loss, "driven wild" by the sudden, imagined materialization of his beloved "as a living child." The fourth stanza drifts back as "Her present image floats into the mind," transformed by time but still beautiful, "Hollow of cheek as though it drank the wind." The momentary self-indulgence of the drafts— "And I/ ... Have wrongs to brood upon" — is revised into a pained awareness of what the children really see, and an impatient gesture:

> And I though never of a Ledaean kind
> Had pretty plumage once—enough of that,
> Better to smile on all that smile, and show
> There is a comfortable kind of old scarecrow.

The fifth stanza modulates away from the scene, public inspection and private memory becoming speculation, as ideas of childhood lead to thoughts about motherhood and its pains:

What youthful mother, a shape upon her lap
Honey of generation had betrayed,
And that must sleep, shriek, struggle to escape
As recollection or the drug decide,
Would think her son, did she but see that shape
With sixty or more winters on its head,
A compensation for the pang of its birth,
Or the uncertainty of his setting forth?

Yeats's note refers "recollection or the drug" to Porphyry's theory that the soul longs to return to prenatal harmony, and the drafts emphasize "the soul's betrayal into flesh," making this stanza Yeats's version of Section VII of the Immortality Ode. But "Among School Children" does not need Porphyry any more than the Ode needs Plato; or, rather, we do not need them to understand the issues and feelings of the poems. "Honey of generation," is marvelous for semen and the proper location of the stanza is the maternity ward not the cave of the nymphs, the pangs of birth and disappointment as children change "shape" from foetus to infant to scarecrow. These speculations and the earlier parable lead him back to Plato, to three ways of locating reality—in the Ideal, in Nature, and in Art and Numbers—and to the inevitable conclusion that the Great Thinkers, and even their theories, decline into decrepit age.

The seventh stanza begins to gather the poem's themes. Reality and relationship are referred to lovers (romantic and maternal) and worshipers, not philosophers:

Both nuns and mothers worship images,
But those the candles light are not as those
That animate a mother's reveries,
But keep a marble or a bronze repose.
And yet they too break hearts—O Presences
That passion, piety or affection knows,
And that all heavenly glory symbolize—
O self-born mockers of man's enterprise;

the punctuation is abrupt and the syntax difficult and controversial. The clearest reading is that the Presences are the images — both bronze and mental—known by lovers (passion), nuns (piety), and mothers (affection). They symbolize "all heavenly glory" because of their ideal perfection and because of the transfiguring love which their worshipers bring to them. They are self-born in two senses. Like the purified souls of *A Vision* and "Byzantium" they have achieved a permanent and unified existence out of time. However, they are also born out of the self who worships, and so in their very ideality and permanence, their marble "repose," they mock the inescapably defeated, the merely human endeavors. The magnificent concluding apostrophe addresses those Presences, now the poem's only conceivable audience, and offers to them, in some ways against them, two concluding images of Unity of Being:

> Labour is blossoming or dancing where
> The body is not bruised to pleasure soul,
> Nor beauty born out of its own despair,
> Nor blear-eyed wisdom out of midnight oil.
> O chestnut-tree, great-rooted blossomer,
> Are you the leaf, the blossom or the bole?
> O body swayed to music, O brightening glance,
> How can we know the dancer from the dance?

The difficult movement of "Among School Children" is organized around a series of more or less parallel trinities which become antinomies and then finally a unity. There are three locations: the schoolroom, the mind (memory, imagination, speculation), the visionary conclusion out of space and time; three Yeatses (son, lover, public man and artist); three Maud Gonnes (child, beloved—or Helen, daughter of Leda, gaunt elderly woman); three kinds of worshipers (nuns, lovers, mothers); three kinds of worship (piety, passion, affection); three ways of locating reality. The defining quality of the experiences of the poem until the last stanza is that they all have to do with the process of Becoming rather than a state of Being. The children and nuns, mothers and lovers are all partial and incomplete. With its shifts and juxtapositions the poem sees life in pieces not as a whole, explores the process of life and the trials of life, returns to another old thought, "that the world was now but a bundle of fragments." The worshiped presences may be permanent and unified and so, like the great dome of "Byzantium," mock the mere complexities of living; but they too are fixed, static, inert. But Tree and Dancer are ideal *and* alive. They have the fluidity and energy of life and the permanence and self-containment of images, of art. They do not have to labor like lovers, nuns, philosophers, and mothers (or like the beautiful women, lovers, and artists of "Adam's Curse"). They simply are: whole and fluid, containing within themselves unity and process, permanence and life, Yeats's most resonant embodiment of the emblem of his quest for Unity of Being.

There are many difficulties to that quest and several in this poem. Is the movement of mind, especially into the last stanza, convincing? Does

Yeats make it—rhetorically and spiritually—from the schoolroom to the vision? These questions raise others, mostly about the irony of "Among School Children." It is certainly there. He is mildly and affectionately ironic about the nuns teaching "In the best modern way" and about the uncomprehending children. He is urbane and sardonic about the public man, smiling but abstracted and ill at ease. He is a good deal more bitter about scarecrows and old sticks, the fate of thinkers and poets for all their paradigms and golden thighs (Yeats quoted the stanza as "a fragment of my last curse upon old age"). The irony of ideal and so mocking Presences is cosmic, and deeper ironies cluster around that "where" of stanza VIII. For Yeats knows—knows from all his experience—that body is bruised, that beauty is born out of despair at its possession, and that there is no wisdom without toil.

Thomas Parkinson's skillful study of the drafts shows that the last stanza was a late addition, that a sense of loss and age dominates the early versions as it does the first part of the poem, though Yeats is more urbane than usual, closer to the tone of his letters than most of his poems. "Among School Children" originally had "a sorrowful and disillusioned conclusion," and the slowly evolving final hymn suggests desire rather than fulfillment. This does not mean that the last stanza is an afterthought or a forced addition, but that, as usual, Yeats discovers both thought and feeling in the process of composition. The final quatrain forms a genuine question. How can we separate the living tree into its parts? "How can we know the dancer from the dance?" The "know," rather than the more obvious "tell," refers to the "Presences/ That passion, piety or affection knows" in the penultimate stanza. It is a reminder that Yeats addresses the presences and that there is no more sense that he masters them than that nuns and mothers do.

The question is as crucial as Keats's "Fled is that music: —Do I wake or sleep?"—and with the same edge of desperation. In both poems the answer matters. Here the answer is that we cannot know, do not have to, and that only rarely do we have this sort of epiphany, a vision of reality where vision and reality are indistinguishable. The tree of "Vacillation" defines the antinomies and allows for creative joy; this tree resolves them and is joy. But it is a fleeting fullness and separate from the being of the poet. "Among School Children" does not return to its opening scene like the major Romantic odes. "It is not a bridge," John Wain has said, "but a pier. It leads nowhere; its purpose is to afford us, before we turn and retrace our steps, a bleak and chastening glimpse into the deep waters," though the glimpse is heroic and enlarging as well.

Yeats was altogether self-conscious about the issues. A diary entry in 1929 records a conversation with Ezra Pound and his resistance to Pound's skepticism, which could also be the skepticism with which this poem must regard the Presences:

> I agree with Ezra in his dislike of the word belief. Belief implies an unknown object, a covenant attested with a name or signed with blood, and being more emotional than intellectual may pride itself on lack of proof. But if I affirm that such and such is so, the more complete the affirmation, the more complete the proof, and even when incomplete, it remains valid within some limit.... The one reason for putting our actual situation into our art is that the struggle for complete affirmation may be, often must be, that art's chief poignancy. I must, though the world shriek at me, admit no act beyond my power, nor thing beyond my knowledge, yet because my divinity is far off I blanch and tremble.

In *The Trembling of the Veil* he had recorded again his discovery "that certain thoughts sustain us in defeat, or give us victory, whether over ourselves or others, and it is these thoughts, tested by passion, that we call convictions." In "Among School Children," tree and dancer are those thoughts. But the *Autobiographies* goes on to say that "the victory is an intellectual...re-creation of all that exterior fate snatches away" and to the famous sentence: "We begin to live when we have conceived life as tragedy." The irony in "Among School Children" is a tragic irony, one that Yeats at his most honest and exalted shares with Melville, Sophocles, and Shakespeare. The irony is existential in life and structural in the poem, certainly not verbal at the close, as there is nothing ironic about the language of that final stanza. Yeats takes images and visions seriously and, as "A Prayer for my Daughter" and "The Tower" establish, makes self-birth one of those passionate, sustaining convictions.

The centrality and resonance of "Among School Children" can be suggested by a brief look at three major concerns—familial, philosophical, political—which illuminate and complement the poem. We have already seen some of the ways in which Unity of Being derives from his father's theories of personality and that the image of the dancer as both self-contained and expressive may go back to JBY's enraptured description of Isadora Duncan in New York. The image also appears in *A Vision* where it represents both the *Thirteenth Cone* ("It becomes even conscious of itself ..., like some great dancer, the perfect flower of modern culture, dancing some primitive dance and conscious of his or her own life and of the dance") and the "complete beauty" of Phase Fifteen ("Thought and will are indistinguishable, effort and attainment are indistinguishable; and this is the consummation of a slow process; nothing is apparent but dreaming *Will* and the Image that it dreams."). A more satisfying link between poem and system occurs at the end of *A Vision* where Yeats sits "turning a symbol over in my mind, exploring all its details, defining and again defining its elements, testing my convictions and those of others by its unity, attempting to substitute particulars for an abstraction like that of algebra." That approximates the movement of "Among School Children," from paradigm through passion to symbol of conviction. *A Vision* too confronts that old thought—"But nothing comes"—and also resolves it with a symbol, the *Thirteenth Cone*, and—far more persuasively—with an image, the reconstituted Heracles walking among the gods, something intended and complete, a truth that cannot be known and must be embodied.

Another extension of the world of the poem is into Irish life and history. The Arnoldian role in the Senate led not only to "Among School Children" but to his advice, formulated two years before the poem was written, on national education. "The Child and the State" offers "a philosophy on which it is possible to base the whole life of a nation" and urges his country to follow "Berkeley and the great modern idealist philosophy created by his influence" and "Burke who restored to political thought its sense of history.... Berkeley proved that the world was a vision, and Burke that the State was a tree, no mechanism to be pulled in pieces and put up again, but an oak tree that had grown through centuries." Yeats had been reading Berkeley since 1922. The text he read most often and closely, and praised most frequently, was *Philosophical Commentaries*, which he knew as Berkeley's *Commonplace Book* and claimed was the "Irish Salamis"— Ireland's declaration of intellectual independence from English empiricism and materialism. Entry Number 796 reads: "Hobbes in some degree falls in with Locke saying thought is to the mind or him self as dancing to the dancer. Object." "Among School Children's" assertion of the unity of being and becoming postulates the same kind of inseparability of mind and self, experience and perception, and with the same image.

A tradition, Yeats wrote in the diary entry recording his need for affirmation, "is not a belief or submission, but exposition of intellectual needs." Poets "do not seek truth in argument or in books but clarification of what we already believe"—so with Bishop Berkeley whom Yeats read idiosyncratically, waywardly, and profitably. Studying Berkeley's philosophy in the midst of a general rediscovery of and controversy about its true nature and import, he saw it as both commonsense realism and subjective idealism. He championed the young Irish realist and iconoclast who destroyed the abstractions of Locke, Newton, and Descartes, refuted

English materialism, and gave birth to the national intellect. He responded more deeply to the subjective idealist who proved that the world was a dream and brought spirituality back into European thought. Berkeley and immaterialism sanctioned his own subjectivism and his belief in the powers of the imagination, and so gave authority to the resolutions and affirmations they permitted.

"What is the right, the virtuous feeling, and consequent action," Coleridge asked, "when a man having long meditated & perceived a certain Truth finds another, foreign Writer, who has handled the same with an approximation to the Truth, as he had previously conceived it?" He answered "Joy! — let Truth make her voice audible!" That is the joy of recognized affinity, of authority and sanction, and Yeats delighted to make it audible, as he delighted to find those sustaining thoughts, tested by passion, he called convictions. The unity he celebrates in "Among School Children" embodies conviction and is Berkeleyan and Burkean — philosophical and political—as well as experiential and lyrical. He has in mind the education of the Irish Commonweal as well as the enlargement and completion of his own vision.

3

"We begin to live when we have conceived life as tragedy." It is the best known sentence of the *Autobiographies* and an idea that defines much of Yeats's most valuable work from the time he wrote it until the end of his life. The tragedy is the ultimate incompatibility of the antinomies. Imaginative life and poetic vocation is to confront them, as in "Vacillation," and occasionally, fleetingly to resolve them, as in "Among School Children." The structure of Yeats's poetic thought is determined by them. During the twenties he completed the first edition of *A Vision* and *The Trembling of the Veil*. He was revising all his earlier poetry and writing many of his major poems and plays. As he too knew that poetry is a vale of soul-making, he was also reconstituting a self. The "self-possession and power" which *A Vision* justly claims is the creative power to continue working in spite of the inevitable loss and transience, to write—even to rejoice—in the face of tragedy, to be reborn. The pun on "conceived" in the *Autobiographies,* like the one on "labour" in "Among School Children," is deeply deliberate. Sometimes the reference is personal and the expression direct: "Three days ago I spat a little red and that roused me to defy George and begin to work. ... How strange is the subconscious gaiety that leaps up before danger or difficulty. I have not had a moment's depression—that gaiety is outside one's control, a something given by nature." Sometimes he is more general and oracular, as when he wrote to Sturge Moore that "the one heroic sanction is that of the last battle of the Norse Gods, of a gay struggle without hope," or to Dorothy Wellesley, "to me the supreme aim is an act of faith and reason to make one rejoice in the midst of tragedy. An impossible aim; yet I think it true that nothing can injure us."

"Lapis Lazuli" is the poem that most fully contains Yeats's convictions about life as tragedy. It apparently originates, like "A Dialogue of Self and Soul," with a gift:

> I notice that you have much lapis lazuli; someone has sent me a present of a great piece carved by some Chinese sculptor into the semblance of a mountain with temple, trees, paths and an ascetic and pupil about the climb the mountain. Ascetic, pupil, hard stone, eternal theme of the sensual east. The heroic cry in the midst of despair. But no, I am wrong, the east has its solutions always and therefore knows nothing of tragedy. It is we, not the east, that must raise the heroic cry.

He completed the poem a year later, in July 1936, writing more easily and rapidly than usual and with more immediate satisfaction, calling it "almost the best I have made of recent years." It begins, according to Yeats's note on the manuscript, with the remark "some woman" made "yesterday, I am sick of ... poets that seem always gay," reminding him of Dowson's "Villanelle" — "Unto us they belong,/ Us the bitter and gay,/ Wine and women and song"—which he had just quoted in his B. B. C. broadcast on "Modern Poetry," and of the "hysterical patriots" of the old Abbey fights, who "used to repeat as often as possible that to paint pictures or to write poetry in this age was to fiddle while Rome was burning":

> I have heard that hysterical women say
> They are sick of the palette and fiddle-bow,
> Of poets that are always gay,
> For everybody knows or else should know
> That if nothing drastic is done
> Aeroplane and Zeppelin will come out,
> Pitch like King Billy bomb-balls in
> Until the town lie beaten flat.

The occasion for that anxiety may be the widely feared prospect of aerial warfare, or the German reoccupation of the Rhineland, or Italian invasion of Abyssinia, or the new weapons being tested in Spain — the condition of life in 1936. The anxiety is legitimate and the poem attacks hysteria, not concern. Yeats would have liked that story from World War I, the German commander reporting that the situation was serious but not hopeless, the Austrian that it was hopeless but not serious. "Lapis Lazuli" mimes and mocks hysteria: the off-hand prosody, absence of punctuation, anachronism of Zeppelin, forced elision of King William and the Battle of the Boyne with modern warfare. Yeats himself is often shrill and sometimes hysterical in *A Full Moon in March* and *Last Poems,* but not in this poem. He does not shrug (as in "Politics") or spit (metaphorically in "The Leaders of the Crowd," dramatically in the "Prologue" to *The Death of Cuchulain*), but chooses his terms very carefully, or allows them to choose him, as stanza II embodies his deepest convictions and provides the poem's first answer to the fears and agitation of contemporary life:

> All perform their tragic play,
> There struts Hamlet, there is Lear,
> That's Ophelia, that Cordelia;
> Yet they, should the last scene be there,
> The great stage curtain about to drop,
> If worthy their prominent part in the play,
> Do not break up their lines to weep.
> They know that Hamlet and Lear are gay;
> Gaiety transfiguring all that dread.
> All men have aimed at, found and lost;
> Black out; Heaven blazing into the head:
> Tragedy wrought to its uttermost.
> Though Hamlet rambles and Lear rages,
> And all the drop-scenes drop at once
> Upon a hundred thousand stages,
> It cannot grow by an inch or an ounce.

The importance of that highly compressed stanza is illustrated by the way in which it resounds backwards and forwards in Yeats's work. In 1910 he wrote about "The Tragic Theatre" under the pressure of Synge's death and of the inadequate response to Synge's last play, *Deirdre of the Sorrows,* both shattering events, different in kind and scope from the prospect of war, but still liable to hysterical response. As he knew from experience and from an unsympathetic reading of *In Memoriam,* the personal is often felt as the apocalyptic. In the essay he argued that genuine tragedy confounds the conventional distinctions between playwright and player and audience and at certain moments ascends "into that tragic ecstasy which is the best that art—perhaps that life—can give.... we too were carried beyond time and persons to where passion, living through its thousand purgatorial years, as in the wink of an eye, becomes wisdom; and it was as though we too had touched and felt and seen a disembodied thing." In the 1930 *Diary* Yeats reaffirms his conviction that without a sense of personal immortality, "we can no longer write those tragedies which have always seemed to me alone legitimate—those that are a joy to the man who dies," a belief that goes back to Lady Gregory and forward to his last formulation of tragic ecstasy: "The arts are all the bridal chambers of joy. No tragedy is legitimate unless it leads some great character to his final joy. Polonius may go out wretchedly, but I can hear the dance music in 'Absent thee from felicity awhile,' or in Hamlet's speech over the dead Ophelia."

The poem enacts what the prose defines, embodies the truths Yeats knows as a critic. It creates the sensation of enormous imaginative pressure with the abrupt syntax and reckless rhythms. It is as if Yeats had not enough time for poetic style or linear organization, and had grown too masterful to care. In "Easter, 1916" the subject was people but the stage metaphor likened them and their actions to high art. Here the process is reversed. The stanza is "about" Shakespearean tragedy, but the metaphor extends to life. Synge and O'Leary, Pearse and O'Higgins, also know tragedy and exit gaily, secure in their knowledge that after a peak of intensity, "It cannot grow by an inch or an ounce." In both poems Yeats restores body to the idea of tragedy and affirms its pertinence to the way life is lived. Hamlet says "The rest is silence" and dies — "All men have aimed at, found and lost;/ Black out;" but he has also said "Absent thee from felicity awhile" and Horatio adds "Good night Sweet Prince and flights of angels sing thee to thy rest." The hero dies but the dance music continues, the abundant and intense life he represents is affirmed: "Heaven blazing into the head." Lear and Cordelia die, but the idea of Lear and Cordelia — and of Lear and Cordelia united — continues. Tragedy cannot grow beyond this intensity, yet it is heroic and redemptive—"We too had touched and felt and seen a disembodied thing"—and it leaves no room for hysteria.

The justifications for tragic gaiety come from Shakespearean tragedy and Eastern contemplation. Yeats, always the synthesizer, joins them with a stanza about history:

On their own feet they came, or on shipboard,
Camel-back, horse-back, ass-back, mule-back,
Old civilisations put to the sword.
Then they and their wisdom went to rack:
No handiwork of Callimachus,
Who handled marble as if it were bronze,
Made draperies that seemed to rise
When sea-wind swept the corner, stands;
His long lamp-chimney shaped like the stem
Of a slender palm, stood but a day;
All things fall and are built again,
And those that build them again are gay.

It is another rhetorical triumph. The impatient energy and rapidity of the first sentence mimes the process it describes. The movement slows for a long periodic sentence (to the second semicolon), a leisurely pause at Callimachus's spot in time, what *A Vision* called "a momentary dip into ebbing Asia." The epigrammatic conclusion has a terminal *click* not characteristic of Yeats, and very effective. The rebuilders have learned the lessons of "The Tower," "Two Songs from a Play," "A Dialogue of Self and Soul," and "Vacillation." It is both necessary and possible to rejoice in the face of loss, to accept the inevitable transience of things, because all worthwhile, creative endeavor does begin in the human heart. It is that precarious humanism, at the edge of solipsism but redeemed by its historicity, of Yeats's most powerful affirmations. Time destroys and man rebuilds. If we are to cast out remorse and learn to rejoice, we must accept our immersion in time and our mortality.

Callimachus may dip into Asia, but Yeats jumps, too impatient and confident to bother with transitions:

Two Chinamen, behind them a third,
Are carved in lapis lazuli,
Over them flies a long-legged bird,
A symbol of longevity;
The third, doubtless a serving man,
Carries a musical instrument.

"*Doubtless* a serving man" is a little off-putting, but Yeats had long dreamed of an alliance among artist, aristocrat, and peasant, and the casual *hauteur,* like the Nietzschean bravado, seems a small price to pay for such energy and equanimity. The bird signifies longevity, not eternity, an accurate reading of Chinese iconography, and more significantly of the poem's central premise. The Chinamen are in time, not detached from it. They are not escaping from life but participating and evaluating:

> Every discoloration of the stone,
> Every accidental crack or dent,
> Seems a water-course or an avalanche,
> Or lofty slope where it still snows
> Though doubtless plum or cherry-branch
> Sweetens the little half-way house
> Those Chinamen climb towards, and I
> Delight to imagine them seated there;
> There, on the mountain and the sky,
> On all the tragic scene they stare.
> One asks for mournful melodies;
> Accomplished fingers begin to play.
> Their eyes mid many wrinkles, their eyes,
> Their ancient glittering eyes, are gay.

It gives body to "gay" as the second stanza restores body to "tragedy." There is nothing facile or evasive about those glittering eyes. They ask for "mournful melodies" appropriate to the "tragic scene," the wreck of civilization they survey. In "The Tragic Theatre," Yeats contemplates Deirdre's "reverie of passion that mounts and mounts till grief itself has carried her beyond grief into pure contemplation." In the "civility of sorrow," an acute phrase, passion can become wisdom. The Chinamen are gay because they have behind them an ancient tradition, with them a sense of ceremony, and because they *understand*. They understand hysteria and tragedy, Aeroplane and Zeppelin, destruction and transience. They understand because they take part in experience and because they distance and order it; they apprehend it aesthetically and formally. They can see flux and the larger pattern that contains it, what *A Vision* describes as the vast design resolving itself into the single image, and breaking up again into the vast design. They recognize wholeness and form and the artist's ability to create both. They see the semi-circle of life amid the full circles of eternity, history, and art.

"Lapis Lazuli" declares that art is animate: birds fly, men climb, fingers play, eyes glitter. As Yeats moves into the scene of the medallion, like Keats entering the Urn, he dwells upon its ambiguity. Every discoloration, crack or dent "*seems* a water-course or an avalanche." The sweetening tree *may* be a plum or a cherry. Art and life are composed of multiple perceptions, of the interplay between observer and object, consciousness and the scene. As Yeats enters the medallion he also possesses it, and the gaiety becomes his, a gaiety which counters ravage and loss, but does not deny them or their causes. The poem asserts and demonstrates that there is a larger and more harmonious vision, that the imagination can transform the self and its experience. "A Dialogue of Self and Soul" found the rhetoric for ecstatic transformation and the possibility of vision, "Among School Children" the symbols. "Lapis Lazuli" embodies the whole drama, the full play of consciousness and the world it contemplates in grief and in joy.

It is a marvelous moment, for Yeats and for us. As all his mature poetry testifies, it cannot last. Six months later, recovering from the fatigue of age and ill-health, Yeats imitated a Japanese haiku he liked. It is a slight enough poem, though pleasing for the way that Yeats informs the clichés with meaning and feeling. He called it "Imitated from the Japanese," and it immediately follows "Lapis Lazuli," in *Collected Poems,* a rueful footnote:

> A most astonishing thing—
> Seventy years have I lived;
>
> (Hurrah for the flowers of Spring,
> For Spring is here again.)
>
> Seventy years have I lived
> No ragged beggar-man,
> Seventy years have I lived,
> Seventy years man and boy,
> And never have I danced for joy.

8

Valediction

While Yeats was alive *Last Poems* was *New Poems,* an uneven though impressive collection. Yet now the poems collected and published posthumously seem not so much a departure as another consolidation, as *The Wild Swans at Coole* had been in 1919. They do imaginatively what repose did psychologically and spiritually: "Rest is a great instructor, for it brings the soul back to itself. We sink down into our own soil and take root again." He mines old topics and renews old themes in an attempt to enact the bold prescriptions of the "General Introduction," to make nature more intelligible, to be reborn as an idea, to embody that post-Romantic claim that "the world knows nothing because it has made nothing, we know everything because we have made everything." On occasion he recapitulates to the point of parody or even caricature. He is unusually attentive to the visual arts, especially sculpture, and the monuments of "The Statues" are not touched by the irony that attaches to those of "Sailing to Byzantium." This respectful attention probably expresses a double impulse. It fixes experience in a timeless, or at least relatively permanent, mould; it compensates for the sense of loss he frequently expresses in verse and letters, "all my personal experience having in some strange way come to an end." He gathers energy in order to face the inevitable, enclosing end. He records some moving expressions of a final sense of resolution and a wide range of valedictions.

What seems most new about *Last Poems* is its manner. The diction is unconventional, often wild, and so are the syntax and grammar. The rhymes are impatient and the rhythms hard-driving. The wit is earthy and aggressive, deliberately offensive to various orthodoxies. The mastercraftsman, traditionalist and endless tinkerer has become incredibly nonchalant. There is a consummate and self-conscious mastery that almost reaches arrogance (the prose equivalent is Chapter Seventeen of *Ulysses* where Joyce says "see, these are the materials, in all their flattened reality, with which I have enthralled you for so long"). *Last Poems* is for Yeats what the last plays are for Shakespeare where, as MacNiece's fine poem says, the old master hardly bothered even to be a dramatist. What seems most familiar about the collection is the renewed fury against his time and his body. Some of these poems make *The Tower* look sanguine. One, clearly autobiographical, laments "time's filthy load"; another, decidedly historical, assaults "this filthy modern tide." In both cases the adjective carries the attitude. The letters are punctuated by pain and anxiety:

> 1928: Probably I have made my last Senate appearance. A little speech, three sentences, was followed by a minute of great pain.
>
> 1935: I was holding my own until I collapsed, spitting blood, panting, shivering, too exhausted to stay still for a moment.
>
> 1936: I have had an unexpected attack, breathing became difficult and painful.
>
> 1937: I have had a poor time since I returned, convinced, as my doctor (no cheerful man) was, or seemed, that the rest of my life would be a daily struggle with fatigue.

Physical decay and political disillusion largely account for the "lust and rage" that so notoriously characterizes some late poems, plays, essays, and letters. Yeats prays to be "a foolish, passionate man," and with his spokesman Ribh studies "hatred with great diligence." The reach for new energy, experience, commitment, and the hoarding exhilaration when they come, are often desperate. The public causes and manifestations of such feelings have already been considered. The more strictly personal are dramatized in "An Acre of Grass," a poem of 1936 which begins with accepted diminution and ends with yet another Yeatsean version of Romantic striving. The acre belongs to Riversdale, the "little plain eighteenth-century house" in suburban Dublin which was Yeats's last home. In the first stanza, the tidy smallness ("At first I was unhappy, for everything made me remember the great rooms and the great trees of Coole, my home for nearly forty years") corresponds to diminished imaginative expectations.

The second recalls the conclusion of "Anima Hominis," but places Yeats where the younger poet had derisively placed Wordsworth, "withering into eighty years, honoured and empty witted."

In the third stanza he violently turns to old heroes and monitors, incorporates the old boast about revisions ("It is myself that I remake") and the new boast about poetry as the completed self: "Myself I must remake." The last stanza of this small poem of huge hopes finds a new hero and pleas for a new definition of self. It was for no slight reason that Yeats was known, *en famille,* as "the eagle":

> A mind Michael Angelo knew
> That can pierce the clouds,
> Or inspired by frenzy
> Shake the dead in their shrouds;
> Forgotten else by mankind,
> An old man's eagle mind.

The lines ring with a kind of desperate heroism. Still, the Lear most insistently instructive to Yeats is Lear on the heath, *hysterica passio,* and *A Vision* tells us that in Phase Sixteen "there is always an element of frenzy... for the being must brag of its triumph over its own incoherence." The bragging in *A Full Moon in March* and *Last Poems,* the insistence that "we have made everything," takes more from Nietzsche than from Blake, and is often frenzied in the more conventional sense, that is shrill, the imagination under pressure, the destructive (and self-destructive) impulses nearly out of control. Fortunately it is not the only note. Yeats is still capable of self-parody, even of comedy. "News for the Delphic Oracle," which follows the high seriousness of "The Statues" in *Last Poems* and was probably written about the same time, is a surprise—a very funny poem. Yeats plays with one of his "favourite quotations," Stephen MacKenna's translation of Porphyry's account of the Oracle's description of Plotinus arriving in heaven. The news is that heaven contains such wonders as never occurred to the Oracle, or Plotinus, or Porphyry, or MacKenna. Instead of breathless sages this paradise is peopled by "golden codgers" who lay around, stretching and yawning and sighing. Old friends, Oisin and "Man-picker Niamh," have incongruously and marvelously joined the classical Immortals. Dolphins carry the innocents across purgatorial waters again; but they are sporting rather than bloody, as they unceremoniously "pitch their burdens off" into "some cliff-sheltered bay/ Where wades the choir of love." The last stanza reflects Yeats's delight in Poussin's "Marriage of Peleus and Thetis" and probably his recollection of the "Saphoistic" drawing at Coole which "got into my dreams" and made a racket but still suggested spiritual things. It extravagantly corrects and completes the disembodied paradises of both the Oracle and "Byzantium," yoking the tender delicacy of Poussin to the language and perceptions of Crazy Jane.

"News for the Delphic Oracle" does not really exorcise the Wild Old Wicked Man, but it does mock and so tame him by showing lust and rage in the comic mode and by insisting that the transcendental world thrives on the physical rather than escaping from it or even sublimating it.

2

In 1935 Yeats wrote to Ethel Mannin that Harvard had made a generous offer for him to give the Norton lectures, but that he had decided to refuse in order to concentrate on whatever poetry was left. He wanted "to cut myself adrift, as far as I can, from all external circumstance. ... I want to plunge myself into impersonal poetry, to get rid of the bitterness, irritation and hatred my work in Ireland has brought into my soul. I want to make a last song, sweet and exultant, a sort of European geeta, or rather my geeta, not doctrine but song." However, Yeats was never an impersonal poet and he could not get rid of Ireland. Close to the end and knowing it, he is self-consciously valedictory, hence inclusive, hence Irish. He remembers the old desire to "preserve that which is living and help the two Irelands... so to unite that neither shall shed its pride" as well as the burden of that desire, the alternating hatred and love "that can still make us wag between extremes and doubt our sanity." No matter how tortured, that sense of nationality, what Burke called the "little platoon" and Yeats the clan, is a strength as well as a burden. In the "General Introduction" he asserts that his "Subject-matter" is Ireland, discovered through O'Leary and the poets of *The Nation,* that he knew they were not good poets, but that "they had one quality I admired and admire: they were not separated individual men; they spoke or tried to speak out of a people to a people; behind them stretched the generations." In the short "Introduction" for a new *Collected Works,* he makes the same point, now adopting the language and historical sense of Burke:

> This subject matter is something I have received from the generations, part of that compact with my fellow men made in my name before I was born. I cannot break from it without breaking from some part of my own nature, and sometimes it has come to me in super-normal

experience; I have met with ancient myths in my dreams, brightly lit; and I think it allied to the wisdom or instinct that guides a migratory bird.

In *Last Poems* the compact gets renewed in poems celebrating Irish men and women ("Beautiful Lofty Things," "The Municipal Gallery Revisited"), rehearsing old themes ("The Circus Animals' Desertion"), and taking root in Irish soil ("The Man and the Echo," "The Black Tower," "Under Ben Bulben") for his final explorations. The many late ballads express the same impulse, and so does the return of Crazy Jane (no more exorciseable than Ireland) and Cuchulain. He had earlier reintegrated Irish subject matter and resolved some of the tensions in the Coole Park poems and in the haunting twentieth poem of *Words for Music Perhaps:*

> '*I am of Ireland,*
> *And the Holy Land of Ireland,*
> *And time runs on,' cried she.*
> '*Come out of charity,*
> *Come dance with me in Ireland.'*

The lady, who is not so much of Ireland as Ireland and herself, begins with the imperative language of her predecessor, Cathleen Ni Houlihan. But she has no Michael Gillane to march off after her. Her audience diminishes from a crowd to "One solitary man" who is at first evasive and then preoccupied. He has his own pressing sense of Irish confusion and personal apocalypse. Her refrain, repeated three times, becomes frail rather than commanding, then finally defeated, and very moving. In "Remorse For Intemperate Speech" Yeats contemptuously dismisses Republican politics and the Celtic Twilight, claims his attachment to the Anglo-Irish Augustans, and accepts the "fanatic heart" created by such "Great hatred, little room." Here, without sacrificing any of the impatient energy of the late ballads, he finds the right voice for all the pathos and heroism of Irish nationalism. And the generations do stretch before and after. Yeats took his refrain from an early fourteenth-century lyric read to him by Frank O'Connor. His speaker joins hands with the "Unfortunate Lady" of Swift's first Irish tract, the "Dark Rosaleen" of the Gaelic Munster poets—sad and lovely, victimized but transcendent, waiting for the lover who will rescue her, usually a legendary Gaelic hero or a disguised Stuart king—or the analogous figure in the nineteenth-century lyrics of Allingham and Moore. She shares the accent of Grattan's lament for his country and for the constitution that he and the Patriot Party almost created in 1780: "Yet I do not give up my country. I see her in a swoon but she is not dead; though in her tomb she lies helpless and motionless, still on her lips is the spirit of life and on her cheeks the glow of beauty." Her modern cousins include Juno, Deirdre, and Pegeen Mike, Cathleen and Crazy Jane, Anna Livia Plurabell and the brave and ironic women of *States of Ireland,* O'Brien's brave and tragically ironic book of 1969. These battered, persisting ladies have different faces and different voices, but they are alike enough to substantiate Yeats's claims for a living tradition and a national audience. Their creators, for all their differences, are not "separated individual men"; they do "speak out of a people to a people"; and they all, in their various ways, love her.

"Beautiful Lofty Things" is the most straightforward of Yeats's Irish valedictions, and one of the most successful. It is one of the few poems of Yeats which, like so many of Hardy's, invites the critic simply to recite and admire. It is not difficult to understand, but it is not easy to do, as Yeats, paralleling the section on "Subject-Matter," finds a diction and syntax which mimes the qualities he admires and here memorializes. The summonings—especially of JBY, Lady Gregory, and Maud Gonne—dramatize the rhetorical and evocative power of "things," that is of images, and so authenticate the pride and plangency of the last line, "All the Olympians; a thing never known again." "The Municipal Gallery Revisited" is more complex and problematical. It begins with the enacted moment of "Beautiful Lofty Things" as Yeats contemplates, at the Gallery, "the images of thirty years" and expands the context to include all of modern Ireland, "'an Ireland/ The poets have imagined, terrible and gay.'" It is not he says, "'the dead Ireland of my youth'" (and of "September, 1913") but the tragic Ireland created by the Uprising and by his own consciousness of that event and its consequences. The poem is public in its origins as well as in its reference and rhetoric. In 1937 a Testimonial Committee had been formed in America to raise enough money to guarantee Yeats financial comfort for the rest of his life. He accepted with the proviso that he announce the gift publicly, which he did at a banquet in Dublin in August, adding "I think, though I cannot yet be sure, that a good poem is forming in my head—a poem I can send them. A poem about the Ireland we have all served, and the movement of which I have been a part." Both the speech and the poem were privately printed, signed, and sent to the subscribers. Yeats was understandably touched by the "gift which gave my declining years 'dignity and ease,'" by allowing him, he added as example, to visit the Gallery by taxi. He was unusually pleased with the poem—"one of my best" which "for the moment I like exceedingly."

There is nothing wrong with either a generous gift or a gracious acknowledgement. But some of the lines are not only public discourse, but a particular kind of public discourse, that given after large dinners. It is the accent of Yeats that Joyce liked to parody as he perhaps does in Gabriel Conroy's ample lubrications in "The Dead." In the speech Yeats said that when he returned to the Gallery after long neglect he "was restored to many friends. I sat down, after a few minutes, overwhelmed with emotion." In the poem that sincere and reticent speech becomes a little theatrical and a little self-indulgent:

> Heart-smitten with emotion I sink down,
> My heart recovering with covered eyes.

A later line — "My mediaeval knees lack health until they bend" —is meant as a tribute to Lady Gregory, but rings false and reveals a pose rather than a mask. The speech refers to "the movement of which I have been a part," the poem to "My permanent or impermanent images," which claims too much, possession rather than participation. The sixth stanza

> We three alone in modern times had brought
> Everything down to that sole test again,
> Dream of the noble and the beggar-man

revises Lady Gregory's favorite advice from Aristotle — "'to think like a wise man, but express oneself like the common people'"—in the direction of snobbery, and hardly conveys Synge's desires or his achievement. It is "baptism of the gutter" as well as the Municipal Gallery that is being revisited.

In his last "Introduction," also written in 1937, Yeats argued that "a poet is justified not by the expression of himself, but by the public he finds or creates," and that the "first business" of an artist is "to paint, or describe, desirable people, places, states of mind." Both assertions are at work in "The Municipal Gallery Revisited," but the claims are vitiated by a complacency and self-indulgence which it is one of the chief glories of Yeats's last work to avoid. Nevertheless, like "Shepherd and Goatherd" twenty years earlier, the poem attempts something fine, and indeed, after several missteps, achieves it in the resonant and justly admired conclusion:

> You that would judge me, do not judge alone
> This book or that, come to this hallowed place
> Where my friends' portraits hang and look thereon;
> Ireland's history in their lineaments trace;
> Think where man's glory most begins and ends,
> And say my glory was I had such friends.

As Yeats was a European as well as national poet, not all the resolutions and valedictions are Irish. "Long-Legged Fly," written in late 1937 or '38, defines the self-possession and power of the creative moment, the equanimity and equilibrium of the creative mind, and does it with a triumphantly ordinary image. Caesar saves a civilization but, alone in his tent, "His eyes fixed upon nothing" rather than his maps,

> *Like a long-legged fly upon the stream*
> *His mind moves upon silence.*

Helen destroys a civilization, or at least initiates the events that destroy one, but she is caught by the omniscient and protective poet in unself-conscious reverie. The "tinker shuffle" she practices conflates recollections of both Maud Gonne "singing upon her road" and Iseult dancing upon the beach in Normandy.

Michael Angelo makes a civilization. Unlike Caesar and Helen his action is simultaneous with his reverie, but the poet is still protective, again issuing a command preceded by the reasons for that command:

> That girls at puberty may find
> The first Adam in their thought,
> Shut the door of the Pope's chapel,
> Keep those children out.
> There on that scaffolding reclines
> Michael Angelo.
> With no more sound than the mice make
> His hand moves to and fro.
> *Like a long-legged fly upon the stream*
> *His mind moves upon silence.*

The artist has to labor while the soldier and beauty simply act. But his achievement is greater. Michael Angelo creates God creating Adam and so creates a defining type of western civilization. Life follows art in an even more extreme statement than "The Statues." "An Acre of Grass" had claimed Michael Angelo as the hero of aging creators, and "Under Ben Bulben" returned to the argument with language strained into crassness; but the "purpose set/ Before the secret working mind" is the same: "Profane perfection of mankind." Yeats told Edith Heald that "Long-Legged Fly" is "about the necessity of silence and peace to people of creative energy"; but it is hardly a pastoral poem. The stream of silence upon which the mind moves is also Other. Creative power is not separated and solitary but in touch with a life force outside the self, whether it is called national tradition, anima mundi or the collective unconscious. Caesar and Helen instinctively follow; Michael Angelo recreates out of a deep awareness and imaginative intensity.

While "Long-Legged Fly" "moves upon silence," "High Talk," written a few months later, enacts noise — all kinds of noise and incredible amounts. The last Romantic had been given to unguarded outbursts against modern realism, such as the assaults on the dancers of Degas, which are disappointing lapses from the son of a painter. Now the claims for high mimetic art, no less cranky, are redeemed by exuberance. The first stanza recalls the fine boast on hearing of Swinburne's death—"now I am King of the Cats"—and the contemptuous dismissal of imitators in "A Coat," but with even more vehemence and extravagance. It combines bravado and self-parody in a way only possible for a master, and perhaps only for an Irish master. The Yeats dynasty, upon which so much pride had been spent, has become a circus. The fit audience claimed in "The Municipal Gallery Revisited" and the introductions has become clamoring children and shrieking women. The commitment to statuary and fixed types has been replaced by a renewed respect for his brother's wild paintings. The poet too can claim that "his style fits his purpose, for every sentence has its own taste, tint, and smell." The second stanza shouts that it is "All metaphor," self-possession and power in a different key; but metaphor gives way to nature, nature untamed and unredeemed, dwarfing the poet now off his stilts but still stalking on like those giant presences at the end of "The Statues," "through the terrible novelty" of yet another apocalypse:

> Malachi Stilt-Jack am I, whatever I learned has run wild,
> From collar to collar, from stilt to stilt, from father to child.
> All metaphor, Malachi, stilts and all. A barnacle goose
> Far up in the stretches of night; night splits and the dawn
>   breaks loose;
> I, through the terrible novelty of light, stalk on, stalk on;
> Those great sea-horses bare their teeth and laugh at the dawn.

Within a few months Yeats wrote his most fully recapitulative poem.
It too builds upon the ironic representation of work held dear—shows and
stilts, wild animals and screaming women—and adopts a nonchalant tone
for deeply serious matters. "The Circus Animals' Desertion" begins with a
different terror, searching for lost poetic matter and imaginative energy,
and concludes with a similar sense of walking naked before experience.
Tentative titles—"Despair," "On the Lack of a Theme"—indicate that it is
Yeats's Dejection Ode, and the first stanza starts with frustration ("sought
...sought...sought") moves through reluctant resignation, and ends with
an invocation of past images almost contemptuous in its dismissive infor-
mality. The next three stanzas, printed as section II, "enumerate old
themes." Oisin, "that sea-rider ... led by the nose," is treated with the
affectionate raillery *Last Poems* reserves for the great, the legendary, and
the poet's own creations. His three centuries of "dalliance with a demon
thing" remind Yeats of the sexual yearning and frustration in which his
first major poem was completed:

> But what cared I that set him on to ride,
> I, starved for the bosom of his faery bride?

The whole section rehearses a rich and deliberate confusion of life
and art, friends and imaginings. *The Wanderings of Oisin,* a poem, makes
him think of *The Countess Cathleen,* a play, which does provide a sort of
counter-truth as the Countess elects sacrifice, character, and responsibility
(the values, later, of *Soul*) while Oisin chose fulfillment, personality, and
dream (the virtues of *Self*). The recollection is of the play and of Maud
Gonne, the figure for whom it was written, who informs and is informed
by it:

> I thought my dear must her own soul destroy,
> So did fanaticism and hate enslave it,
> And this brought forth a dream and soon enough
> This dream itself had all my thought and love.

The pronouns are tricky. Is "this" the play or the person? Which dream is
"this dream?" Is "dream" mere compensation or wish-fulfillment or, more
usually the case with Yeats, "a kind of vision of reality which satisfies the
whole being?" "The Circus Animals' Desertion" insists upon the simultaneous presence of a fiction, pity-crazed Cathleen, and a figure, fanatical

Maud; upon the inseparability of personal pain and artistic achievement, the accident of life and the completion of poetry. The second stanza is also a counter-truth because the reflex of the first stanza is from art ("Oisin") to life (sexual starvation) while the reflex of the second is from life (Maud) to art *(The Countess Cathleen)*. The third stanza seems to complete the movement, to register the triumph of art over life, but with Yeats it is never that simple or that comfortable. It recollects *On Baile's Strand*, a play which juxtaposes sordid degradation and overwhelming passion:

> And when the Fool and Blind Man stole the bread
> Cuchulain fought the ungovernable sea;
> Heart-mysteries there, and yet when all is said
> It was the dream itself enchanted me:
> Character isolated by a deed
> To engross the present and dominate memory.
> Players and painted stage took all my love,
> And not those things that they were emblems of.

The dream enchants because Yeats is a poet for whom writing it down and getting it right is the supreme fact of life. But the dream is defined as "character isolated by a deed," exactly the achievement of some late poems, plays, and *Dramatis Personae,* the long section of *Autobiographies* completed in 1935. Its function is "To engross the present and dominate memory," art as a mode of action, the poet speaking, as he had said about some favorite models, "sword in hand," playing his part "in a unique drama ... with the whole soul." The opposition of "players" and "things" is not a *symboliste* contrast between transcendent art and dreary life but animated art set against abstract qualities. So, "when all is said," the enchanting dream is also a deed, a way of being in the world. Even at this late date and under duress, he will not choose perfection of the life or of the work.

The last section continues the exploration, gathers energy and intensity, and then returns to the self:

> Those masterful images because complete
> Grew in pure mind, but out of what began?
> A mound of refuse or the sweepings of a street,
> Old kettles, old bottles, and a broken can,
> Old iron, old bones, old rags, that raving slut
> Who keeps the till. Now that my ladder's gone,
> I must lie down where all the ladders start,
> In the foul rag-and-bone shop of the heart.

The heart is a relatively late addition in the process of composition, replacing the mere "fact" with which the old poet would have had to content himself. Its presence enriches the poem and relates it to the argument of "Self and Soul" and "Vacillation." An early version of the stanza was more explicitly preoccupied with impending death, strained for the counter impulse of tragic gaiety, and concluded with the sentiments and accents of "Under Ben Bulben": "Tension is but the vigour of the mind,/ Cannon the god and father of mankind." Its removal chastens the poem; Yeats's best instincts are at work and the purging is evidence of moral as well as poetic tact. As a theory of art the accepted stanza is developmental and autobiographical, a proud assertion that "the bundle of accident and incoherence" has been "reborn as an idea, something intended, complete." It is also a confession or an acknowledgement. He must accept the decrepit and occasionally muddled old man that he has become. He must accept Ireland and its fanaticism, the land of "hot-faced bargainers and money changers" along with the isle of saints and heroes. He must accept Maud Gonne and her career, the heart and its defects, the fecund ditch that "Self and Soul" had presented as the image and consequence of their relationship. *Must* not *will;* necessity rather than election. "An Acre of Grass" said that

> Neither loose imagination,
> Nor the mill of the mind
> Consuming its rag and bone,
> Can make the truth known.

which should remind us that the image of this poem does not register triumph. The first stanza wonders if "maybe" he "must be satisfied with my heart"; now there is no choice. It is a testament with more than an edge of bitterness and resignation. But Yeats often presents the tragic without despondency, even with exhilaration. The conclusion of "Among School Children" could be wistful or grim, but it is radiant. Here the lingering, sour sense of defeat, as the marvelous energy of the stanza demonstrates, is overcome by delight — delight in experience, and in surviving it and transforming it.

3

Some of his final statements are cosmic, panoramic, prophetic and oratorical: "Meru," "The Gyres," "Under Ben Bulben." Some are more personal and experiential, limited in range of feeling and reference, characterized by questions rather than answers. They are remarkable for their intensity, vulnerability, and honesty, a manifestation of integrity more convincing and moving than the late poems of the Grand Statement. "I think," Yeats wrote in 1936, perhaps reaching all the way back to "the terror that alone could check my wandering mind" of his childhood, that

> profound philosophy must come from terror. An abyss opens under our feet; inherited convictions, the pre-suppositions of our thoughts, those Fathers of the Church Lionel Johnson expounded, drop into the abyss. Whether we will or no we must ask the ancient question: Is there reality anywhere? Is there a God? Is there a Soul? We cry with the Indian Sacred Book: 'They have put a golden stopper into the neck of the bottle; pull it! Let out reality!'

A series of short poems written between that cry and his death face the abyss. He had seemed to long for death's release in the Byzantium poems and had been able to declare, in all the bitter confidence of 1927, that "Man has created death." Not now, as the end really does draw near. He told Stephen Spender that "the final reality of existence in Shakespeare's poetry is of a terrible kind" which echoes what he learned from the death of Synge: "the knowledge of reality is always in some measure a secret knowledge. It is a kind of death."

In "What Then?," a companion poem to "An Acre of Grass," he rehearses his own seven ages of man—toil, fame, money, settled domesticity and a circle of admirers—and with some of Shakespeare's spiced wit. But there is nothing playful about the refrain which comes from one of the old scarecrows of "Among School Children," who now mocks in his turn. "'What then?' sang Plato's ghost. 'What then?'" Hard pressed, the poet offers another definition of the integrity of his career, but the ghost is implacable:

> 'The work is done,' grown old he thought,
> 'According to my boyish plan;
> Let the fools rage, I swerved in naught,
> Something to perfection brought';
> *But louder sang that ghost, 'What then?'*

The ghosts return in "The Apparitions," but they are not Platonic, or literary, or occult. They are natural, the poem having begun in dreams of death, and terrifying, the terror of the actual and the inexplicable. The short poem recapitulates some central impulses, and then challenges them. The first stanza serves as a summary of the caginess and mystification with which he chose to present his unusual experience and odd theories.

But the nightmare allows no charming obfuscation:

> Fifteen apparitions have I seen;
> The worst a coat upon a coat-hanger.

The next stanza returns to friendship as the final compensation for all difficulties, the idea of "In Memory of Major Robert Gregory" and "Meditations in Time of Civil War," and with the same yearning; but the repeated refrain, increasingly eerie and disembodied, jolts him back to fear and solitude. The last stanza is the most urgent and moving as he attempts to gather his resources, as Ellmann has said, to go forth "like Antony to meet darkness as a bride, with passion and befitting fear," only to be again assaulted by the dream, heart mysteries rather than pure mind.

Ghosts make their most mysterious, haunting appearance in "Cuchulain Comforted," his second-to-last poem, which grew out of his last play, The Death of Cuchulain. The play is not an inviting conclusion to the great saga or to Yeats's dramatic career. It was finished in January 1939 but unrevised and, unlike most of his work for the theater, not tested by performance. As drama it is marred by compression, confusion, and an uncontrolled rage at a world incapable of appreciating the heroic, a world of "sciolists ... pickpockets and opinionated bitches." Olivia Shakespear had just died, and the loss can be felt in the solitary fury of the "very old man looking like something out of mythology" who opens the play. It has only one scene, but it tries to present Cuchulain's relationship to the five women who passionately love or hate him: his wife Emer, his mistress Eithne Inguba, Aoife whose son he had begotten and killed, his old antagonist Maeve, and the Morrigu, goddess of War. It also wants to incorporate the resonance between the Cuchulain myth and the tragedy and legacy of the Uprising. It is as uncompromising about filling in the expository details as Purgatory. The climactic moment, however, is breath-taking, as "strange and ... moving" as Yeats thought. Cuchulain, mortally wounded, has tied himself to a post, with Aoife's help and with her veil, so that he may die on his feet. He is approached by that antithetical creature of sordid greed, the Blind Man of On Baile's Strand, who has been promised twelve pennies by Maeve for Cuchulain's head. Knife out, he fumbles his greasy way from the warrior's feet up to his neck. Cuchulain is indifferent:

> There floats out there
> The shape that I shall take when I am dead,
> My soul's first shape, a soft feathery shape,
> And is not that a strange shape for the soul
> Of a great fighting-man?

As the Blind Man begins to cut, Cuchulain continues: "I say it is about to sing." The stage darkens and lights again. The Morrigu arranges a dance to the dead Cuchulain which Emer dances. *"Then she stands motionless. There is silence, and in the silence a few faint bird notes."*

At three in the morning on January 7, 1939, Yeats dictated to his wife a prose draft of a poem which came from a dream, which in turn derived from *The Death of Cuchulain*. Perhaps it was finally true that he needed to write plays in order to write lyrics out of dramatic experience because personal experience had come to an end. "Cuchulain Comforted" is Yeats's only poem in Dante's *terza rima,* and the shrouds are Virgil, or Brunetto Latini, to Cuchulain's pilgrim. It is Dante with a difference, however; for Dante perfection comes from denial and ascent; for Yeats "profane perfection" derives from immersion and intensification. The poem continues the action of the play. Cuchulain arrives in Purgatory to be greeted by "certain Shrouds"—"Eyes stared out of the branches and were gone." Cuchulain would "meditate on wounds and blood," but "A Shroud that seemed to have authority" shyly gives him "A bundle of linen" and mysterious instructions:

> 'Your life can grow much sweeter if you will
>
> 'Obey our ancient rule and make a shroud;
> Mainly because of what we only know
> The rattle of those arms makes us afraid.
>
> 'We thread the needles' eyes, and all that we do
> All must together do.' That done, the man
> Took up the nearest and began to sew.

The shrouds are "Convicted cowards all," but that does not matter as they, too, are transfigured:

> They sang, but had nor human tunes nor words,
> Though all was done in common as before;
> They had changed their throats and had the throats of birds.

Harold Bloom is just right about the tone: "'Cuchulain Comforted' will always have the authority of mystery about it ... a tone of revelation imperfectly apprehended, a half-light that darkens into religion." Cuchulain has his arms, wounds, and blood, the Shrouds their linen, sewing, and singing. They are the opposites he must seek, cowards who define his heroism. They know more than he does because they know their own past and the purgatorial process that dissolves it. They can experience their own true death, soul and body embracing. Cuchulain's comfort is his acceptance of their communion and his chosen fate, the purgatorial process and his place in it. Yeats's comfort—after the rant of the prologue and straining for relevance of the final song, it is an extraordinarily quiet poem —is his acceptance of the dream, the play, the full Cuchulain cycle, his own cycles, and at least for the moment his own condition.

Cuchulain is not the only embattled hero and Yeats cannot always accept his condition with—in both senses of the word—grace. "The Black Tower," his last poem, written a week before he died, goes back to "The Curse of Cromwell," written about two years earlier. Yeats had said that he was "expressing my rage against the intelligentsia by writing about Oliver Cromwell who was the Lenin of his day" and the poem is animated by reactionary bitterness and the fierce, lonely pride of extremity:

> They have schooling of their own, but I pass their schooling by,
> What can they know that we know that know the time to die?

The third stanza seems to accept as inevitable that Yeatsian role, the poet in service of an audience long gone and now unimaginable:

> But there's another knowledge that my heart destroys,
> As the fox in the old fable destroyed the Spartan boy's,
> Because it proves that things both can and cannot be;
> That the swordsmen and the ladies can still keep company,
> Can pay the poet for a verse and hear the fiddle sound,
> That I am still their servant though all are underground.
> > *O what of that, O what of that,*
> > *What is there left to say?*

"The Black Tower" answers that question with an imperative "Say that" — commanding an unspecified auditor to recognize and legitimate the impossible circumstances and unshakable loyalty of the embattled remnant:

> Say that the men of the old black tower,
> Though they but feed as the goatherd feeds,
> Their money spent, their wine gone sour,
> Lack nothing that a soldier needs,
> That all are oath-bound men:

Both discourse and drama change after the colon, as the men interrupt the poet and shout their defiance to an unnamed enemy: "Those banners come not in."

Yeats abruptly shifts to the disembodied, objective ballad refrain, another Rocky Voice. But the refrain is not simply choric. It furthers the drama as well as commenting on it, ballad acting as interior monologue. As Daniel Harris says, "this deliberately incongruous merging of objective and subjective elements results in a strange, eerie resonance. Two voices consider the same event from radically different perspectives, experiential and omniscient; both say the same thing: 'There in the tomb the dark grows blacker.' The dying warrior shares the commentator's omniscience; the commentator, the warrior's tragedy."

The next stanza again changes discourse, beginning with a description of the situation and switching to contemptuous questioning of the enemy: "Why do you dread us so?" The third stanza explicitly includes the poet among the ancient warriors and introduces the comic, pathetic figure of the cook.

The cook may be a materialist, like the Boy in *Purgatory*, desperately needing proof and so inventing it; unlike the boy he is one of us, not the new man but the old retainer. He loyally serves a necessary function. The poet could say of him, as he does of the "old beggar" in "The Curse of Cromwell," "His fathers served their fathers before Christ was crucified." So the "lying hound," while it dismisses his forlorn hopes, is affectionate, not contemptuous (all the contempt in this poem is reserved for the enemy). He remains with the "oath-bound men" as the final darkness descends:

> *There in the tomb the dark grows blacker,*
> *But wind comes up from the shore:*
> *They shake when the winds roar,*
> *Old bones upon the mountain shake.*

Whose bones are these, and do they shake in fear, death, defeat, defiance, or all four? Who are the brave and enigmatic men in this last Yeatsian tower? In the early drafts the warriors were definably Celtic. In one cancelled line the wind "blows from the black pig's dike," an allusion to folklore Yeats had long ago written about, "The Valley of the Black Pig," where Irishmen fight a great battle and finally defeat their enemies. The dead "stand upright," are buried vertically, in tales of the heroic period, and the poem may find one source in O'Grady's *Finn and His Companions* and another in Mallory's account of Arthur and his court, asleep in their castle, awaiting the blast on the horn to call them to battle. The allusions would indicate that the soldiers are Irish, the enemy England, and the poem traditional Irish nationalism, a late *Cathleen Ni Houlihan*. But Yeats cancelled such particularity of reference and in the completed poem both heroes and enemy are less historically defined, and more deeply personal, and more mythic. The carriers of alien banners will bribe, threaten, whisper; they are not warriors but politicians, knowing no loyalty without a pay-off and no tactics but manipulation. They could be the new Irish excoriated in "The Leaders of the Crowd." They could represent "the English mind" which, Yeats said in *On the Boiler,* "excited by its news-paper proprietors and its schoolmasters, has turned into a bed-hot harlot." In either case they embody the new politics (Mrs. Yeats said that the poem is "on the subject of political propaganda"), the murderousness and man-ipulation of which so enraged Yeats. The enemy is temporal not national, "this filthy modern tide" wherever encountered.

But the last enemy is the enveloping darkness, a darkness that is unpolitical and inevitable and which the poem faces with an urgent and angry heroism. "He knew he was dying," Mrs. Yeats told Jon Stallworthy, and death, as Hannah Arendt has said, "whether faced in actual dying or in the inner awareness of one's own mortality, is perhaps the most antipoliti-cal experience there is" because it separates the individual from both time and community. In "Vacillation" he had told himself to "begin the prepara-tion for your death

> And call those works extravagance of breath
> That are not suited for such men as come
> Proud, open-eyed and laughing to the tomb.

"The Black Tower" does not laugh, though there is some gallows humor about the cook and the cowardice of the enemy, but it surely meets the test of pride and, finally, of self-knowledge. In those remarkable sentences at the end of *Anima Hominis* Yeats had written, "I shall find the dark grow luminous, the void fruitful when I understand I have nothing, that the ringers in the tower have appointed for the hymen of the soul a passing bell." That passage begins, as we have seen, with the "old artist" who was his father. In one of the cancelled passages of this poem, the old poet thinks of his father and his son, and David and Absalom, and so counters the Oedipal fury of *Purgatory:*

> Do you hear (   ) father
>   no no
>   not yet   not yet
> But (   )
>   soon soon my   son

As he now faces the luminous dark of the blackening tomb, preparation over, his own nothing grudgingly accepted, he knows what the Oldest Pupil had to learn in *The King's Threshold,* that earlier study of political manipulation and heroic response:

> Not what it leaves behind it in the light
> But what it carries with it to the dark
> Exalts the soul.

Yeats is most truly heroic when most defenseless, and the increasing Night receives its most powerful expression in the "cleft that's christened Alt" of "The Man and the Echo," originally placed at the end of *Last Poems,* just before "The Circus Animals' Desertion." The cleft may be on Knocknarea, near Queen Maeve's grave, or on Ben Bulben, near Yeats's. It draws on "the carved stone head, high in the S. E. wall of Thoor Ballylee" as well as on the Delphic Oracle, the piece of Lapis Lazuli, Ahasuerus, and Ben Jonson's "rockie face," all the "stony recessions of history" and art. The situation reverses that of "Lapis Lazuli" and "The Gyres." The man is shrouded in darkness and looks into the mountain rather than out from it. He is questioner rather than prophet or sage, unaccommodated man, the poor, forked, naked creature of Lear, Swift, and the Crazy Jane poems:

> In a cleft that's christened Alt
> Under broken stone I halt
> At the bottom of a pit

That broad noon has never lit,
And shout a secret to the stone.
All that I have said and done,
Now that I am old and ill,
Turns into a question till
I lie awake night after night
And never get the answers right.
Did that play of mine send out
Certain men the English shot?
Did words of mine put too great strain
On that woman's reeling brain?
Could my spoken words have checked
That whereby a house lay wrecked?
And all seems evil until I
Sleepless would lie down and die.

History and literature again—the stanza refers to *Cathleen Ni Houlihan,* Margot Ruddock, and Coole Parke—but with a difference: remorse of conscience is unabated. The drafts wonder more baldly if he and his work "have done but harm," the opposing proposition to Seanchan's and most of Yeats's poems and plays. The echo's reply is a mocking and terrifying injunction: "Lie down and die."

The man is roused to counter-statement, a compressed definition of the integrity of age and the poetic intellect. Behind it stand Blake and Shelley, Swift and Shakespeare ("Shakespeare's persons, when the last darkness has gathered about them, speak out of an ecstasy that is one-half the self-surrender of sorrow, and one-half the last playing and mockery of the victorious sword before the defeated world"), and the assertiveness of "The Tower," even more urgent now in the presence of death:

That were to shirk
The spiritual intellect's great work,
And shirk it in vain. There is no release
In a bodkin or disease,
Nor can there be work so great
As that which cleans man's dirty slate.
While man can still his body keep
Wine or love drug him to sleep,
Waking he thanks the Lord that he
Has body and its stupidity,
But body gone he sleeps no more,
And till his intellect grows sure

That all's arranged in one clear view,
Pursues the thoughts that I pursue,
Then stands in judgement on his soul.
And, all work done, dismisses all
Out of intellect and sight
And sinks at last into the night.

Again the echo mocks, offering only all that is left: "Into the night." The man desperately confronts and questions:

O Rocky Voice
Shall we in that great night rejoice?
What do we know but that we face
One another in this place?

"An abyss opens under our feet"—of history and of the self. Long ago Yeats had asked, "Why should we honour those that die upon the field of battle? A man may show as reckless a courage in entering into the abyss of himself." More recently he had wondered if subjective men caught up in the world of action, like Robert Gregory, "hesitated before they plunged into the abyss." Now, an agonizing pause follows "place." The voice could answer "rejoice" as it does in "The Gyres," but that seems impossible here. It could answer "in this place," which would be aptly enigmatic and terminal. But in fact it answers not at all, a moment of enormous reticence, not even the comfort of an echo. Instead the man—he is surely Yeats—is hurtled away from the dialogue, now a monologue, by one of nature's most painful, final sounds.

But hush, for I have lost the theme,
Its joy or night seem but a dream;
Up there some hauk or owl has struck,
Dropping out of sky or rock,
A stricken rabbit is crying out,
And its cry distracts my thought.

The rest is silence.

But not really. There is a graffito on the basement wall of the library at the college where I work (or used to be until a zealous janitor removed it) that scrawls: "Yeats lives!" The pleasure it gave me was no doubt sentimental and self-indulgent. Yet, no matter to what school of critical theory

we subscribe, or fashion we endorse, we generally agree that "the text" —
poems and stories, plays and essays — has a life of its own. Most of us
believe that behind the text is a lived life that we can discover, intuit,
approximate. For several generations of practicing poets, beginning with
his own and continuing today, Yeats has been a model of dedication and
hard work, of commitment to "this craft of verse." He is a moral example
as well as a literary influence. The endless curiosity, the athletic intellect,
the repeated struggle, and continual growth are proper objects of our
wonder and our admiration. No modern poet has as fully developed a
sense of history or of reality; none has become so wholly synonymous with
his age, culture, and nation. There are moments when Yeats passes beyond
time, when he achieves a stance, vision, and language that are remarkable
equally for their scope and their intensity. For him such moments are
costly, fleeting, and ecstatic; for us they are chastening and sustaining. He
undertook to do a great deal, and he did, truly and concretely, bring it
to pass.

Notes

I have largely restricted the notes to citation of direct quotations and references. The notes list page and line number, followed by a word or phrase from the quoted or annotated material. Articles and books not dealing with Yeats or Ireland and cited only one time are given in the notes but not included in the bibliography. A few general acknowledgments and references precede the notes to each chapter. Names, abbreviations, and short titles given in the notes are fully cited in the bibliography. I have tried to cite only the most easily available edition or reprinting.

INTRODUCTION

There is an increasing body of criticism about Yeats and literary influence. Three of the most influential are Ellmann, *Eminent Domain;* Bate, *The Burden of the Past;* and Bloom, *The Anxiety of Influence.* My own view is found in "Yeats's Encounters: Observations on Literary Influence and Literary History," *New Literary History* 1, no. 3 (1970): 439–69, and "The Words upon the Window-pane and Yeats's Encounter with Jonathan Swift," in O'Driscoll and Reynolds.

xi, 15 die at top.' Edward Young, *Conjectures on Original Composition,* ed. Edith J. Morley (Manchester: The University Press, 1918), p. 29.
xii, 6 half-symbolic image." E&I, 397.
xii, 22 dynasty...." Ex, 295.
xii, 25 expression of himself." *Plays and Controversies,* 95.
xii, 27 mythic identification." Thomas Mann, "Freud and the Future" in *Freud, Goethe, Wagner* (New York: Knopf, 1939), pp. 3–45; Ellmann, *Identity,* p. 267.
xiii, 6 discipline." Ex, pp. 343–45.
xiii, 22 and eaten." Ex, pp. 301–03. I have reversed the order of the second and third entries.
xiii, 31 *Thou....* Martin Buber, *I and Thou,* 2nd ed., trans. R. G. Smith (New York: Charles Scribner and Sons, 1958), p. 128.
xiii, 32 personal intimacy." T. S. Eliot, *The Egoist* 6 (July 1919): 39–40.
xiv, 13 hatred and pride. Ex, pp. 293–94.

CHAPTER 1

My reading of "Frost at Midnight" and my general sense of Coleridge is indebted to Bate's *Coleridge* and to Parker and Abrams.

5, 18 extreme simplicity." L, 30.
5, 30 *ottava rima....*" Kermode, *Romantic Image*, p. 38.
6, 24 space and time." Kermode, *Romantic Image*, p. 2.
6, 37 independent of his will." Donoghue, 85.
8, 1 public... occasions. Lyons, pp. 380–436; Harris, p. 138.
10, 14 paternal generosity. Parker, pp. 127–33, and Abrams, pp. 264–77.
11, 13 foam upon the deep." The phrases quoted in this paragraph are from E&I, pp. 78, 79, 146, 148, 155, 157, 159, 162, 163, 164, 195.
11, 34 Song of Sixpence. L, 922.
12, 12 that is all." A, 298–99.
12, 18 what I looked for." Myth, 63.
12, 19 spiritual loss...." M, 171.
12, 25 never happens." A, 106.
12, 27 unseen reality." Ex, 170.

CHAPTER 2

Murphy's splendid biography of J. B. Yeats provides the fullest account. Lynch is interesting about father and son. My *J. B. Yeats,* a short introduction, has a bibliography which includes a list of his fugitive writings and all the published editions of his letters.

13, 6 hung with slime...." see note to p. 87, 19.
13, 17 argument of metaphysics. JBY, *Letters,* pp. 291–92.
14, 26 monkish hate." A, 25, 82.
15, 19 Tell Willie...." JBY, *Letters,* p. 50.
15, 26 my father's studio." Ellmann, *M&M,* p. 14.
15, 32 another matter." JBY, *Letters,* pp. 52–53.
15, 34 a father's feeling.'" Hone, p. 50.
15, 41 off my mind." Hone, p. 58.
16, 6 Henly and Morris...." Reid, p. 494.
16, 22 doing and thinking." Ellmann, *M&M,* p. 94.
17, 12 a man and a poet." JBY, *Letters,* pp. 97–98. JBY was fond of italics and I have retained them throughout.
17, 19 decadent verse." JBY, *Letters,* pp. 93–94, 102.
17, 30 infirmity of will." Reid, p. 493.
17, 39 black beetles." JBY, *Letters,* pp. 78, 121.
18, 16 years ago." Hone, p. 334.
18, 28 forthcoming autobiography." JBY, *Letters,* pp. 274, 280.
18, 35 Please tell me...." JBY, *Letters,* p. 282.
18, 39 domestic emotion." L, 502.
19, 8 animal and primitive." JBY, *Letters,* p. 283.

19, 28 poetry of life." JBY, *Letters*, p. 281.

20, 12 "'Ripeness is all.'" JBY, *Letters*, pp. 262, 280.

20, 20 dignity and love." Erik H. Erikson, *Identity: Youth and Crisis* (New York: Norton, 1968), p. 139.

20, 25 see her grown up?" JBY, *Letters*, p. 273.

20, 28 under my skin.'" Padraic Colum, "My Memories of John Butler Yeats," *Dublin Magazine* N.S. 32, no. 4 (Oct.–Dec. 1957):9.

21, 21 details and applications." L. 548–49.

22, 8 back into the tapestry...." E&I, p. 517.

22, 19 would have put it." Wade, p. 88.

22, 29 her or the music." JBY, *Letters*, p. 116.

23, 14 averted their eyes." JBY, *Letters*, p. 163.

23, 25 thinking and feeling." L, 583.

24, 3 the great reaction." JBY, *Letters*, pp. 191–92.

24, 31 a passing bell." JBY, *Letters*, p. 161; Myth, pp. 331–32; cf. Bloom, pp. 178–84, who admires the passage and deletes JBY.

25, 2 presence of any sufferings." JBY, *Letters*, p. 221.

25, 11 thinking and writing." L, 678.

25, 32 from meeting it." JBY, *Letters*, pp. 169–79; L, 586–87, 607.

26, 3 for his dreams...." JBY, *Letters*, p. 189.

26, 20 this kind of humor." *Further Letters of John Butler Yeats*, ed. Lennox Robinson (Churchtown, Dundrum: The Cuala Press, 1920), p. 48.

27, 1 possible to men." A, 190, 344; V-B, 88.

27, 13 the whole being," JBY, *Letters*, p. 185; L, 588.

27, 15 and to Pelham.... JBY, *Letters*, p. 48; L, 922.

27, 27 money changers." A, 461.

27, 29 passion for self-expression...." JBY, *Letters*, p. 125.

28, 7 I did enjoy it. JBY, *Letters*, p. 214.

28, 11 forgot them." A, 483.

CHAPTER 3

For Lady Gregory I have relied on her own writings and the studies by Adams, Coxhead, Harris, and Saddlemeyer. For Maud Gonne I have relied on *A Servant of the Queen* and the biographies by Cardozo and Levenson.

29, 3 one has to choose.'" L, 838.

30, 7 something intended, complete. E&I, 509.

30, 21 and exultation?" M, 155.

30, 28 complete arcs." M, 158; A, 475.

30, 41 man and poet." M, 9–11; Holloway in Donoghue and Mulryne.

31, 18 were incestuous." Weintraub, Reade, and especially Easton.

32, 30 I think very good." L, 574–75; Lady Gregory, *Seventy Years*, pp. 487–91; the line on the Rhymers is from "The Grey Rock."

35, 35 the looker-on." A, 330.

36, 14 rage against iniquity!" M, 92; A, 331.

36, 23 play of mind." A, 325–36.
36, 25 sanctity in theology." V-B, 130.
37, 15 hatred of life." A, 323, 331–33, 368–87; V-B, 129–30; L, 819.
37, 30 could not draw. Easton, pp. 115, 206.
38, 16 shadows and hollow images." L. 434.
38, 19 sentimental sensuality. . . . " A, 326.
39, 28 known again. A, 123; "No Second Troy"; "Beautiful Lofty Things."
39, 36 so laborious. M, 141–42; cf. the poem "Words."
40, 4 avoid thought. MacBride, p. 308.
40, 11 one-ideaed. . . . " MacBride, p. 158.
40, 40 Paris clothes. . . . " Gwynn, p. 17.
41, 9 Irish people. . . . " MacBride, p. 104.
41, 18 lived among." MacBride, p. 332; Levenson, p. 308.
41, 23 kings' visits." MacBride, pp. 332–33.
42, 1 old caubeen. . . . " L, 110.
42, 5 any thought?" M, 60.
42, 12 the troubling. . . . " M, 40.
42, 20 dark and still." M, 85.
43, 25 crowd of stars. "When You Are Old."
43, 35 Irish Victor Hugo. . . . " M, 41.
43, 38 Christian Ireland." Jeffares, *Plays*, p. 1.
44, 10 than Maud Gonne. Bloom, p. 119.
44, 21 mortal infirmity." Jeffares, *Plays*, pp. 29–30.
44, 30 blind / With lightning. . . . " "Reconciliation."
45, 8 head to foot. "Friends."
46, 5 her recollection. . . . " MacBride, pp. 328–30.
47, 21 Pre-Raphaelite passion." Ellmann, *Golden Codgers*, p. 107; M, 45–48, 133.
48, 14 do no more.' M, 131–34.
48, 21 stone doll. A, 504; M, 192.
49, 3 bomb or rifle. . . ?" A, 368.
49, 17 criticism from politics." L, 612–613.
50, 13 to Ireland.'" L, 613.
50, 28 Cathleen Clarke. . . . " Gwynn, pp. 31–32.
50, 36 German plot. . . . " MacBride, pp. 289–90.
51, 16 President Cosgrave." L, 312, 313, 631, 739.
51, 30 with the people." Jeffares and Cross, *Reverie*, p. 6.
52, 1 clinking brood mare.'" M, 43, 49, 59–61.
52, 9 daughter still." Sean O'Casey, *Inishfallen, Fare Thee Well* (London: Macmillan, 1949), 244.
52, 28 night come." "That the Night Come."
53, 9 does not create." M, 247.
54, 22 a dozen poems: M, 101–02; A, 457; V-B, 170; "Beautiful Lofty Things" and "The Municipal Gallery Revisited."
55, 16 Barrington's *Memoirs*. . . . " A, 393.
55, 22 strict Orangism. . . . " quoted Coxhead, 5.
56, 8 lesser mortals. . . . " Lady Gregory, *Seventy Years*, p. 430; A, 408; JBY, *Letters*, pp. 152, 186.
56, 19 that ever lived.'" A, 395.
56, 41 so much to dread. *Journals*, 33.

57, 29 bitterness of feeling. ... " *Seventy Years*, p. 542; *Journals*, p. 310.
57, 35 thinking Democracy." A, 456; Adams, *Gregory*, 35.
58, 7 keep it open." *Journals*, pp. 20, 131, 188, 340.
58, 22 and banishment. ... " Coxhead, p. 217.
58, 24 men of letters. ... " L, 716.
59, 2 merit is mainly hers." UcP, II, 299; Myth, 1.
59, 24 and benediction." *Seventy Years*, p. 390.
59, 27 Nobel Prize Speech. ... " A, 559–72.
60, 30 Urbino or Versailles." A, 473–74.
61, 7 repetition of those words." L, 795–96.
61, 23 all the house I have." A, 472–73, 477–78; M, 154; L, 796. The thought is incorporated into the poem, "A Friend's Illness."
62, 22 of the multitudes." A, 473.
63, 7 intense depression. ... " Jeffares, *Poems*, pp. 153–55.
64, 6 into good hands." L, 633; *Seventy Years*, p. 551.
64, 29 wrote of Sidney. ... " L, 647–48.
65, 37 courageous letters." L, 646.
67, 12 is not Gregory's." The passages are Yeats, A, 318; a letter from Henry James to Yeats, quoted in *Seventy Years*, p. 184; Yeats's "Appreciation" of Gregory in *The Observer*, reprinted UcP, II, 429–31. The commentary includes Kermode, *Romantic Image*, pp. 30–42; Harris, pp. 126–37, and Marjorie Perloff, "The Consolation Theme in Yeats's 'In Memory of Major Robert Gregory,'" *MLQ* 27:306–22.
68, 9 grave distinction. ... " UcP, II, 430.
68, 27 their admiration." L, 647.
69, 4 will and desire. UcP, II, 430–31.
70, 29 historical crisis." Harris, pp. 223–24.
70, 30 almost pathetic." Adams, *Gregory*, p. 27.
71, 23 to what creditor." A, 381.
71, 32 died too. ... " L, 796.
72, 18 under anasthesia. ... " A, 388–89; *Journals*, pp. 35–36.
73, 39 lament for its passing." Whitaker, p. 221.
74, 14 modified by religion." L, 808.
74, 27 members of her class." Harris, p. 24.
75, 19 bitterness of feeling. ... " *Journals*, p. 310.
75, 25 before they die." "Parnell's Funeral."

CHAPTER 4

For the political and literary history I have relied mainly on Lyons, Marcus, Fallis, and Yeats's prose. The best essay on "The Wanderings of Oisin" is Michael J. Sidnell's in the *Colby Library Quarterly* 15, no. 2 (June 1979):137–51.

76, 9 except 'the arts.'" "Mr Yeats's Autobiographies," *Dial* 83 (August 1927):93–97.
77, 2 to the tomb." A, 7–17, 19–22, 55, 138; "Vacillation."
77, 11 poet and dreamer." Hone, p. 9; JBY, *Letters*, p. 5.
77, 23 it is enticing." *Further Letters of John Butler Yeats*, ed. Lennox Robinson (Churchtown, Dundrum: The Cuala Press, 1920), p. 74.

79, 19 ingenuity of man." Hoffman and Levack, p. 501.

80, 4 head of a needle." Ex, 337; A, 376–77.

80, 31 doubt our sanity." E&I, 518–19.

81, 9 into the tapestry...." E&I, 517.

82, 13 without literature." Yeats, *Letters to the New Island,* 75–76.

82, 21 get a style." E&I, 4.

83, 10 romantic and poetical." A, 559–60.

84, 28 immortal things." E&I, 179.

85, 10 tradition of Ireland." Ex, 79, 93.

84, 34 there in the end." Ex, 156.

86, 5 express themselves." Marcus, p. 188.

86, 18 things invisible and ideas." L, 255.

86, 24 to write...." A, 376.

86, 17 day and night." L, 87, 786.

87, 7 autobiographical. Ellmann, *M&M,* pp. 51–53; *Identity,* p. 18.

87, 19 orgasm incarnate...." Morton I. Seiden, "A Psychoanalytic Essay on W. B. Yeats," *Accent* (Spring 1946):178–90.

87, 33 between the episodes." Marcus, p. 243 f.

88, 27 melt into one another," E&I, 148.

89, 8 the paper." L, 87–88.

89, 26 haunted me." L, 111; Ex, 392.

89, 30 circle joined." Ex, 401.

90, 30 the critic scholar.... L, 87; Sidnell, 145–47.

91, 7 more likely candidate." L, 106; UcP, II, 148.

93, 16 blessings on your head?" L, 798.

93, 23 no meaning for him." Ex, 24.

96, 30 more salt in it." L, 63; letter to AE, Ellmann, *M&M,* p. 153.

98, 34 at present." Ex, 74, 99, 101, 107, 112.

99, 6 amounts to anything." Ex, 191, 201; A, 488.

99, 28 instinct for excellence." L, 254.

100, 12 wistful alienation." Ex, 83, 147; A, 233, 473–74.

100, 15 have to live in...." Ex, 204.

100, 25 between 1902 and 1912. The quotations in this paragraph are from E&I, 221–383.

101, 21 conceived ourselves." M, 251.

101, 37 as the dawn.'" "The Fisherman."

102, 17 service of a cause." A, 473, 508; Ex, 107.

103, 15 true to the cast." A, 485.

104, 13 minds without culture." Var, pp. 818–19.

104, 18 exultant slaughtermaster." Henn, p. 97.

104, 40 teeth of Murphy...." Jeffares and Cross, p. 236.

105, 10 a kind of joy." L, 876.

105, 20 all kinds of fear." E&I, 246, 260.

106, 39 onto the roads." M, 247.

CHAPTER 5

I have relied, again, on Lyons for history and Ellmann and Hone for biography. Conor Cruise O'Brien's essay, in Jeffares and Cross, set the terms for all subsequent discussions of Yeats's politics. I have discussed "Edmund Burke and the Conservative Imagination" in the *Colby Library Quarterly* 12, no. 4 (December 1976):191–204, and 13, no. 1 (March 1977):19–41.

108, 6 hope of success." Var, 820.
108, 13 born again.'" L, 613.
109, 12 bear the Gael." Dangerfield, p. 220.
110, 6 and the glory. T. S. Eliot, *The Use of Poetry and the Use of Criticism* (London: Faber and Faber, 1933), p. 106.
111, 6 sour and argumentative. L, 675.
111, 25 a cultivated man." Ex, 263.
111, 39 Unity of Being." Ex, 280; Ellmann, *M&M*, pp. 216, 238.
113, 26 hatred and abstraction. Donoghue and Mulryne, p. 75.
114, 9 The drafts. ... Stallworthy, *Lines*, 16-25.
114, 25 of the Left. Bloom, 317–25 who establishes the sources.
114, 38 ecstatic destruction." A, 185–86; Ex, 393.
115, 13 the next age. ... " Jeffares, *Poems*, p. 241.
115, 34 interior Lucifer." Whitaker, p. 53.
116, 17 State of the World. ... " Bradford, p. 72.
116, 32 never to many." Ex, 246, 254, 257.
117, 14 no more war. ... " Torchiana, pp. 317–18.
120, 25 early version. ... " Bradford, p. 70.
121, 17 give way to worse." "Notes" to CP, 448, 455.
121, 25 women love shows." Bradford, 76–78.
121, 41 Juno's peacock." V–B, 268; Whitaker, p. 232.
123, 4 perhaps the sole theme. ... " L, 729, 733, 798.
123, 10 intellectual nationalisms. ... " L, 738, 747, 779.
124, 13 riot for it." UcP, II, 433–36; L, 682, 690, 693.
124, 24 into this House." SS, 30, 152.
125, 2 done what I have. ... " Ex, 338; UcP, II, 482, 484; L, 727, 809.
125, 14 to make a nation." "Notes" to CP, 452.
125, 38 through the centuries." SS, 171–72.
126, 6 rhetoric of agitation." Ex, 292-93; UcP, II, 489.
126, 39 mind of Burke." V–B, 297; E&I, 411; Ex, 337.
127, 2 in the earth." *Moore Corr*, p. 114.
127, 16 into the tapestry. ... " E&I, 517.
127, 26 if it is rejected." L, 678.
130, 8 given them the bridge," "Notes" to CP, p. 455.
130, 33 the irrational cry. ... " V–B, 268.
132, 21 of the moment." A, 562, 580.
133, 21 by candle light." L, 690–91. Yeats is apparently conflating Black and Tan atrocities of The Troubles with atrocities committed by both sides during the Civil War.
133, 31 our expectations." Ex, 161–62.
133, 33 modern Ireland. Lyons, title page.
134, 15 various kinds." "Notes" to CP, 455.
135, 1 Women and Unicorns. ... " L, 865; Henn, 255.

135, 8 Yeats's note.... CP, 455.
136, 13 some bitter crust." Myth, 342; Whitaker, 186, also notes this passage; Ellmann, *Id*,
   223, sees Wordsworth; Harris, 183–84, defines limits.
137, 8 foolish body decays." *Letters to the New Island*, 94; Henn, 39.
137, 20 no art at all." Harris, 185.
138, 10 might quiet him." Jeffares, *Poems*, 259–60.
138, 27 blushes in her cheeks...." A, 561.
138, 37 in her face...." Myth, 24–25.
139, 30 poem was written." "Notes" to CP, 453–54.
140, 7 he possesses them. Whitaker, 195–97; Jeffares, *Poems*, p. 264; "Death."
141, 23 gloomy bird of prey...." "Notes" to CP, 455.
142, 15 freedom or virtue." Ex, 336.
142, 37 Eternal Man...." Bradford, 84–87.
143, 8 made it lucid." E&I, 402, 411.
145, 1 cannot know it." L, 922.
145, 20 and Christianity." Bradford, pp. 87–99.
145, 29 egg to dust?" V–B, 214.
145, 32 Song of Sixpence." L, 922.
146, 34 practical tasks." L, 761.
147, 31 things I care for. L, 805, 812–14.
147, 33 commentaries upon them.... Var, 543–45, 835–37.
149, 4 done for years," L, 816–29, 855, 860.
149, 17 mob violence." L, 871, 885.
149, 34 passionate and cold. L, 837, 873; A, 463.
150, 4 distrust of England...." Lady Gregory, *Our Irish Theatre*, 41.
150, 13 powerful air-force." Jeffares and Cross, 266–70.
150, 40 final destroying horde." L, 819, 838, 869-76; "Speech after Long Silence."
151, 19 photographic plates." L, 827.
152, 25 once a year." L, 897–912; Bradford, 377–85; Bloom, 158.
153, 3 eagle mind...." "An Acre of Grass."
153, 24 in prison." Jeffares, *Poems*, 232.
154, 34 set up a wall." M, 77.
155, 34 feelings to explode. L, 913–15; Bradford, 294–304.
155, 41 *mesalliance*.... Hone, 283–84; Jeffares, *Plays*, 275–80; Bradford, 296.
156, 9 lover's night...." C Plays, 630.
156, 38 Irish folklore.... see, e.g., "Theologians" in *The Celtic Twilight*.
158, 26 of such politics." Jeffares, *Plays*, 275; the dates are provided by Torchiana, 359–60;
   his allegory is not convincing.
158, 33 ancient sanctities." A, 54; Jeffares, *Plays*, 275.
159, 6 in reality, sacred...." Ex, 369.
159, 15 imagination at work." Vendler, 197 f.; this paragraph is indebted to her reading.
159, 20 of eugenics." Jeffares, *Plays*, 275.
159, 24 perpetuates it." This is Whitaker's reading, 271–72; I think he posits too sharp a
   distinction between Yeats and the Old Man.
159, 35 distraught protagonist. Bradford, 297.
160, 15 and continuity." Russell Kirk, *The Conservative Mind* (Chicago: Henry Regnery
   Company, 1960), p. 547.
160, 23 to be immortal." Harper, *Occult*, 84, 107.
161, 37 human equality." Both Auden (136–45) and Orwell (187–93) are reprinted in
   Pritchard.

162, 25 newspaper office...." A, 225.
163, 4 totalitarian shadow." Whitaker, 73.
163, 30 pragmatic assertions." Kermode, *Ending*, 103–113.
163, 41 of John O'Leary...." L, 921.
164, 16 Junto of Robbers...." Hoffman and Levack, 501, 503.
164, 38 in my imagination." SS, 88.
165, 16 test of government. Morley, Cobban, and Pocock are, in different ways, persuasive about this aspect of Burke's thought.
165, 28 singular condition." Swift's phrase: *Works,* ed. Herbert Davis (Oxford: The Shakespeare Head Press, 1955) vol. XII, p. 65.
166, 8 life of a nation." Ex, 337 f.; SS, 172.
166, 11 riches of convention...." Hoffman and Levack, 471.
166, 29 conservative thought...." Ex, 292–93.
167, 4 work of the imagination. E&I, 215.
167, 20 civilisation renewed." Ex, 412–14, 425.

CHAPTER 6

169, 16 all that I write...." Ellmann, *M&M,* 94–95.
170, 20 again in 1937. Harper finds only thirty-six manuscript books: *Occult,* 6; I follow the usual distinction between V–A (1925) and V–B (1937).
170, 25 his horoscope. SS, 11.
170, 31 saving skepticism." Pound in Harper, *Occult,* 12; Orwell in Pritchard, 189; Auden in Hall and Steinmann, 345; Wilson in *Axel's Castle,* 26–63; Virginia Woolf, *The Sickle Side of the Moon: Letters 1932–35* (London: The Hogarth Press, 1979), p. 341 & n.
170, 32 neutral scholarship...." I have relied upon Ellmann (both books), Harper (both books), and David Clark in Skelton and Saddlemeyer.
171, 3 eshcatology as art. Frye, Vendler, Whitaker, Sidnell in Harper, *Occult,* Langbaum. All are necessary to the argument of this chapter.
171, 7 infernal nuisance...." Frye in Donoghue and Mulryne, 14.
171, 23 three stories.... Myth, 267–315.
172, 28 two polemical essays.... Harper, *Golden Dawn,* pp. 259–68; E&I, 28–52.
174, 29 Florence Farr's. Wade, 52.
174, 38 of literature." L, 766–77.
175, 8 Desolate Places...." Ex, 30–70 for the quotations of this and the next paragraph.
175, 41 human life." Frye in Donoghue and Mulryne, 12.
176, 4 convictions." Myth, 319.
176, 18 Hic and Willie. Ellmann, *M&M,* 197.
176, 27 and beyond me." Myth, 325–26.
176, 32 and self-realisation...." Myth, 333.
177, 24 violent passion. Myth, 326–30.
178, 2 somehow inseparable!" L, 731.
178, 9 paraphrase of Dante.... George Bornstein, "Yeats's Romantic Dante," *Colby Library Quarterly* XV, no. 2 (June 1979):93–113.
178, 26 famous things." Myth, 334, 342; Hone, 295.
179, 4 that other Will." Myth, 336–37.
179, 35 to the void." Myth, 332; Moore Corr, 254.

180, 14 of the brutes." Myth, 337, 339, 340, 341, 361.

181, 27 branches in the air." Myth, 340, 348, 352, 359; A, 272.

181, 33 single moment." Myth, 357.

182, 13 burn up time." Myth, 364–65.

182, 27 impish humor...." V–B, 8; Russell, 254.

183, 13 each other's death...." L, 709; V–B, 68.

184, 4 of the plot." V–B, 83–84, 92.

184, 7 act of thought." V–B, 81.

184, 37 all that I am." Ex, 305.

185, 29 last of a dynasty." V–B, 79, 214, 234; Ex, 295, 307, 356; A, 355.

186, 14 time and space." V–B, 187, 192, 193, 200, 209, 212; L, 712.

187, 11 mass of Eden." V–B, 187, 210–11, 263; Ex, 320; L, 785.

187, 16 phaseless sphere...." V–B, 210.

188, 39 most unfinished...." L, 781; V–B, 23.

189, 19 harsh, surgical." V–B, 248, 263.

189, 38 vision of history.... Ex, 289, 336, 397; Whitaker, 93–97.

190, 41 that the soul's." V–B, 255, 271; V–A, xi.

191, 23 shod with gold....'" V–B, 301–02; A, 106.

191, 37 *of that phase.*" V–B, 23, 91; L, 888–89, 898.

192, 22 with the future." L, 727, 812; Ex, 315; Orwell in Pritchard, 91; Ellmann, *M&M*, 96–97; Harper, *Occult*, 105.

192, 39 private philosophy...." V–B, 120, 147, 158, 239, 299; L, 916.

193, 24 generative grammar." V–B, 23; Donoghue, 23; Ellmann, *Identity*, 155.

194, 3 reality and justice. V–B, 24–25.

194, 8 explained the world." V–B, 81; Kermode, *Ending*, 105.

194, 22 Song of Sixpence." JBY, *Letters*, 281; L, 781, 922.

194, 37 lasting attachments. V–A, xi; V–B, 5, 8, 24, 207, 214.

195, 6 has had a vision...." A, 298–99; V–B, 8.

196, 2 Events of Time. ... " V–B, 268; Jeffares, *Poems*, 296; Ellmann, *Identity*, 176; Whitaker, 106.

196, 11 winding arcs." Myth, 340.

196, 23 revisions.... Ellmann, *Identity*, 176–77; Parkinson, *Later Poetry*, 136–42.

197, 13 of the supernatural...." Ex, 398; Ellmann, *Identity*, 260–63, for the details of the historical parallels.

198, 27 Christmas dinner.... Ellmann, *Eminent Domain*, 9–27; Gordon, 81–89.

198, 38 single image. V–B, 279–80.

199, 17 wistful tone...." Vendler, 113; for an example of Yeats's juggling, see V–B, 281; the terms of this paragraph come from Yeats and from Engelberg.

199, 33 live on love.... Stallworthy, *Lines*, 86f.; Bradford in Unterecker, 93–130.

200, 37 joy of eternity. ... " CP, 453; V–B, 214; Bradford in Unterecker, 95; Whitaker, 111–12.

200, 14 of the Law...." Myth, 301.

200, 19 speech on Divorce.... SS, 97–98.

200, 34 Roman decay." V–B, 274–75, 279; Bradford in Unterecker, 96, 102.

202, 23 to Paradise. Moore Corr, 162; Ex, 290; I have added the dolphins as have Bradford and Stallworthy.

202, 28 for some time...." Ex, 290; Jeffares, *Poems*, 352; Moore Corr, 164.

203, 5 point in the Zodiac.... " Ellmann, *Identity*, 221; this paragraph is indebted to Bornstein, *Transformations*, 81–83.

203, 14 Blake's London.... Stallworthy, *Lines,* 117 among others.
204, 9 of complexity.'" Myth, 268f., 354; V–B, 231, 233.
204, 31 but symbiotic." Jeffares, *Poems,* 353; Stallworthy, *Lines,* 127; Vendler, 117.
205, 4 back into life...." Jeffares, *Poems,* 351.

CHAPTER 7

206, 3 series of antinomies...." V–B, 187.
207, 3 whole being." L, 588.
207, 8 through intensity." V–B, 140, 180, 183.
208, 20 autumnal tint." L, 729, 785.
208, 32 and Truth...." V–B, 141–42; Bloom, 376; Keats, letter of Dec. 21, 27, 1817.
209, 14 vacillated all day...." L, 788, 790.
210, 11 of joy. E&I, 176; Ellmann, *Identity,* 172, 268–74; Parkinson, *Later Poetry,* 220–28.
210, 26 expression of himself." Ex, 147.
211, 14 one single moment." E&I, 321, 350; myth, 347.
213, 2 in my youth." L, 788–90.
213, 23 of the land. Isaiah, VI, 6–12.
213, 32 stricken dumb." Ex, 294.
214, 11 early draft.... Bradford, 129.
214, 26 honeyed comb." A, 207; Samson's riddle is Judges XIV, 5–18.
215, 9 hammered gold. L, 798; Moore Corr, 114; Ellmann, *Identity,* 268–74; "Ribh at the Tomb of Baile and Aillin."
215, 14 very near me." L, 715.
216, 3 mental excitement...." L, 785–86, 814.
216, 29 energy and daring...." "Notes" to CP, 457.
217, 7 replace illusion. Henn, 42.
217, 21 excrement instead...." Ex, 325.
218, 2 not so innocent...." L, 725–26, 818–19.
219, 30 clamant sexuality...." Ellmann, *Identity,* 167.
220, 7 the old thought...." Jeffares, *Poems,* 299; Parkinson, *Later Poetry,* 93.
220, 29 to brood upon...." Parkinson, *Later Poetry,* 92–113.
221, 11 into flesh...." CP, 455–56; Parkinson, *Later Poetry,* 96–97.
222, 28 bundle of fragments." A, 189.
223, 9 last curse...." L, 719.
223, 19 disillusioned conclusion...." Parkinson, *Later Poetry,* 104.
223, 38 deep waters...." Pritchard, 250.
224, 13 blanch and tremble. Ellmann, *Identity,* 239–40.
224, 21 life as tragedy." A, 189; cf. Myth, 319.
225, 7 of algebra." V–B, 135, 240, 301.
225, 30 dancing to the dancer...." SS, 171–72; Ex, 333–34; *The Works of George Berkeley,* ed. A. A. Luce and T. E. Jessop (London: Thomas Nelson & Sons, Ltd., 1949), vol. I, p. 96.
225, 36 already believe." Ellmann, *Identity,* 240; Ex, 310.
226, 11 voice audible." *Notebooks,* ed. Kathleen Coburn (New York: The Bollingen Foundation, Pantheon Books, 1961), vol. II, p. 2546–47.

227, 8 nothing can injure us." L, 733, 838; Moore Corr, 154.

227, 18 heroic cry. L, 837.

227, 28 Rome was burning." L, 859; Ex, 492; E&I, 232, 239; Stallworthy, *Revision,* 45.

228, 1 occasion for that anxiety...." Stallworthy, *Revision,* 44; Jeffares, *Poems,* 441–43.

229, 16 the dead Ophelia." A, 167, 313, 342; E&I, 239, 523; Ex, 333, 449.

230, 17 ebbing Asia." V–B, 270.

231, 1 Chinese iconography.... Donoghue, 61; Langbaum, 228–30.

231, 24 civility of sorrow...." E&I, 239.

231, 32 vast design. V–B, 279–80.

CHAPTER 8

233, 2 impressive collection. *New Poems* included the poems that now appear in CP from "The Gyres" through "Are You Content." The remaining, twenty-two poems, completed during the last year of Yeats's life, were first published as *Last Poems and Two Plays.* CP does not adopt Yeats's ordering and has created some false impressions about his sense of the shape of his final work. When it is significant, I refer to Yeats's plan. See Curtis Bradford, "Yeats's Last Poems Again," *Dolmen Press Yeats Centenary Papers,* vol. VIII (Dublin: Dolmen Press, 1965) and Jeffares, *Poems,* 435.

233, 19 to an end." L, 819, 904; E&I, 509–10.

234, 8 modern tide." "The Results of Thought" and "The Statues"; Henn, Ellmann, and Parkinson all write well about the manner of *Last Poems;* MacNiece's poem is "Autolycus."

234, 32 forty years." L, 745, 799, 802, 831, 847, 901; "The Spur," "A Prayer for Old Age," "Ribh Considers Christian Love Insufficient."

234, 36 empty witted." Myth, 342.

235, 18 made everything...." V–B, 138–39; E&I, 510; Ellmann, *Identity,* 209; Donoghue, 61f., 123, 139.

235, 38 spiritual things. E&I, 409; L, 715; Henn, 235–36.

236, 3 migratory bird. E&I, viii, 510, 519; Ex, 337; L, 836.

237, 32 Frank O'Connor. Ellmann, *Identity,* 280; Jeffares, *Poems,* 385.

238, 4 glow of beauty." *The Speeches of the Right Hon. Henry Grattan* (Dublin: James Duffy, 1865), p. 286.

238, 42 like exceedingly." L, 891–97.

239, 22 common people.'" Ex, 371.

239, 29 states of mind." E&I, x.

240, 19 in Normandy. "Against Unworthy Praise"; V–B, 219–20.

241, 7 creative energy...." Stallworthy, *Revision,* 115.

241, 29 and smell." Ex, 450; "Prologue" to *The Death of Cuchulain;* Hone, 230.

242, 7 of a Theme...." Stallworthy, *Lines,* 221; Parkinson, *Later Poetry,* 174–76; in Yeats's ordering "The Circus Animals' Desertion" rather than "Under Ben Bulben" concludes (except for the short "Politics") *Last Poems,* giving it the testamental location to match its tone.

242, 15 demon thing...." "The Wanderings of Oisin."

242, 34 whole being?" L, 588.

243, 24 whole soul." Ex, 301.

244, 16 money-changers. ... " A, 461; E&I, 509; Parkinson, *Later Poetry*, 174; Brad-
    ford, 158.
245, 15 out reality.' E&I, 502–03; A, 57.
245, 23 kind of death." Ellmann, *Identity*, 206; A, 482.
246, 16 befitting fear. ... " Ellmann, *Identity*, 214.
246, 35 strange and ... moving. ... " L, 922.
247, 21 profane perfection. ... " "Under Ben Bulben"; L, 810; Henn, 338; Jeffares, *Poems*,
    513; Bloom, 462–65; Langbaum, 234–35; George Bornstein, "Yeats's Romantic
    Dante," *Colby Library Quarterly* vol. XV, no. 2 (June 1979):111–13.
248, 6 into religion." Bloom, 462; L, 916–18.
248, 22 Lenin of his day. ... " *Wellesley Letters*, 131.
249, 21 warrior's tragedy." Harris, 248; my reading is indebted to his.
250, 10 call them to battle. Stallworthy, *Revision*, 222–42; Patrick Diskin, "A Source for
    Yeats's 'The Black Tower,'" *N&Q* (March 1961):107–8; W. J. Keith, "Yeats's Arthu-
    rian Black Tower," *MLN*, 75 (1960), 121.
250, 22 political propaganda. ... " Ex, 443; Saul, 176.
251, 12 soon my son." Stallworthy, *Revision*, 232; Myth, 332; Hannah Arendt, *Crises of the
    Republic* (New York: Harcourt, Brace Jovanovich, 1972), p. 164.
251, 27 stony recessions. ... " Whitaker, 296; Stallworthy, *Revision*, 37, 60.
252, 27 defeated world. ... " E&I, 254; Stallworthy, *Revision*, 62, 68.
253, 22 surely Yeats. ... Ellmann, *M&M*, 6; UcP, II, 431; A, 55; "The Death of the Hare."

Bibliography

WORKS BY YEATS   ABBREVIATIONS

Autobiographies. London: Macmillan, 1955, 1961.   A

The Celtic Twilight. London: Lawrence and Bullen, 1893.

Collected Poems. New York: Macmillan, 1956.   CP

Collected Plays. London: Macmillan, 1960.   C Plays

Essays and Introductions. London: Macmillan, 1961.   E&I

Explorations. London: Macmillan, 1962.   Ex

The Letters of W. B. Yeats. Edited by Allan Wade. London:
     Rupert Hart-Davis, 1954.   L

Letters on Poetry from W. B. Yeats to Dorothy Wellesley. Edited by
     Dorothy Wellesley. London: Oxford University Press, 1940.

Letters to the New Island. Edited by Horace Reynolds.
     Cambridge, Mass.: Harvard University Press, 1934.

Memoirs. Edited by Denis Donoghue. London: Macmillan, 1972.   M

Mythologies. New York: Macmillan, 1959.   Myth

Plays and Controversies. London: Macmillan, 1923.

The Senate Speeches of W. B. Yeats. Edited by Donald R. Pearce.
     London: Faber and Faber, 1961.   SS

Uncollected Prose, I, Edited by John P. Frayne. New York:
     Columbia University Press, 1970.   UcP I

Uncollected Prose, II. Edited by John P. Frayne and Colton Johnson.
     New York: Columbia University Press, 1976.   UcP II

The Variorum Edition of the Poems of W. B. Yeats. Edited by Peter Allt
     and Russell K. Alspach. New York: Macmillan, 1957.   Var

A Vision. London: T. Werner Laurie, 1925.   V-A

A Vision. New York: Macmillan, 1938, 1961.   V-B

W. B. Yeats and T. Sturge Moore: Their Correspondence 1901–1937.   Moore
Corr
> Edited by Ursula Bridge. London: Routledge & Kegan
> Paul, 1953.

WORKS ON YEATS

Adams, Hazard. *Blake and Yeats: The Contrary Vision.* Ithaca, N.Y.: Cornell
University Press, 1955.
Bloom, Harold. *Yeats.* New York: Oxford University Press, 1970.
Bornstein, George. *Yeats and Shelley.* Chicago: University of Chicago Press, 1970.
———. *Transformations of Romanticism in Yeats, Eliot, and Stevens.* Chicago:
University of Chicago Press, 1976.
Bradford, Curtis B. *Yeats at Work.* Carbondale: Southern Illinois University
Press, 1965.
Clark, David R. *W. B. Yeats and the Theatre of Desolate Reality.* Dublin: Dolmen
Press, 1965.
Donaghue, Denis. *William Butler Yeats.* New York: Viking, 1971.
———, and J. R. Mulryne, eds. *An Honoured Guest: New Essays on W. B. Yeats.*
London: Edward Arnold, 1965.
Ellmann, Richard. *Eminent Domain: Yeats among Wilde, Joyce, Pound, Eliot and
Auden.* New York: Oxford University Press, 1967.
———. *Golden Codgers: Biographical Speculations.* New York: Oxford University
Press, 1973.
———. *The Identity of Yeats.* New York: Oxford University Press, 1954.
———. *Yeats: The Man and the Masks.* New York: Macmillan, 1948.
Engelberg, Edward. *The Vast Design: Patterns in W. B. Yeats's Aesthetic.* Toronto:
University of Toronto Press, 1964.
Frye, Northrop. *Fables of Identity: Studies in Poetic Mythology.* New York:
Harcourt, Brace, & World, 1963.
———. *The Stubborn Structure.* New York: Methuen, 1980.
Gordon, D. J., ed. *Images of a Poet.* Manchester: Manchester University
Press, 1961.
Gwynn, Stephen, ed. *Scattering Branches: Tributes to the Memory of W. B. Yeats.*
London: Macmillan, 1940.
Hall, James, and Martin Steinmann, eds. *The Permanence of Yeats: Selected
Criticism.* New York: Macmillan, 1950.
Harper, George M. *Yeats's Golden Dawn.* New York: Barnes and Noble, 1974.
———, ed. *Yeats and the Occult.* Toronto: Macmillan, 1975
Harris, Daniel A. *Yeats: Coole Park and Ballylee.* Baltimore: Johns Hopkins
University Press, 1974.

Henn, T. R. *The Lonely Tower: Studies in the Poetry of W. B. Yeats.* London: Methuen, 1950.

Hone, Joseph. *W. B. Yeats: 1865–1939.* London: Macmillan, 1962.

Jeffares, A. Norman, ed. *A Commentary on the Collected Poems of W. B. Yeats.* London: Macmillan, 1968.

———, and A. S. Knowland, eds. *A Commentary on the Collected Plays of W. B. Yeats.* London: Macmillan, 1975.

———, and K. G. W. Cross, eds. *In Excited Reverie: A Centenary Tribute to William Butler Yeats, 1865–1939.* London: Macmillan, 1965.

Lynch, David. *The Poetics of Self.* Chicago: University of Chicago Press, 1981.

Marcus, Phillip L. *Yeats and the Beginning of the Irish Renaissance.* Ithaca, N.Y.: Cornell University Press, 1970.

Maxwell, D. E. S., and S. B. Bushrui, eds. *W. B. Yeats, 1865–1965: Centenary Essays on the Art of W. B. Yeats.* Nigeria: Ibadan University Press, 1965.

Nathan, Leonard E. *The Tragic Drama of William Butler Yeats: Figures in a Dance.* New York: Columbia University Press, 1965.

O'Driscoll, Robert, and Lorna Reynolds, eds. *Yeats and the Theatre.* Toronto: Macmillan, 1975.

Parkinson, Thomas. *W. B. Yeats Self-Critic: A Study of His Early Verse.* Berkeley: University of California Press, 1951.

———. *W. B. Yeats: The Later Poetry.* Berkeley: University of California Press, 1964.

Pritchard, William H., ed. *W. B. Yeats: A Critical Anthology.* Middlesex: Penguin, 1972.

Ronsley, Joseph. *Yeats's Autobiographies: Life as Symbolic Pattern.* Cambridge, Mass.: Harvard University Press, 1968.

Saul, G. B. *Prolegomena to the Study of Yeats's Poems.* Philadelphia: University of Pennsylvania Press, 1957.

Skelton, Robin, and Ann Saddlemeyer, eds. *The World of W. B. Yeats.* Seattle: University of Washington Press, 1965.

Stallworthy, Jon. *Between the Lines: Yeats's Poetry in the Making.* Oxford: The Clarendon Press, 1963.

———. *Vision and Revision in Yeats's Last Poems.* Oxford: The Clarendon Press, 1969.

Stock, A. G. *W. B. Yeats: His Poetry and Thought.* Cambridge: Cambridge University Press, 1961.

Torchiana, Donald T. *W. B. Yeats and Georgian Ireland.* Evanston: Northwestern University Press, 1966.

Unterecker, John, ed. *Yeats: A Collection of Critical Essays.* Englewood Cliffs, N.J.: Prentice-Hall, 1963.

Ure, Peter. *Yeats the Playwright: A Commentary on Character and Design in the Major Plays.* London: Routledge & Kegan Paul, 1963.

———. *Yeats and Anglo-Irish Literature: Critical Essays by Peter Ure.* Edited by C. J. Rawson. New York: Barnes and Noble, 1974.

Vendler, Helen. *Yeats's Vision and the Later Plays*. Cambridge, Mass.: Harvard University Press, 1963.

Wade, Allen. *A Bibliography of the Writings of W. B. Yeats*. London: Rupert Hart-Davis, 1958.

Whitaker, Thomas R. *Swan and Shadow: Yeats's Dialogue with History*. Chapel Hill: University of North Carolina Press, 1964.

Wilson, F. A. C. *W. B. Yeats and Tradition*. London: Gollancz, 1958.

———. *Yeats's Iconography*. London: Gollancz, 1960.

OTHER WORKS

Adams, Hazard. *Lady Gregory*. Lewisburg, Pa.: Bucknell University Press, 1973.

Abrams, M. H. *Natural Supernaturalism: Tradition and Revolution in Romantic Literature*. New York: Norton, 1971.

Archibald, Douglas. *John Butler Yeats*. Lewisburg, Pa.: Bucknell University Press, 1974.

Bate, Walter Jackson. *The Burden of the Past and the English Poet*. Cambridge: Mass.: Harvard University Press, 1970.

———. *Coleridge*. New York: Macmillan, 1968.

Beckett, J. C. *The Anglo-Irish Tradition*. Ithaca: Cornell University Press, 1977.

Bowra, C. M. *The Heritage of Symbolism*. London: Macmillan, 1943.

Bloom, Harold. *The Anxiety of Influence: A Theory of Poetry*. New York: Oxford University Press, 1973.

Cardozo, Nancy. *Lucky Eyes and a High Heart: the Biography of Maud Gonne*. New York: Bobbs-Merrill, 1978.

Coxhead, Elizabeth. *Lady Gregory: A Literary Portrait*. London: Macmillan, 1961.

Cobban, Alfred. *Edmund Burke and the Revolt against the Eighteenth Century*. London: Allen & Unwin, 1929, 1960.

Curtis, Edmund. *A History of Ireland*. London: Methuen, 1936.

Dangerfield, George. *The Damnable Question: A Study in Anglo-Irish Relations*. Boston: Little, Brown, 1976.

Easton, Malcolm. *Aubrey and the Dying Lady: A Beardsley Riddle*. Boston: Godine, 1972.

Eliot, T. S. *On Poetry and Poets*. London: Farrar, Strauss and Cudahy, 1957.

Fallis, Richard. *The Irish Renaissance*. Syracuse: Syracuse University Press, 1977.

Ferguson, Oliver W. *Jonathan Swift and Ireland*. Urbana: University of Illinois Press, 1962.

Gregory, Lady Isabella Augusta. *Lady Gregory's Journals 1916–1930*. Edited by Lennox Robinson. London: Putnam, 1946.

———. *Our Irish Theatre: A Chapter of Autobiography*. New York: Putnam's, 1913.

————. *Seventy Years, Being the Autobiography of Lady Gregory.* Edited by Colin Smythe. Gerrards Cross: Colin Smythe, 1974.

Harrison, John R. *The Reactionaries: A Study of the Anti-Democratic Intelligentsia.* New York: Schocken, 1966.

Hoffman, Ross J. S., and Paul Levack, eds. *Burke's Politics: Selected Writings and Speeches of Edmund Burke on Reform, Revolution, and War.* New York: Knopf, 1959.

Hough, Graham. *The Last Romantics.* London: Duckworth, 1949.

Howarth, Herbert. *The Irish Writers, 1880–1940.* New York: Hill and Wang, 1958.

Kermode, Frank. *Romantic Image.* London: Routledge and Kegan Paul, 1957.

————. *The Sense of an Ending: Studies in the Theory of Fiction.* New York: Oxford University Press, 1967.

Langbaum, Robert. *The Mysteries of Identity: A Theme in Modern Literature.* New York: Oxford University Press, 1977.

Lecky, W. E. H. *A History of Ireland in the Eighteenth Century.* Abridged and with an Introduction by L. P. Curtis, Jr. Chicago: University of Chicago Press, 1972.

————. *Leaders of Public Opinion in Ireland.* London: Longmans, Green, 1871.

Levenson, Samuel. *Maud Gonne.* New York: Reader's Digest Press, 1976.

Lyons, F. S. L. *Ireland Since the Famine.* New York: Scribner's, 1971.

MacBride, Maud Gonne. *A Servant of the Queen.* London: Gollancz, 1938.

Miller, J. Hillis. *Poets of Reality: Six Twentieth Century Writers.* Cambridge: Mass.: Harvard University Press, 1965.

Morley, John. *Burke.* London: Macmillan, 1879.

Murphy, William, M. *Prodigal Father: The Life of John Butler Yeats, 1839–1922.* Ithaca, N.Y.: Cornell University Press, 1978.

O'Brien, Conor Cruise. *States of Ireland.* New York: Pantheon, 1972.

Ó Tuathaigh, Geróid. *Ireland Before the Famine, 1798–1848.* Dublin: Gill and Macmillan, 1972.

Parker, Reeve. *Coleridge's Meditative Art.* Ithaca, N.Y.: Cornell University Press, 1975.

Pocock, J. G. A. *Politics, Language and Time: Essays on Political Thought and History.* New York: Atheneum, 1971.

Pyle, Hilary. *Jack B. Yeats: A Biography.* London: Routledge and Kegan Paul, 1970.

Reid, B. L. *The Man from New York: John Quinn and his Friends.* New York: Oxford University Press, 1968.

Russell, George [AE]. *The Living Torch.* Edited by Monk Gibbon. London: Macmillan, 1937.

Saddlemeyer, Ann. *In Defense of Lady Gregory, Playwright.* Dublin: Dolmen, 1966.

Symons, Arthur. *The Symbolist Movement in Literature.* London: Heinemann, 1899; rev. eds., 1908, 1919.

Weintraub, Stanley. *Beardsley: A Biography.* New York: Braziller, 1967.

Wilson, Edmund. *Axel's Castle.* New York: Scribner's, 1931.

Yeats, John Butler. *Early Memories: Some Chapters of Autobiography.* Church-town, Dundrum: Cuala Press, 1923.

———. *Essays Irish and American.* Dublin: Talbot, 1918.

———. *Letters to His Son W. B. Yeats and Others.* Edited by Joseph Hone. New York: Dutton, 1946.

Index

275

YEATS

was composed in 10-point Merganthaler Sabon and leaded two points,
with display type in Sabon and Erbar by Partners Composition,
printed on 50-pound, acid-free Glatfelter Smooth Offset,
Smythe-sewn and bound over binders boards in Joanna Arrestox B
by Maple-Vail Book Manufacturing Group, Inc.
and published by

SYRACUSE UNIVERSITY PRESS
SYRACUSE, NEW YORK 13210